Violence to Eternity

In this volume **Grace M. Jantzen** continues her groundbreaking analysis of death and beauty in western thought by examining the religious roots of death and violence in the Jewish and Christian tradition, which underlie contemporary values.

She shows how man's fear of the female is often implicated in religious violence and in her critique of the Hebrew Bible and the Christian New Testament she examines a range of themes that show the western pre-occupation with necrophilia. She examines the relation of death to the Jewish covenant, the nature of monotheism, Holy War and the Christian covenant and kingdom. However, Jantzen recognizes that submerged beneath these themes in Judaism and Christianity are traces of an alternative world of beauty and life.

Jantzen's internationally recognized feminist philosophy of religion puts forward a powerful analysis of patriarchy and violence and reveals the hidden power of natality. Her work is a searching challenge for our times and one that gives hope in a violent world. This work is the first of two posthumous publications to complete her impressive genealogy of death and beauty in western thought.

The late **Grace M. Jantzen** (1948–2006) was Professor of Religion, Culture and Gender at Manchester University and a widely respected feminist philosopher and theologian.

Jeremy Carrette is Professor in the Department of Religious Studies at the University of Kent and is the author of *Selling Spirituality* (Routledge, 2005) and *Religion and Critical Psychology* (Routledge, 2007).

Morny Joy is University Professor in the Department of Religious Studies at the University of Calgary. She is author of *Divine Love: Luce Irigaray, Women, Gender and Religion* (MUP, 2007).

Violence to Eternity

Death and the Displacement of Beauty,
Volume 2

Grace M. Jantzen

Edited by
Jeremy Carrette and Morny Joy

Routledge
Taylor & Francis Group

LONDON AND NEW YORK

First published 2009
by Routledge
2 Park Square, Milton Park, Abingdon, Oxon. OX14 4RN

Simultaneously published in the USA and Canada
by Routledge
270 Madison Ave., New York, NY 100016

Routledge is an imprint of the Taylor & Francis Group, an informa business

© 2009 Grace M. Jantzen; Jeremy Carrette and Morny Joy for editorial material

Typeset in Times New Roman by
Taylor & Francis Books
Printed and bound in Great Britain by
TJ International, Padstow, Cornwall

British Library Cataloguing in Publication Data
A catalogue record for this book is available from the British Library

Library of Congress Cataloging in Publication Data
Jantzen, Grace.
    Violence to eternity / Grace Jantzen; edited by Jeremy Carrette and Morny Joy.
        p. cm.
    Includes bibliographical references (p.) and index.
    1. Violence – Religious aspects – Christianity – History. 2. Feminist
theology. 3. Violence in the Bible. 4. Bible – Feminist criticism. I. Carrette,
Jeremy R. II. Joy, Morny. III. Title.
    BT736.15.J36 2008

ISBN10: 0-415-29034-1 (hbk)
ISBN10: 0-415-29035-X (pbk)
ISBN10: 0-203-89092-2 (ebk)

ISBN13: 978-0-415-29034-0 (hbk)
ISBN13: 978-0-415-29035-7 (pbk)
ISBN 13: 978-0-203-89092-9 (ebk)

Contents

Preface

Grace Jantzen (1948–2006) was Professor of Religion, Culture and Gender at the University of Manchester from 1996 to 2005 and Emeritus Professor until her untimely death. Using French continental philosophy, and the work of Luce Irigaray in particular, she sought to challenge the patriarchal Western symbolic, built around a preoccupation with death, by providing a new imaginary of birth and natality. After working on a series of studies in philosophy of religion from *God's World, God's Body* (DLT, 1984) to *Power, Gender and Christian Mysticism* (CUP, 1995), she recognized the need to provide alternative models to counter the Western symbolic of death and violence. Her initial theoretical mapping of this project appeared in her innovative work *Becoming Divine: Towards a Feminist Philosophy of Religion* (Manchester, 1998), which was published in her Manchester University Press series on Religion, Culture and Gender.[1]

Volume 1 of *Death and the Displacement of Beauty* was an impressive *tour de force* through Western philosophy in the Greco-Roman period in terms of her necrophilia and natality model of Western thought. The proposed multi-volume project was not intended as a 'history' of Western philosophy, but a genealogy – in the best senses of Foucault's Nietzchean idea. It was one that followed 'discourses' through a particular conceptual strand and highlighted the body and social and political institutions, with as much concentration on the present as the past. Jantzen was always careful to identify the context of her selective readings as being determined through a particular critical concern or 'purpose' (49, 50, 189, 288, 317). In this regard, she respectively qualified her work alongside other scholars, carefully marking out how she engages – or not – with existing scholarship in each historical period and in relation to each philosopher. It would be wrong therefore to dismiss her work in terms of its choice of texts, because the 'evidence', or 'inventory of our violent cultural habitus' (50), is in what is presented and in the political hermeneutic, which demands our attention.

In the first volume the massacred and burnt bodies of innocent civilians and soldiers in Iraq, Afghanistan and Bosnia were interwoven with classical Greco-Roman philosophical texts. Homer, Socrates, Plato, Seneca and Plotinus have, according to Grace Jantzen's critical genealogy, contributed to the symbolic foundations of a necrophilic and violent culture, which links the horrors of modernity to a violent past. The preoccupations with the eternal, immortal and the ever-lasting soul have all created 'death, violence and mastery' as the story of Western culture (91). As Jantzen indicates, we are all heirs of the tragedy of Athens (129) and the violence of Rome (254). Following Bourdieu's idea of a cultural 'habitus', Jantzen believed we were educated through the stories of heroic death, suicidal honour and military manliness, and uphold the epics of Alexander the Great and Julius Caesar in support of contemporary colonial and imperial power (129, 288–89). The strength of Jantzen's first volume was how she forged the vital links between the philosophical past and the brutality of the contemporary world, weaving, as she did, a complex network of ideas around gender, violence and death. But, as Jantzen constantly asked, 'should humans be *defined* by death?' (59). The key part of her 'patient investigation and analysis' of Western philosophy was to show that 'the present is not inevitable' (21); and hidden in the violent history are 'voices of dissent' (98, 255, 298) where beauty, creativity and flourishing and an affirmation of a new life can be found – the world of natality.

Grace Jantzen's first volume was no archaic intellectual reading of ancient philosophy, but rather an engagement with a problem that required a response in the present. In doing so it raised questions – as Foucault himself did – about the nature of the intellectual today. Throughout the work, Jantzen brought each Greco-Roman philosopher back into the historical– political location and showed the correlation between abstract thinking and political struggle, including – as it happens – the running away from political involvement. Her work was, as she stated, what an intellectual can 'offer' in a 'death-dealing' time (4); and in the discussion of Seneca and Ovid speaking out under the despotic rule of the Roman Empire, there is clear historical link between the violence of Rome and the violence of contemporary America (129, 343). According to Jantzen, philosophers can either 'speak truth to power' or 'they can redefine intellectual endeavour as no longer a threat, no longer in active engagement with public life' (343). In bringing philosophy to life, Jantzen was seeking to make philosophy not only relevant but also to add a different voice to the philosophical collusion with death and violence. *Foundations of Violence* was not a 'call to arms', but rather a rejection of the combat and conflict metaphors that litter the language of philosophy. By opening up a counter-discourse Jantzen was seeking to find alternative ways to think and flourish.

The critical edge of Jantzen's work revealed 'the real locus of the problem' of Western violence within the representation and relationship towards 'the maternal body and female sexuality' (17). Indeed, the most compelling part of Jantzen's study is the philosophical excavation of a very disturbing reality in the Western cultural symbolic. It is the way gender is embedded in the notions of death and violence and how this relates to a profound fear and unconscious hatred of the female body. The combination of death, darkness and the female – as displayed in the Pythagorean table of opposites and 'acted-out' through history – relates to a combination of themes that Diane Jonte-Pace discovered in her reading of Freud's writing around mothers, death and religion; which Freud saw but avoided (Jonte-Pace *Speaking the Unspeakable*, California, 2001). This constellation of themes enables us to recognize that the male response to the female body is caught in an entire series of uncomfortable associations from birth itself and a fundamental fear of the forces that give life. Jantzen takes us to some of the disturbing philosophical truths of this question and offers in response a powerful political reordering of the way we think. The change she demands – while necessary – will not be easy. It will mean that in order to come back to life we have not only to change our thinking but also our political system of democracy built on death, something which Jantzen, like Agamben – also following Foucault – recognized as a disturbing feature of our so-called democratic peace (Agamben *Homo Sacer*, Stanford, 1998). Jantzen disentangles the complex knots that create such a violent and gendered constellation in the West and opens resources, with Foucault, for 'thinking differently'. The debt to Foucault is evidenced throughout her study, but it might be that Jantzen provides one of the key genealogical insights Foucault avoided by showing how our preoccupation with death and violence relates to how we understand and are terrified of our birth and life, which is itself determined by our views of the female body.

Due to her death, Grace Jantzen's project for a six-volume work on *Death and the Displacement of Beauty* was never completed and only Volume 1 appeared before she died. However, in the last months of her life she gathered together as much as she could for two volumes and requested that we complete the project as far as possible. The trajectory of her genealogy of death and beauty included material for studies of the Judaic-Christian period, the medieval period, the seventeenth century, modernity, psychoanalysis and post-modernity. The magnitude of the project only confirmed the enormity of the intellectual loss and the complex historical and philosophical unravelling that her projected required. However, it was evident that the two volumes she attempted to bring together for posthumous editing and publication, could be published with different levels of editorial work. The present volume on the Judaic-Christian tradition, *Violence to Eternity* and *A Place of Springs*, gathers up her final assessments of beauty from the seventeenth century. Both volumes continued the searching of philosophical history and showed how the violence within the contemporary world echoes narratives and images deep in the layers of the Western cultural inheritance. But as Jantzen shows, despite the violence, marked out as it was in relation to the female body, there were choices and alternatives from which a new political vision of life could be rescued. The final two volumes bring the project forward by offering another foundational study of biblical material, and make one important step in the modern period by considering material close to her own Quaker tradition.

The request to complete the work was in equal measure a great honour and a difficult challenge. In honouring Grace Jantzen's request to complete *Violence to Eternity* we have tried to keep to her own words as far as possible and resisted attempts to fill in the gaps or supplement incomplete sections, not least because of the limits of our own specialist knowledge. Our editorial input has been to make structural changes to bring consistency and coherence. One difficulty was to assess different working versions of each respective volume, something that was more of a problem for Volume 3. We attempted to respect the most recent versions and at the same time bring to light as much of the remaining material as possible. In Volume 2, we have moved material from different sections and rearranged and reintegrated incomplete material, originally meant for introductory sections, into subsequent chapters. In Part 3 in Chapters 11 and 12, we have used two extraneous articles to replace a chapter that we deemed too incomplete for publication. The structural changes honour the line of argument by keeping to the order of material. The changes we have made are principally to make the argument more accessible. In consequence, some chapters are shorter in length, but we hope the different parts of the work are more balanced as a result of our editorial shaping. We have footnoted all our editorial changes in the text. We have also tried to follow up all outstanding references in the text, but where these were unfinished or unclear we had to make some judgement about the source material. Although these selected sources appear to correspond to the best of our knowledge, there may be cases where they may not have been those originally intended. In addition to the two most complete volumes – which Jantzen had marked out for specific publication – there were notes and chapters for subsequent volumes. These notes and papers were too incomplete for publication.[2] The publication of the remaining two volumes thus reflects Grace Jantzen's final efforts to rescue as much as possible in two final works before she died. We believe her project is substantial and important in the critical history of ideas and, given the issues Jantzen's work explores, our knowledge and understanding of such themes may literally be a matter of life or death for the Western world.

Jeremy Carrette and Morny Joy
February 2008

Acknowledgements

We would like to thank Grace Jantzen's partner Tina Macrae for helping us in this project. Without her assistance and support during our respective times working on Grace Jantzen's notes and papers in 2007, this project would not have been possible. Her hospitality and sensitivity to the work was vital. Completing this project during a period of grief and loss has been difficult, but we hope we have honoured her request to the best of our ability under the given constraints. Above all we hope the project will be a fitting tribute to our friendship and appreciation of Grace Jantzen and her philosophical project.

We thank Lesley Riddle and Routledge, Taylor and Francis, for supporting the work and agreeing to complete the original six-volume proposal with the two final volumes following Grace's untimely death. Thanks to members of the Department of Theology and Religious Studies at Manchester University for their support, particularly George Brooke and Elaine Graham, who have helped with specific issues along the way. Papers for Volume 2 contained notes of suggested texts from various members of the Manchester department, and Grace's appreciation of her colleagues for their respective expertise in Judaic and Christian history is evident. Jeremy would like to thank the British Academy for a small grant to support travel and administrative assistance for his part of the project. Morny would like to thank John King for his generous help in editorial matters. Finally, we are grateful to a number of journals for permission to use material that helped complete the unfinished parts of the volume and provide material for our preface. Chapter 11 originally appeared as 'A Reconfiguration of Desire: Reading Medieval Mystic in Postmodernity' in *Women's Philosophy Review* 29 (2002): 11–22; Chapter 12 originally appeared as 'Feminism and Flourishing: Gender and Metaphor in Feminist Theology' in *Feminist Theology* 10 (1995): 81–101; a part of our preface was taken from Jeremy Carrette's 'Bringing Philosophy to Life: A Review Article in Memory of Grace M. Jantzen (1948–2006)' in *Literature and Theology* 20, no. 3 (2006): 321–25. We thank Soran Reader of SWIP, UK, Julie Clague and Andrew Hass for assistance in seeking these permissions.

Introduction

Was it 'very good'?

> ... A scene of light and glory, a dominion,
> That has endured the longest among men ...
>
> (Samuel Rogers in Norwich 2003:3)

I am not the first person for whom these words encapsulate the ambiguities of Venice: its breath-taking beauty built on violence, its opulence as assertion of power, its artistic creativity exercised in a celebration of death. When my partner and I visited the city recently, we were repeatedly drawn back to the golden glow of the mosaics in the Basilica of San Marco, to the delicate stone tracery of the Doge's Palace, to the water of the canals lapping gently at the ancient pastel houses. It is easy to fall in love with Venice, impossible to resist its beauty and the creative energy that achieved such magnificence.

It is easy, too, to be drawn into the religious validation of its beauty. Was not San Marco built to honour the evangelist and blessed by the miracle of the rediscovery of his bones on the occasion of its dedication? Does it not tell all the stories of the Bible in its glowing mosaics and innumerable sculptures and ornaments? And was not all this wealth achieved and celebrated in the defence of Christendom against the Muslim 'infidel'?

But with those questions the ambiguities can no longer be avoided. If there can be no doubt of the intermingling of religion and beauty in the making of Venice, neither can it be denied that their interconnection is an assertion of power. The wealth that built San Marco was not innocently acquired. Much of the gold, silver and marble came from Byzantium and the Arab world, sometimes through friendly trade but often as tribute or plunder in the looting that characterized the Crusades. The four great bronze horses that stand above the main door of San Marco were taken as booty in the sack of Constantinople. An intricately carved pillar, probably a work of sixth-century Syrian art, was looted from Acre in Palestine. Even the relics of St Mark which the Basilica was built to house had been smuggled out of Alexandria. San Marco exists because of warfare, plunder, and violence, and stands as an assertion of power: it was from the first the Doge's chapel, the place of state where soldiers and sailors were given divine blessing and validation at the start of their expeditions. At whose expense is this beauty?

My discomfort increased as the gendered nature of the power of San Marco became more insistent, its masculinity implicit and explicit in the carvings and mosaics. By far the greater number of portrayals are of men, ranging from elegant marble renditions of Christ and the evangelists to exquisite cycles of carvings representing Venetian trades and allegories of the months of the year. Where women are portrayed they are for the most part depicted as either submissive or seductive: Noah's wife and daughters-in-law stand by their menfolk; holy women – perhaps nuns – lean towards Christ in the jewel-encrusted Pala d'Oro; the mosaics of the first pair show Eve presenting Adam with the fatal apple. The great exception is Mary, mother of Jesus, repeatedly shown in a golden glow of dignity, the masculine fantasy of virgin mother, an impossible ideal for actual women. San Marco is not unique in its depiction of gender inequality of course; the themes are repeated with variations in churches throughout Christendom. But should that make us less uncomfortable, or more?

Moreover, the beauty and power of San Marco, as of Christendom more generally, is deeply invested in death. The Basilica was erected to house the dead bones of the evangelist. Its treasury contains sumptuous reliquaries of gold and silver finely wrought and inlaid with priceless jewels, made to contain drops of the precious blood of Christ, or an arm or finger or skull of some venerated saint or martyr. In the glowing gold of the mosaics the themes of Christ crucified and Christ Pantocrator are inextricably connected: his death is precisely the basis of his power. And all points forward to a world beyond this one, a heavenly world of which this splendour is a pale reflection. The gateway to that world is death.

There could hardly be a more telling instance than San Marco of the complex interpellation of beauty, gender, violence and death as these themes have shaped and been shaped by Christendom. Its beauty draws forth endless wonder, but it is not innocent. The more its history and its symbolism is probed, the greater the ambiguities of creativity and violence. Perhaps it is particularly apposite for its contemporary impact that the enemy, the feared 'other' against whom the power of Venice was asserted, was Islam. Against this dreaded menace the whole force of church and state was arrayed, even while its wealth was derived in no small measure from its Crusades against the 'infidel' who served as the reason or excuse for the full assertion of its power.

The dissonances of beauty and violence, creativity and an investment in death, that characterize San Marco echo those which have resonated through Christendom from its earliest religious history. From the first words of the Bible as we have it today, religion in the West is linked with creativity and beauty that quickly gives way to violence.

> In the beginning God created the heavens and the earth ... And God
> saw everything that he had made, and behold, it was very good ...
>
> (Genesis 1.1, 31)

God creates order out of chaos, and then systematically brings into existence
earth and sea, the sun, moon and stars, plants and animals, and finally the
first human pair. Repeatedly God examines his handiwork, and each time
'God saw that it was good', until at the end of the creation week when he
looks at his completed work, 'behold, it was very good'. The Hebrew word
for 'good' here is *tob*; the translators of the Greek Septuagint rendered it as
kalon. It means both 'good' and 'beautiful'. In the story, it indicates more
than just that God was satisfied with the results of his labour, seeing it as
adequate or utilitarian; and more, too, than an ethical appraisal. Besides
these, there is an aesthetic dimension. God saw that the world, the product
of his creative effort, was beautiful.

On the face of it this creative beauty seems at the furthest remove from the
destructive violence which quickly follows. The Genesis story is a story of
the creation of a garden, in which all things flourish together in harmony.
And yet only a few pages later we find God engaging in what could be
described as the first military act: he sends an angel with 'a flaming sword
which turned every way' (Genesis 3.24) to do guard duty to keep humankind
out of the paradise which had been created for them. They forfeited such
bliss by their disobedience, and were punished by an existence of labour and
pain. Although God offers redemptive possibilities as the story continues,
men and women repeatedly fail to grasp them. From this point on it has
been a besetting temptation to Christian theologians to tell the story of religion in the West as a narrative of the struggle of the destructive impulses of
sinful humanity over against the redemptive creativity of the divine, the
conflict between violence and beauty.

But of course to tell the story in that way is to leave out the ambiguities
which make the telling worthwhile. Even the Genesis account is more complicated. There are hints that the violence is not just a result of human sin,
but is present before the first human pair is made. Indeed there is the barest
whisper of a suggestion – a whisper that will become a roar in the story of
the flood – that violence originates in God himself, his masculinity of a piece
with his self-assertion as a God of Battles who demands obedience on pain
of destruction. All this will become more apparent in later chapters, but
already from the beginning of the creation myth, things are not as peaceful
as they seem; and when we dig more deeply into it, we can find destabilizing
precursors of divine violence alongside divine creativity.

This is not what has been taught in Sunday School. As later Christian
theology would have it, God created the world out of nothing. He did not
shout or raise his voice. 'Let there be light', God says calmly, 'and there was
light' (1.3). In the Genesis myth the divine imposition of order upon chaos is

represented as a benign Spirit hovering, bird-like, over the waters; and creation is portrayed as a steady succession of events, the activity as orderly as the results which it produced. Yet even a bright Sunday School child will insist on the question: where did the chaos come from? And scholars, like children, must face the issue. Should the story of creation really be read as an account of calm creation *ex nihilo*, or is it in fact a story of divine struggle against chaos, similar to other violent creation myths from the ancient near east with which the Genesis story has much in common?

In the Babylonian *Enuma Elish*, for example, primordial chaos is personified as Tiamat, mother of gods; she is killed by Marduk who forms the ordered world out of her corpse. Egyptian creation stories are similarly violent: a battle of re-creation is enacted daily in which Re, the sun god, battles against Apophis, the dragon-like god of chaos. The writer (or editor) of Genesis chooses to leave out any reference to struggle; but the acknowledgement of chaos is like a barely repressed hint that all is not as calm as it at first seems. Moreover, elsewhere in the Bible there are references to the monsters of chaos which inhabit other near-eastern creation stories: Leviathan, Behemoth, Yam. Is it the case that the biblical writers have left all this behind? Or is it rather, as Timothy Beal has argued, that 'these chaos monsters are part of a divinity that is deeply divided within itself about the future viability of the cosmos and of life as humankind knows it?' (Beal 2002:22).

Whatever we say about the creation story itself, divine violence quickly asserts itself in the Genesis text. Even though God is portrayed at the outset as transforming chaos into paradise without struggle, before six chapters are complete, God is so frustrated with what he has made that he plans and carries out genocide. He is displeased with humans because they are 'only evil continually', and he wishes he had never made them.

> So the Lord said, 'I will blot out man whom I have created from the face of the ground, man and beast and creeping things and birds of the air, for I am sorry that I have made them.'
>
> (Genesis 6.7)

The story of the flood, like the creation story, has parallels in other near-eastern texts, especially the *Epic of Gilgamesh*, in which the primordial waters of chaos overwhelm the world and destroy all living things. The Genesis writer, like the author of Gilgamesh, chooses to focus on the one man (with his family and selected animals) upon whom God decides to have mercy. Accordingly, the biblical story of the flood is usually read as the story of the marvellous rescue of Noah and his family in the ark, along with the animals who come two by two for their preservation. But on the other side of that story is an act of unimaginable violence, inflicted not by sinful human beings but by God, in which all humankind is exterminated together with all animals except those kept safe in the ark.

> All flesh died that moved upon the earth, birds, cattle, beasts, all
> swarming creatures that swarm upon the earth, and every man ... [God]
> blotted out every living thing that was upon the face of the ground, man
> and animals and creeping things and birds of the air; they were blotted
> from the earth ...
>
> (Genesis 7.21–23)

What could the animals possibly have done to deserve wholesale drowning?
And even if the people had been sinful, could God not think of any methods
to correct them and teach them to do better? As the Bible represents it, God
did not even try. His immediate reaction was to decide to kill everyone and
everything. Violence, the text implies, must be at the heart of the divine.
God's actions are astonishing in their gratuitous cruelty.

Just as astonishing is the fact that the story has regularly been read in
Christendom as an account of divine mercy to the few in the ark, not as a
story of horrific divine brutality to the many who perished. It is as though
someone today planned and carried out nuclear holocaust which exterminated all life on earth except for one family and their livestock: should the
perpetrator of this deed be venerated for his great mercy? If Hitler had
managed to kill all Jews except for one small group that he set apart, should
he be revered because he saved them? How we read the Bible reveals as
much about ourselves as about what the Bible actually says. What do we
think we are doing if we airbrush out the violence, ignore the ambiguities,
and read the story of the flood as a story of divine care and compassion?

I am of course not making claims about the historicity of the flood or of a
six-day creation, but about the ways in which God is portrayed by the writer(s)
of these stories and accepted by their readers. I shall have more to say in a
later chapter about narratives and their afterlife, the way in which a foundational myth or narrative shapes the self-identity and subsequent behaviour
of a culture. What I wish to emphasize here is the depiction of the divine
within a thematic of violence, a thematic which is continued in such narratives as the Passover, the drowning of the Egyptians in the Red Sea, the
extermination of the inhabitants of the 'promised land', and in the New
Testament the representation of God as the sort of father whose wrath can
be appeased only by the torture and death of his innocent son. As God is
portrayed in the Bible, his cruel, brutal and bloodthirsty characteristics are
shown as vividly as are his mercy, love and compassion. Yet Christians (and
Jews) who have accepted these narratives as scripture and thus as revelatory
of God have often managed to ignore or repress representations of divine
violence and have contrived to develop a theology of God as unambiguously
loving and compassionate. The violence is hidden in plain sight in the biblical texts, hidden only because its religious readers have for centuries averted
their eyes and repressed their consciousness of the central place it occupies in
the configurations of religion in the West.

One of the techniques of this repression is implicit identification of the reader with those who are in divine favour, and the readers' enemies with those on whom the destruction is visited. Thus Christian readers read themselves into the flood narratives as those who were with Noah in the safety of the ark: the Church was the 'Ark of Salvation'. All those outside the Church would utterly perish. And if theologians could not quite permit themselves to gloat over such wholesale destruction of their enemies, they could disguise their delight as rejoicing in the justice of God, who saves his own and damns the rest. Again, the Church saw itself as God's Chosen People, liberated from the oppressive 'Egypt' of this world and carrying out God's work in subduing its enemies. All such interpretations depend upon a set of reader identifications of 'us' and 'them': 'we' are the good on whom God's favour is rightly showered, 'they' are the evil who deserve violence and destruction. Of course if we were once to identify ourselves with those on whom God visits his violence in narratives like that of the flood or the conquest of Canaan or the visions of heaven and hell we would read the passages very differently. But for the most part they are written to encourage reader identification with those who are chosen, loved and blessed; and centuries of theological writing and popular religion have reinforced this reassuring stance.

In consequence, not only is attention not focused on the ambiguities of divine creativity and divine destruction, but those who take upon themselves the status of the people of God can easily convince themselves that their own violence is done in God's name and at God's behest. How many wars have been fought in the West, from Constantine's conversion to the American-led occupation of Iraq, under the explicit or implicit banner of a Crusade or Holy War? How much violence has been done to 'indigenous' or 'primitive' peoples because they are 'idolators' who do not obey divine laws or structure their societies according to the patriarchal system of the Bible? How many times has the notion of being a chosen people with a promised land been the basis of unspeakable atrocities towards those who, inconveniently, were already in the land in question, from the Europeans' appropriation of the Americas and the genocide of the indigenous population, to the Vortrekkers' claims in South Africa, and continuing in the present in the displacement of contemporary Palestinians? It would hardly be possible to overstate the interconnection of religion with the intense and escalating violence of the West, or the extent to which the perpetrators of violence have represented themselves as carrying out God's work: bringing civilization, democracy, or liberation, in comparison with which atrocities could be glossed over in silence, and plunder or booty – whether the bronze horses of San Marco, the gold of the Incas, or the oil of Iraq – is a just reward. Whether or not any of these activities were or are legitimate is not my present point: my point is only the simple and obvious one that Christendom in the West is fathoms deep in violence and supports this violence by its reading of its foundation texts. This is of course not to say that other religions are not also involved in violence: obviously they have been and still are. My concern, however, is not to analyse specks in the eyes of others but to shift the log jam in our own perceptions. Only in that way can we hope to find resources for change.

Some of these resources are in the foundation texts themselves, often in the very ambiguity which has too often been flattened out by subsequent readers. Even in the utter catastrophe of the flood, for example, an alternative to violence presents itself. God sends a rainbow, whose translucent beauty shines with the divine promise that God will never do it again, will never send another flood that will destroy all humankind. God promises that when he sends clouds and rain upon the earth, then 'when the bow is in the clouds I will look upon it and remember the everlasting covenant' which God makes with humankind (Genesis 9.16). Beauty stands against violence as a reminder to God himself not to indulge in the violence which has characterized him up to that point in the narrative. It is not an innocent beauty: without the rain there would have been no rainbow. Nevertheless, godly killing is held in check by beauty. Its potential to transform the violent world arches over the earth and makes its creatures sing.

Yet in spite of the rainbow, in the pages of the Hebrew Bible and its Christian sequel which follows and claims this story, violence regularly comes to the fore. Destruction and creativity, death and beauty appear and reappear in undecidable tension. It is true that the killing is not usually attributed to God in the same direct way as it is in the story of the flood; nevertheless the slaughter of animals for blood sacrifices, the slaughter of people to exterminate them from the land claimed by God's people, even the slaughter of Jesus as the 'lamb of God' are all represented as the enactment of the divine will. Ever and again, violence displaces beauty as central to religious thought and practice. Yet ever and again beauty stands as a challenge to destruction, even when it is built upon the spoils of violence. The rainbow arches over the desolation left by the flood; the temple of Jerusalem, opulent as San Marco with the spoils of plundered peoples, is to be a house of prayer for all nations; even the lamb of God 'slaughtered from the foundation of the world' is also simultaneously the prince of peace. The biblical writings and the history of early Christendom can indeed be read as a struggle between violence and beauty, but not in simplistic terms of divine beauty and creativity against sinful human destructiveness. The task, rather, is to discern *both* how Christendom from its foundational texts has legitimated and valorized violence *and* how it provides resources for creativity and peace. How does beauty serve as a sign, like the pledge of the rainbow, of creative and life-giving alternatives?

Christendom has commonly held as one of its central concerns, questions of death and the possibility of life after death. Death, the last judgement, heaven and hell have been depicted in graphic terms by theologians and artists throughout the West, their imaginations often more fertile in portraying the horrors of hell than the beauties of heaven. Significant as all this is, however, I shall show in this volume that much of this preoccupation with death and other worlds in the religious thought of the West is not so much with death as such, death as a natural end to life, but with death as violence: death as punishment, sacrifice, warfare or martyrdom. My overall project, of which this is the second volume, is a genealogy of death, tracing the sediments of death in the Western symbolic and the possibilities of its subversion by beauty. In Volume 1, *The Foundations of Violence*, I traced the constructions of death in the classical worlds of Greece and Rome, with some early indications of how these constructions have shaped Western consciousness through modernity and beyond. In this volume I propose to go back to the other main source of Western thought, its religious roots, and see how religious constructions of death and violence underlie Western values and actions. As in the previous volume, I shall show that these religious constructions of violence are always gendered; and indeed that men's fear of women (or of femaleness) is often implicated in religious violence. Moreover, I shall show again that violence in its various guises represented choices, choices which could have been made otherwise. Running alongside the discourses of death and destruction, and often submerged, are traces of alternative discourses of beauty, creativity and life, which could have been chosen, and which I shall try to lift up. Could they, in some form, be chosen yet?

Is religion inherently violent? Or, since that is impossibly broad, are the monotheistic religions that have shaped the West inherently violent? Is violence an aberration: a deviation from the true path of Judaism, Christianity and Islam, which properly understood are peaceable and creative? Or are both these possibilities undecidedly true? These questions have moved in recent years from merely academic interest to matters of urgent insistence, as ostensibly secular postmodernity is caught up in wars of religion, from 'God Bless America' and 'Jihad' to those who would appeal to the three mono-theisms for the paths of peace. We cannot evade the questions of religious necrophilia, religious preoccupations with godly killing. It is urgent to find alternative paths, paths of life and beauty, which will offer hope and joy against destruction and loss.

In the previous volume I called this celebration of life 'natality', a conceptual category over against the category of 'mortality', which has dominated Western thought. In the chapters that follow I shall explore the concept more fully, especially in its relation to beauty and creativity. Natality is linked to the fact that we are born; but it is not reducible to birth any more than the category of mortality is reducible to death. Natality, rather, is the potential for newness and for hope, the creative possibilities of beginning again that are introduced into the world by the fact that we are all natals. To what extent has Christendom fostered natality in the West, and to what extent has it suppressed creativity and beauty in its necrophilia, its obsession with violence and death?

The preoccupation with death which characterizes modernity, and its expression in multiple forms of violence, is a preoccupation which has many layers in the collective consciousness of the West. In the previous volume I discussed the question of a collective consciousness of a deathly habitus, and began to ponder ways in which it could be subverted. I also discussed some of the layers of violence which have sedimented into Western consciousness from the classical civilizations of Greece and Rome. The beautiful death of the young warrior, immortalized by the poet's song, is still a part of every Remembrance Sunday and still forms part of the rhetoric of military commitment. The Platonic idea that death is the release of the soul from the prison-house of the body, and the Aristotelian notion that the rational soul is most akin to the divine, continue to reverberate in discussions of death and immortality. Meanwhile the death-dealing ideals of the *Pax Romana*, which kept the citizens of Rome fed and content by means of continuous warfare at the edges of empire, and entertained them by games and spectacles of ever-escalating violence, have many echoes in the empires of modernity, from Napoleon to the red map of the British world and to American hyperpower hegemony.

As important as are these sediments of classical necrophilia for the habitus of violence that shapes the West, however, the religious stream runs even more deeply and has deposited sediments which are if anything even more significant than those from classical civilizations. The stories and symbols of the Hebrew Bible and the Christian New Testament, refracted, combined, and divided in countless ways from their origins through medieval thinkers and into modernity, continue to construct thought and behaviour patterns in the twenty-first century.

As I argued in the case of classical civilizations, so too I shall show that in different ways these narratives of religious violence are always gendered, adding layer upon layer to the structures of patriarchy in the West. Moreover they are always related to beauty; indeed what we *mean* by beauty is to a large extent framed by the two sources of classical civilization and religious narrative. Then too, just as we found in relation to the dominant voices and events of Greece and Rome, so again in the Hebrew and Christian accounts there are alternative voices, some of which can still be discerned if we take the trouble to listen for them. Although much has been erased, silenced beyond recall, there are strong strands of counter narrative which celebrate life, natality and flourishing and refuse to define life in terms of death or allow beauty to be appropriated by violence.

This volume, while it can be read on its own, will therefore run parallel to Volume 1. I shall select some of the most dominant and pervasive discourses of death in the Hebrew Bible and early Christendom, discourses which continue to shape twenty-first century thought and action. I will show the gendered nature of these discourses, and their relation to beauty and its displacement. I will also study to find voices of dissent and resistance, voices of hope and natality whose echoes may yet offer redemptive and transformative possibilities, rainbows of hope in a violent world.

Outline of the work

Part 1 provides a theoretical grounding for the project and examines some of the key underlying concepts. Challenging the notions of violence within the biblical material and seeking to question the nature of violence and the displacement of beauty, this section explores theories of violence around the idea of difference and shows how previous models of violence have failed. Chapter 1 questions definitions offered by Hent de Vries (2002) and Regina Schwartz (1997) and seeks to locate these theories in the work of Levinas and Derrida, who see violence in the conceptual and in the nature of desire and sacrifice. These problems are then critically explored in relation to Girard's work on sacrifice. Girard's model is seen as not only as limited in scope, neglecting issues of war and gender and their religious justification, but based on the desire of mimesis, which assumes a basic lack. Resisting such interpretations, an alternative model of desire is built on creativity and difference. Violence is overcome by offering creative alternatives. Chapter 2 offers a narrative understanding of violence, exploring its function rather than its essence. Drawing on the work of Michel Foucault, Hannah Arendt and Adrianna Cavarero, it is not only shown that violence is embedded in narrative and shapes Western identity, but that there are counter-narratives which can empower change. The biblical narrative, whether fiction or history, provides self-identity for a people, even in secular society, but the problem with such narratives is the gendered violence they propagate. While requiring account of this violent history, it is not enough to remain with the negative. There is a need to find an alternative. It is argued that there are different ways of telling the narrative and recovering the hidden narratives of birth, beauty and flourishing within the Judaic-Christian tradition, which is the objective of the book.

After the theoretical mapping, Parts 2 and 3 of the work trace the genealogy of violence and creativity in the Judaic-Christian tradition, providing further assessment of the foundational texts of Western culture. Part 2 documents the Hebrew Bible and its attitudes towards death. Chapter 3 sets the scene and locates the concerns of the biblical material with blood, death and violence inside the problem of scriptural authority, with its patriarchy and misogyny. At the same time, the hermeneutical problems and critical historical studies are seen to allow for new readings that reveal beauty against destruction and creativity against violence; it opens the space for the counter-narrative. Chapter 4 begins a series of specific studies of the Hebrew Bible according to the hermeneutic of necrophilia and natality. It reveals the triangulation of sin, death and gender and uncovers the violence within the covenant, through its exclusion of the other.

The first major theme to be examined as part of God's covenant with Israel in Chapter 5 is that of monotheism. God, in addition to declaring that he has chosen the Jewish people as his elect, also makes a demand of them – that they worship no other gods. These two exclusionary features of the covenant have certain disastrous consequences for those who have not been so favoured. Among the disparate excluded people or rivals who become subject to forms of violent discrimination are the then inhabitants of the promised land, fertility goddesses and foreign women. The basic question is whether the identity of ancient Israel was forged solely in the image of a jealous god who endorses divisions and conquest rather than negotiation and co-existence. The second element of the covenant that merits exploration in Chapter 6 is that of ritual sacrifice which in those days was not only confined to Israel. Nonetheless, the related phenomena of purity and violence raise questions about the legacy of such a mode of honouring and placating a divine figure. The hierarchal system that is thus promoted also results in rules and taboos that serve to reinforce the mores of a patriarchal society. There are, however, countervailing voices to be heard and these are celebrated in Chapter 7. Words praising the beauty and glory of God as well as the wonders do resound in the Hebrew scriptures. The metaphor of flourishing is also often invoked. Yet the contrary metaphor of salvation often intervenes in a manner that portends less harmonious modes of being. This duality gives rise to an inconsistent heritage that still persists where beauty and flourishing are in constant danger of displacement.

Chapter 8 is basically an introduction to Part 3 which analyses Christianity's own ambivalent history. Attention is paid again specifically to the problematic status of beauty and its beleaguered existence during the centuries of Christianity's extensive influence and expansion. The principal challenge that is raised is whether the absence of any strong advocacy for a worldview that promotes wonder and creativity is responsible for the violent outbreaks that have accompanied the spread of Christianity. Investigating this intriguing thesis, Chapter 9 focuses on Jesus's preaching and ministry, and specifically on the term, 'kingdom of heaven'. The issue at hand is not one of determining the most relevant of the various interpretations of this expression, but to assess their respective repercussions. The main point of contention is whether this kingdom was a reference to an otherworldly spiritual realm, divorced from any political entanglements, or a reform movement to change the condition of people's lives on earth. Possibly there will never be consensus on this issue. Unfortunately, however, dire events have resulted from a decision to adopt one as authoritative. Yet such decisions are neither inevitable nor irrevocable. Chapter 10 catalogues the untoward effects that resulted from medieval Christianity's fixation on death and the threat of eternal punishment. This orientation was supported by a form of forensic theology that emphasized sin, guilt and judgement. Such an otherworldly preoccupation also manifested itself in acts of violence, not only against infidels and heretics but also against one's own body in extreme acts of mortification.

In contrast to such concerns with personal salvation, the final two chapters in Part 3 are previously published essays of Grace Jantzen that speak to alternative indications that she has discerned in the Christian tradition. These chapters have been included to provide evidence of the direction in which she had hoped to develop her thoughts on this topic that is crucial for the volume. She detected such alternative voices that professed love for this world and promoted beauty, not just in certain biblical passages, but in the writings of holy men and women. In Chapter 11 Grace Jantzen turns to the work of medieval mystics, in particular to that of Julian of Norwich. Julian provides a vibrant example of the rich resources that are available. She describes her joyful appreciation of the wonders of creation that she reveres as a manifestation of the plenitude of God's love for this world. Then in Chapter 12, an alternate reading of salvation based on a theology of flourishing is presented. Such a proposal encourages a celebration of one's present life, despite the dangers and obstacles inherent in existence, and also supports the creation of a just community where all may flourish. Natality, as conceived by Jantzen, draws together many elements that resonate with ideas she has adapted from Hannah Arendt. Both of these women, despite the destructive violence of their times, responded to their respective contemporary situations with an affirmation of life. They both undertook, in their different ways, to foster the ever-renewing springs of creative responsiveness that bespeaks a cherishing of life in this world.

In her delineation of this vision, Grace Jantzen was adamant that it was not her intention to establish another simplistic binary where beauty and natality were opposed to the forces of violence and death. She viewed life as an inevitable mixture of both. Her purpose was to provide a needed counterbalance to the prominence that has been given to death and certain necrophilic constraints on the fullness of life. It was her hope that by acknowledging specific decisions and turning points, the predominance of destructive violence could be resisted, if never completely erased. Perhaps it is only fitting that Grace Jantzen should have the last word:

> My intention is not to set up binaries: mortality/natality; destruction/ creativity. Instead, I shall be suggesting that the fundamental imbalance of attention and emphasis is part of the violent pattern of the West, and that this imbalance is in urgent need of attention if we are to redeem the present (2004:6).

Part One

Beauty, violence and story

Chapter 1

Violence, desire and creation

The Genesis story in the Hebrew Bible, with its account of a beautiful garden forfeited by a descent into sin and violence, is often taken as the paradigmatic narrative of creation for Christendom. It is not the only biblical account of creation, nor the only one in which we find the ambiguities of violence and beauty. The prophet Isaiah, for example, describes a vision of a new creation, made by God to replace the present world of trouble, destruction and pain. He declares the proclamation of God:

> For behold, I create new heavens and a new earth;
> And the former things shall not be remembered or come to mind.
> But be glad and rejoice forever in that which I create;
> For behold, I create Jerusalem a rejoicing, and her people a joy ...

There follows a description of a Utopian Jerusalem – so different from that conflict-ridden city in Isaiah's time or in ours – in which there is no more distress or violence. It is a beautiful city where people live together in peace and harmony. Even the wolf and the lamb are at peace. All flourish together. Violence has no place, for:

> They shall not hurt or destroy in all my holy mountain, says the Lord.
> (Isaiah 65.17–25)

Similar accounts of a 'new heaven and a new earth' also occur elsewhere in the Bible, notably in the book of Revelation, where the writer describes 'the holy city, new Jerusalem, coming down out of heaven from God, prepared as a bride adorned for her husband' (Revelation 21.2). All God's enemies have been defeated and shut out, and the people of God live with him in unimaginable beauty and splendour. The city has 'the glory of God, its radiance like a most rare jewel, like a jasper, clear as crystal'.

> The wall was built of jasper, while the city was pure gold, clear as glass.
> The foundations of the wall of the city were adorned with every jewel ...

And the twelve gates were twelve pearls, each of the gates made of a single pearl, and the street of the city was pure gold, transparent as glass.

(Revelation 21.18–21)

Through the city flows a 'river of the water of life, bright as crystal', beside which grows 'the tree of life with its twelve kinds of fruit ... and the leaves of the tree were for the healing of the nations' (Revelation 22.1–2).

These visions of a heavenly Jerusalem of peace and beauty stand as parallels to the Genesis story of the first paradise. But whereas the Genesis story represents the beginning of all things, this new creation represents the end. It will not be a scene of sin, disaster and expulsion as was the Garden of Eden; nor will God exert his own violence upon it as he did in the flood that followed the sinfulness of early humanity. Rather, the new paradise will go on forever, with no more sin, pain, or violence, whether inflicted by God or by people. The newness of the new Jerusalem is a cancellation or forgetting of what has gone before: the violence and anguish of the past no longer come to mind, as 'God himself ... will wipe away every tear from their eyes ... for the former things have passed away' (Revelation 21.4).

Nevertheless, it is obvious that the writers of each of these accounts have violence very much on their minds as they write. The ambiguity of the Genesis stories is paralleled by the ambiguities of these new accounts of creation, in which peace and beauty prevails only because of the expulsion of those who would wreak havoc. Isaiah represents the enemies of God's people as utterly crushed; the writer of the Apocalypse has all the opponents of the true believers cast into hell with Satan forever. Just as in the case of the flood, violence and beauty appear in tension: a tension that becomes unbearable if we put ourselves into the position of those who are outside rather than those whom God has favoured.

In the rest of this book I want to explore some of the specific forms which that tension between violence and beauty, necrophilia and natality, took in the Hebrew Bible and in early Christianity, continuing the genealogy of death which I began in Volume I, and showing some of the places of resistance. Before I do so, however, I propose in this chapter to explore some influential theoretical accounts of the relationship between religion and violence, keeping in mind the tension with beauty that keeps reappearing in biblical texts. What is the relationship between creativity and violence? Can there be creation without violence, or is any creative act always already violent? Obviously creativity and beauty are not the same; but if, as seems the case, creativity is needed to bring forth beauty, then must we say that beauty also is necessarily linked to violence? How does newness enter the world, the newness that is needed if there is to be constructive change to the violence of the present world order? Does God bring it about, or do we? Implicit in all these questions are the nagging issues of who is this God and who is this 'we'? What is the gender, race and cultural context that is presupposed, and how might things change if these presuppositions were destabilized? None of the thinkers whose ideas of violence I shall consider has much to say about beauty or creativity. However, I shall argue that although beauty is ignored in their work, and indeed is also pushed to the margins in the Bible and in the theology of Christendom, it still offers a place of resistance from which violence can be challenged. In the final section of this chapter I shall begin an exploration of what that entails.

The violence of creation?

Is creativity itself violent? Could there be creation without violence? At first sight it would seem that creativity is the very opposite of destruction, and therefore is contrary to violence; yet as we saw in the Introduction, the ambiguities are already present in the biblical text. It might be thought, therefore, when influential scholars have defined violence in ways that render creativity itself violent they are in fact closer to the uncomfortable tensions of the Bible than they themselves realize. However, I believe that that is not the case. I propose to begin, therefore, by examining these definitions. I shall argue, in the first place, that they are incorrect or harmful as definitions; and shall show later how creativity is essential if we are to develop alternatives to violence; and that while no human activity is unambiguous, violence is not inherent in creativity itself. What I want to get at is how beauty has been displaced or stood in ambiguous tension with violence; and what are the forms which creativity has taken and perhaps can take again to bring newness into the world?

Everything is violent

I begin with a definition of violence offered by Hent de Vries (2002); but before I address his account directly, I want to pay tribute to the significance and timeliness of his work. Clearly it is enormously important at the beginning of this third millennium, in which God is called upon with increasing regularity to justify or condemn acts of violence that escalate in scope and in cruelty, that we look closely, as de Vries has done, at the relationships between religion and violence.

Until relatively recently, religious scholars, like many others, tended to assume that the world was, for good or ill, becoming increasingly secular, at least in its public face, and that such religious belief and experience as there still is belongs in the private sphere. Religion, it was thought, is not (or should not be) involved in scientific experiments or the stock exchange or the master discourses and disciplines of modernity. But with the violent destruction of the Twin Towers in the name of Allah, and the violent military campaigns against Afghanistan and Iraq in the name of 'God Bless

America', a new era erupted in which it became clear – as it should have been all along – that religion is a potent force in legitimizing violence. Many religious scholars were caught napping, with very little in the way of conceptual resources either to understand the eruption of violence in the name of religion or to see how religion could act as a counterforce. de Vries was one of the few scholars who had seriously focused on the relationship of violence and religion, and was therefore in a position to comment intelligently on what is going on.

Nevertheless, when it comes specifically to de Vries' definition of violence, I have a problem. de Vries says,

> Violence, in both the widest possible and the most elementary senses of the word, entails any cause, any justified or illegitimate force, that is exerted – physically or otherwise – by one thing (event or instance, group or person, and, perhaps, word and object) on another. Violence thus defined finds its prime model – its source, force, and counterforce – in key elements of the tradition called the religious. It can be seen as the very element of religion.
>
> (de Vries 2002:1)

I do not find this definition helpful. If, as he says, violence is involved in *every* exertion of force, even when it is justified and even when it is non-physical; and if moreover this exertion is not restricted to the intentional exertion of force by persons but includes also events and even words, then nothing is left out. Everything is violent. Creation is violent; so is destruction. Religion is violent; but religion is also the 'counterforce' to violence.

Now, although it is important to be aware of ambiguities, it also seems to me that it is vitally important to have tools for discrimination between violence and non-violence, between those exertions of force, physical or not, which are destructive and those which are creative. If we say that *every* exertion of force is violent, then the effect is to evacuate the term 'violence' of all specific meaning, and with it all possibility of moral evaluation. So for example the force of persuasion that a dog-owner exerts in training, all her praise and puppy treats, could not be differentiated from the force she would exert if she were to beat up the puppy instead. The force of an argument and the force of a bomb would be the same, in quality if not in quantity. Since religion, even when it operates only by moral persuasion, exerts a moral force, all religious acts and beliefs are violent. So, obviously, therefore, is any act of creation.

I suggest that if violence is defined so broadly, then rather than being helpful, the definition becomes useless as a way of understanding the function of violence in the paths that religion is taking in the world today. de Vries draws on the work of Levinas and Derrida, among others, to connect the ideas of violence and religion and to explore how repressed violence can be disguised as friendship, and hidden hostilities can distort the face which should be the face of love. Much of what he has to say in his book is profoundly important: I shall return to Levinas and Derrida below. But the definition of violence with which de Vries begins is, I suggest, so wide as to include everything; and thereby becomes unhelpful as a tool to understand the ways in which religion fosters or colludes in the escalating violence of the world, and also the ways in which religion can make for peace. This is not insightful ambiguity; it is rather a matter of tarring everything with the same brush.

Violence as boundary

An alternative definition of violence, which again I find problematic, is given by Regina Schwartz in her recent book *The Curse of Cain* (Schwartz 1997). Again, this is an immensely important book: I shall draw on its insights in a later chapter. However, when Schwartz asserts that 'violence is the very construction of the Other', so that 'imagining identity as an act of distinguishing and separating from others, of boundary making and line drawing, is the most frequent and fundamental act of violence we commit' (5), she thereby defines the term 'violence' in such a way that it indicates every kind of demarcation or exclusion. In her account, even to define a term is already a violent act because it excludes some things from the meaning of the term while including others. Now, if this were correct, then the only path to non-violence would be by collapsing everything into a Sameness, so that all of reality is a thick soup so fully blended that nothing can be distinguished from anything else.

By contrast, I would suggest that it is not the act of distinguishing and separating into self and others which is violent in and of itself; indeed such separation is essential if we are ever to experience the richness which respectful mutual interaction with others who are genuinely different from ourselves can bring. Violence enters, I would argue, not when difference is *defined* but when difference is perceived as *dangerous*, so that hierarchies are imposed and force is exerted to keep the hierarchies in place. Schwartz's important insights on perceived scarcity and competition for resources rather than mutuality and generosity which she explores in the rest of her book can be preserved, I suggest, without holding to her view that the construction of the other is itself violent. In fact, elsewhere in her book she redefines the concept of violence in a more nuanced way, which specifically repudiates her earlier definition (though she does not acknowledge this). She says,

> Violence is not ... a consequence of defining identity as either particular or universal. Violence stems from any conception of identity forged negatively against the Other, an invention of identity that parasitically depends upon the invention of some Other to be reviled.
>
> (Schwartz 1997:88)

In this passage Schwartz is in effect moving from an attempt at a definition of the essence of violence to an analysis of its function, an analysis which she carries through with specific reference to the biblical narratives of ancient Israel; I shall revisit it in a later chapter.

Her earlier definition of violence as differentiation continues, however, to percolate through her book. This definition has a direct bearing on questions of creation. If all forms of differentiation or separation were violent, then to create would be the paradigmatic act of violence. Newness can only arise if it is different from what preceded it: if it were not different it would not be new. So if difference itself indicates violence, then creating anything, making anything new, is a violent act. When we consider the biblical stories of creation, whether the Genesis myth of origins or Isaiah's vision of 'new heavens and a new earth', these are stories of the emergence of newness, where things that are made are separated both from their creator and from anything that had gone before; an ordered cosmos replaces chaos; a world of peace and harmony replaces a world of conflict and destruction. Even if one holds (as I do, see Jantzen 1998:270) to a very strong sense of divine imma-nence in the world, so that all things in some sense participate in the divine, it is still the case that the stars and flowers and birds and mountains are not an undifferentiated soup, a 'night in which all cats are grey'; rather, they are glorious in their vibrant particularity. In their identity, each different from the other, is their beauty; and in their interaction they can flourish.

Thus, so far from this difference indicating violence, it should be under-stood as the very opposite. Creativity, and with it the beauty of particularity, is an antidote to destruction, not its enactment. Creativity invites harmony and flourishing, where the flourishing of one is interdependent with the flourish-ing of all. Although that which has been created can fall all too quickly into violent and destructive behaviour, the violence is not in the creative act itself, the act from which newness and beauty arises. Rather, violence arises when the mutuality of creation is denied, when difference is perceived as threatening rather than enriching, and force is exerted to dominate or stifle the potential of others.

I have not yet mentioned gender, but it is easy to see how the same ana-lysis applies. In the original creation story, God creates Eve out of Adam, giving her a separate identity. Now, suppose one were to hold that the very definition of difference is violent. On such a view, it would follow that vio-lence between the sexes would be built into this creation of male and female. I would argue the opposite: namely that it is precisely because Eve is a person in her own right, separate from Adam, that the two can enter into mutually fulfilling interaction. It is not in their distinctness that violence lies; on the contrary, their distinctness is what makes their relationship possible. Violence arises, rather, when their distinctness is taken as threatening, and made a pretext for the domination of one by the other. To generalize, I would argue (contrary to the implications of Regina Schwartz's definition of violence) that gender difference, like race or class difference, or difference of all other sorts, is not itself violent nor the cause of violence. Violence in gender relations, as in all other relations, arises when difference is treated as a danger rather than as a resource, so that hostility rather than mutuality characterizes the interaction. Creativity is not violent in itself; newness can enter the world in a way that enhances peace and flourishing. Indeed I would argue that creativity and the beauty that can emerge from it is precisely what can stand against violence and destruction. Violence is ugly.

Violence and the face

Both de Vries' definition of violence which gives it universal scope and Schwartz's definition of violence as differentiation can be understood in relation to the work of Levinas and Derrida, since it is in their work that the concept of violence is given a broad remit. Levinas writes self-consciously and deliberately in the shadow of the Holocaust, in which many of his family and millions of his people perished. It has been persuasively argued that the Holocaust was not an aberration of modernity or a reversion to primitive barbarism, but rather was an expression of the 'progress' of modernity and its efficient, bureaucratic rationality; it was, to borrow Zygmunt Bauman's telling image, not like a picture on the wall of normality, neatly framed and separate from the rest of life, but rather a window through which one must view modernity in a much less complacent light (Bauman 1989:vii–viii). How was it, then, that the rationality of modernity could allow for – or even lead to – the horrors of Auschwitz? How must the relationship between rationality and violence be understood? The question had particular poignancy for Levinas because of the unsavoury complicity of Heidegger with Nazism. Heidegger had been Levinas' friend and mentor, his guide into philosophical thinking. If such thinking could lead to, or at least comply with, the Holocaust, how must it be re-evaluated?

Heidegger had contended in his philosophy for the primacy of Being, and for the relation of beings to Being. It would follow, therefore, that to come to a rational understanding of beings one could do so only by seeing them in relation to Being. As Levinas says,

> To comprehend the particular being is already to place oneself beyond the particular. To comprehend is to be related to the particular that only exists through knowledge, which is always knowledge of the universal.
>
> (Levinas 1996:5)

But this will not do when the particular being is a person, an other with whom we come face to face. Our primary task and invitation is not then conceptualization but sympathy and love. If, in encounter with the other, all one does is name them, grasp them in the order of being, then although rationality may be satisfied, Levinas argues that the being of the other has been violated.

> That which escapes comprehension in the other is him [*sic*], a being. I cannot negate him partially, in violence, in grasping him within the horizon of being in general and possessing him … When I have grasped the other in the opening of being in general, as an element of the world where I stand, where I have seen him *on the horizon*, I have not looked at him in the face, I have not encountered his face … To be in relation to the other face to face is to be unable to kill.
>
> (Levinas 1996:9)

Why 'kill'? Why should encounter with the other engender a desire for violence rather than for love? The masculinist assumptions, including the urge to kill, have been rightly challenged by feminist thinkers (Jantzen 1998:238–43; Joy, 1993). Levinas is appropriating the famous master–slave dialectic of Hegel's *Phenomenology*, in which Hegel writes of the desire for recognition and the willingness to struggle to the death to obtain it. For Hegel, and especially for Hegelians like Kojève who influenced twentieth-century French thinkers including Levinas, this master–slave image serves as a model for the progress of philosophy itself (which is also history and politics); new concepts emerge through the violent clash of old concepts opposed to each other. It is in the light of this dialectic that the idea of the violence of the concept takes shape: as Derrida encapsulates Levinas' position, 'Predication is the first violence' (Derrida 1978:147).

If it is indeed the case that philosophical rationality is thus built at every stage upon a scaffold of violence, then it is unsurprising that the rationality of modernity would find expression in Auschwitz. Indeed we can only expect to see violence escalate in extent and brutality; and this escalation is not contrary to rationality but is its outworking. Modernity is built on a desire to know, and to master by knowledge; it thus has violence at its conceptual heart.

Against the 'violence of the concept' inherent in a philosophy of Being, Levinas proposes ethics as first philosophy. This is why, for Levinas, the face is of supreme importance. The face of the other may engender my desire, but it can never be possessed, even conceptually, and still remain other. As Adriaan Peperzak has put it,

> The reduction of particulars to universality is the first theoretical form of violence … It is impossible to get hold of another without reducing her to what she is not, i.e. without killing her. The only way for another to come to the fore is to confront me with the nudity, i.e. the non-universality, of her face. The source of light, due to which we 'know' another, is not to be found in Being, but in the face that looks at me.
>
> (Peperzak 1997:52)

In short, since conceptual knowledge has been defined as knowledge that relates the particular to the universal, and since such reduction is always violent, the 'violence of the concept' characterizes the whole history of Western philosophy. From this perspective it is easy to see how it is that writers like de Vries and Schwartz, influenced by Levinas' thinking, assert the ubiquity of violence. Every concept, every distinction or differentiation, is violent from the ground up.

According to Levinas, the only solution, the path of non-violence, is in face-to-face encounter, an encounter which concerns itself with the particular individual who confronts me in need or distress, and thus puts *me* – rather than a concept – in question.

> There is ... the very uprightness of the face, its upright exposure, without defense ... there is an essential poverty in the face; the proof of this is that one tries to mask this poverty by putting on poses, by taking on a countenance. The face is exposed, menaced, as if inviting us to an act of violence. At the same time, the face is what forbids us to kill.
>
> (Levinas 1985:86)

Leaving aside for a moment the recurrent leap to the idea of killing, we can see that the central burden of Levinas' thought is that ethics must replace ontology. Good must take priority over Being; not some abstract or theorized Good but direct response to the immediate appeal of the face of the other. Violence cannot be overcome by reason; it can only be overcome by Good, a Good which may require self-sacrifice.

> The call of the Other disrupts *and rules* the order of Being ... the ethical is the rejection of murder. This might lead to the torture or sacrifice of the one held hostage to the ethical ... Being sacrificed for Others and subjectivity are one and the same in a being that is a being-for-the-Other.
>
> (Peperzak 1997:225–6)

Levinas' profound summons to ethical response to the violent horrors of modernity deserves thorough consideration, and I will return to it in a later volume. (See also Derrida 1978; Peperzak 1995, 1997.) Here I shall confine myself to two points, both of which are related to the definition of violence.

In the first place, although Levinas connects violence with the conceptual, and seeks to overcome it with the ethical, Derrida has argued convincingly that one cannot escape conceptualization even in ethical response. In 'Violence and Metaphysics' (Derrida 1978), Derrida shows that even to recognize the other, to respond to their particularity, requires that they are in some sense named, seen as individual and differentiated from others, not least in their specific need. But this means that the response is to that extent at least a linguistic and conceptual one; and hence, on Levinas' terms, violent. Levinas' idea of direct, non-violent response to the face of the other, Derrida says,

> would be entirely coherent if the face was only glance, but it is also speech; and in speech it is the phrase which makes the cry of need become the expression of desire. Now, there is no phrase which is indeterminate, that is, which does not pass through the violence of the concept. Violence appears with *articulation*.
>
> (Derrida 1978:147)

Only complete silence could be non-violent; as soon as one speaks, or conceptualizes meaning, even to ascertain need and appropriate response, one has entered the realm of predication. 'One never escapes the *economy of war*' (148).

What this analysis makes apparent, however, even though Derrida does not acknowledge it, is that the language of violence has lost its moorings. Levinas' thought gains its persuasiveness in relation to actual, concrete occasions of violence such as the Holocaust, and the urgency of responding to human need with compassion rather than the disinterested neutrality of rationality. But if *all* predication is violent, then as I argued in relation to de Vries, there is nothing to distinguish ethical from unethical response. Levinas sometimes, indeed, speaks of 'good violence', a violence of appropriate recognition and response to the face of the other (Levinas 1969:25; de Vries 1995:216); and there is reason to ponder his contention that supposedly peaceful responses are often more closely related to hostility than we would like to think. But I suggest that using the language of violence here is confusing. It blurs the very thing that Levinas most wants to lift up: engaged response to the other. If *everything* is violent, if *no* response can escape the economy of war, then the language of violence has effectively been lost as a tool for discriminating between responses.

Levinas, as we have seen, moves quickly to words like killing, murder and war; and given that he is writing very deliberately in the shadow of Auschwitz it is easy to understand why. Nevertheless I think that it is unhelpful. To see why, consider again the biblical accounts of creation. Here, naming is that by which identity is offered and claimed; think of the naming of the animals, or the naming of the first human pair. Although violence is not far in the future in the narrative, the act of naming is not an act of violence but of recognition and respect. The propensity to consider naming as a type of grasping is arguably another aspect of Levinas' unacknowledged masculinism. It is an idea that has much more intuitive plausibility if we think, for example, of the naming that occurs in modern science than if we think of parents naming their long-awaited child when it is born into the world, or learning the name of a stranger as a first step in becoming a friend. By contrast, it is when violence occurs that the name is 'blotted out', whether in the Bible or in modern warfare. It is important – *ethically* important – to be able to distinguish between naming someone (thus conceptualizing them) and killing them; if our language places naming and killing on the same footing, something has gone badly wrong. And this is not a merely linguistic problem which we could overcome by inventing some other term. In the world of the twenty-first century where actual killing and brutality and exclusions occur at an escalating pace, we cannot do without the concept of violence as a way to set these atrocities apart from naming and welcoming the other, whether the newborn or the stranger.

The second point that I wish to draw from Levinas' discussion is his recognition of the fundamental importance of desire and of sacrifice. As already indicated, Levinas' use of the terms of violence – killing, murder, war – is situated historically in the shadow of Auschwitz, but philosophically is indebted to Hegel, especially to his discussion of lordship and bondage. Now, in Hegel the pivotal term of this discussion is desire. It is the desire for recognition that pushes the two subjects into a struggle to the death; and ultimately it is the desire for life, even more than for recognition, that determines that one of them will be a bondsman to the other.[1]

Levinas, as we have seen, takes up these themes of desire, sacrifice, and the violent struggle for life and death, but configures them differently. In Levinas, my desire for recognition must give way to response to the need which I encounter in the face of the other.

> The Other becomes my neighbour precisely through the way the face summons me, calls for me, begs for me, and in so doing recalls my responsibility, and calls me into question.
>
> (Levinas 1989:83)

In Levinas' presentation, rather than struggle for mastery, the face of the other requires me to renounce that desire and the violence it implies, and if need be sacrifice myself. Rather than being the occasion for recognition, the face of the other 'calls me into question'. The face of the other does not summon me to violence, to a struggle to the death as Hegel had said. Quite the contrary: the face forbids me to kill. If that requires self-sacrifice, so be it.

Hegel, as we have seen, used the motif of lordship and bondage as a model not only for subjectivity but for the progress of philosophy and history; for him, negation and violent struggle were central to the idea of philosophical progress. But what price philosophy? Levinas does not challenge Hegel's account of the violence of philosophy or the centrality of desire; instead he argues that this philosophy – ontology – should be subordinate to ethics.

Violence and desire

But is it the case that violence is necessary for progress, as Hegel had said (and which Levinas nowhere disputes)? Can philosophical or historical progress be made without it? And how is this violence related to desire, sacrifice, and creativity? Once the questions are posed in this way, it is impossible to avoid any longer the contribution of psychoanalytic theory to an account of violence. This has been the central theme of the work of René Girard, especially in relation to religion. His writings can be taken both as definition and as explanation of violence, and have been very influential especially among theologians. (See for example Hamerton-Kelly 1992; Redekop 2002.) In my view, however, Girard is fundamentally misguided in the account he gives of violence, not least because he allows no place for creativity. I shall first present his position, and then explain why it will not do.

At least since Freud, desire and its repression has been taken by psychoanalytic theory as central to human behaviour, both at an individual level and at the level of society and civilization. Girard accepts the centrality of desire; but whereas Freud had focused chiefly on the sexual aspect of desire – indeed sometimes seeming to reduce all desire to sexuality – Girard takes a broader view. In particular, Girard pays attention to the imitative dimension of desire. We want what someone else has; more precisely, we want what someone else *wants*. We learn to value things because other people – parents, teachers, peers – value them; this is the basis of education, culture, the development of taste, and much else. All these are founded on imitation, mimetic desire.

But mimetic desire quickly turns to rivalry. Girard gives a simple example: 'place a certain number of identical toys in a room with the same number of children; there is every chance that the toys will not be distributed without quarrels' (Girard 1987:9). Each child can have a toy exactly like the toys the others have; but still they are likely to quarrel, each one wanting not just a toy *like* the others but the very toy that another child has. Girard considers this as characteristic of desire in general. Desire is not just mimetic, it is conflictual and acquisitive.

Moreover, such conflictual mimesis is mutually reinforcing. If I want what you have, value something that you value, then my desire for it causes you to value it even more, in an escalating reciprocity. This feedback process reinforces itself, until the competition becomes rivalry and the frustrated rivalry turns nasty.

> Violence is thus generated. Violence is not originary; it is a by-product of mimetic rivalry. Violence is mimetic rivalry itself becoming violent as the antagonists who desire the same object keep thwarting each other and desiring the object all the more. Violence is supremely mimetic.
>
> (Girard 1996:12–13)

In fact, the mimetic rivalry can quickly intensify in such a way that the ostensible object of desire – the toy both children want – no longer matters; all that matters is their quarrel.

As rivalry becomes acute, the rivals are more apt to forget about whatever objects are, in principle, the cause of the rivalry and instead to become more fascinated with one another. In effect, the rivalry is purified of any external stake and becomes a matter of pure rivalry and prestige ... Only the antagonists remain; we designate them as doubles because from the point of view of the antagonism, nothing distinguishes them.

(Girard 1987:26)

By this time the rivalry can no longer be called acquisitive; the initial object of desire has dropped out. The mimesis is simply conflictual. It is also contagious; before long each of the rivals will have allies, and the violence snowballs and polarizes the contestants.

Of course this mimetic violence can take many forms, from overt force to much more subtle strategies. All of it, however, has its roots in desire, in mimetic rivalry. As Hamerton-Kelly puts it in his interpretation of Girard,

Violence is the whole range of this deformation of desire ... not just the obvious physical coercion. It is the driving energy of the social system. On the level of attitude it is envy and the strategies by which desire attempts to possess itself in the other and the other for itself ... Thus violence is more inclusive than aggression ... Violence describes the deep strategies of deformed desire in pursuit of its ends in all the modalities of culture.

(Hamerton-Kelly 1992:21)

There are obvious resonances here with Hegel's account of the master and the slave, violence between them arising because both desire the recognition of the other. Girard seldom mentions Hegel; and when he does it is usually to dismiss him; but actually both men see desire and the rivalry it generates as the basis of violence and the driving force of history.

Now, animals also display mimetic rivalry. Two puppies will scrap over the same toy even if each is given an identical one, just as children will. But Girard argues that in the case of humans, the contagious effect of mimetic rivalry does not result in two equal groups in conflict with each other, but rather in the formation of one group to which more and more are attracted, and who focus their attention on the other which eventually dwindles to a single victim. Although this victim is the one against whom all the aggression is directed, the very fact that there is such a focus means that all the others unite into a community. Because aggression is focused outward, it becomes possible to develop prohibitions against violence within the community. The other becomes the scapegoat, the sacrifice who must bear the violence of the group. Girard sees this process as the foundation of religion, which develops increasingly formal rituals around the sacrificial victim and increasingly stringent prohibitions on violence within the group itself. Girard sees this whole process as the one that distinguishes humans from animals (who, unlike humans, seldom carry their mimetic rivalries to an actual fight to the death). He puts it bluntly: 'the victimage mechanism is the origin of hominization' (Girard 1987:97). As he explains,

> We can conceive of hominization as a series of steps that allow for the domestication of progressively increasing and intense mimetic effects, separated from one another by crises that would be catastrophic but also generative in that they would trigger the founding mechanism and at each step provide for more rigorous prohibitions within the group, and for a more effective ritual canalization toward the outside.
>
> (Girard 1987:96)

The surrogate victim is thus fundamental to civilization, enabling communities to act out their aggression in increasingly ritualized ways, gradually replacing actual victims with symbols; thus the sacrificial system of ancient Israel gives place to the sacrifice 'once for all' of the Lamb of God, and eventually to the sacrifice of the mass.

> All religious rituals spring from the surrogate victim, and all the great institutions of mankind, both secular and religious, spring from ritual ... It could hardly be otherwise, for the working basis of human thought, the process of 'symbolization', is rooted in the surrogate victim.
>
> (Girard 1977:306)

It is in the gradual substitution of ritual for actual violence that this whole process leads to peace. Rituals are by definition repetitive: by re-enactment of the ritual the community comes to peace with itself as the ritual victim bears its aggression.

> A trace of very real violence persists in the rite, and there is no doubt that the rite succeeds at least partially because of its grim associations, its lingering fascination; but its essential orientation is peaceful. Even the most violent rites are specifically designed to abolish violence.
>
> (Girard 1977:103)

In this way ritually enacted violence permits people 'to escape their own violence ... and bestows on them all the institutions and beliefs that define their humanity' (306).

According to Girard, therefore, violence and religion are inextricable, not in the sense that religion generates violence but rather in the sense that religion is the structure of beliefs and rituals within which the symbolic victim is sacrificed. In his earlier writings Girard believed that religion would die away as 'the rite gradually leads men away from the sacred' and from their own violence (1977:306). In more recent writings he asserts, rather, that Christianity offers the perfect resolution of violence, because it requires that all mimetic desire shall be channelled into the imitation of Christ, the one who gave himself for others and took violence upon himself (Girard 1996:63; 1987:430).

Up to this point I have put aside difficulties that I have with Girard, in order to represent him fairly. I wish now to turn to these, because they help to illuminate aspects of the relations between violence and religion, in particular how creativity enters the context. Girard has virtually nothing to say about creativity or beauty. In his view, peace, and all the values of civilization, are a result of the victimage mechanism; it is thus ultimately through violence, not through creativity, that newness enters the world. By contrast, I hold that violence of itself does not bring peace. Violence repeats itself in escalating patterns; it does not bring newness. The newness that allows for human flourishing requires creativity and beauty, rooted in natality.

To begin with the obvious: in the twenty-first century the form of violence that is much to the fore is indeed religious violence, or at least violence which relies on religion for its justification, but in a very different way than we might have expected from reading Girard. Girard has focused on violence *within* a group, and the way in which that violence can be resolved and the group become peaceable by means of the victimage mechanism. But the violence of freedom fighters and terrorists, landmines and helicopter gunships, ethnic cleansing and genocide, is violence *between* groups, often groups who assume that God or Allah is on their side and that their violence has divine blessing. While it is certainly true that violence can unite a group, it does so by deepening their division from the other: the victims against the perpetrators (who can quickly exchange roles). And while it is true that individual nations can develop greater internal unity by making a 'scapegoat' of another nation, and perhaps deflect internal disquiet or aggression by doing so, it has not been the case historically that all the nations of the world have united to focus on a single victim or scapegoat. In the world wars of the twentieth century each side was composed of groups of nations; and in the first decade of this century we find one hyperpowerful nation attacking a sequence of relatively weak nations. A few others join in, but most of the rest (and much of the population within the aggressive states) watch in paralysed disapproval. Girard's victimage mechanism, in which everyone unites against a single scapegoat, is not in evidence. The ancient history of warfare does not show a scapegoat syndrome any more than does the recent past. Very often we find the same pattern of a very strong nation attacking a weaker one while others look on, unable or unwilling to get involved: the spread of the Roman Empire is an obvious example. Sometimes there is rivalry, as in the wars between the European powers over colonial dominance, but in these instances again, there is no obvious scapegoating.

It will not do for Girard to reply that he has concentrated on violence *within* groups and has left violence *between* groups for others to discuss. This is because it is clear that at least some aspects of violence within a community are very closely related to the warfare it conducts against its external enemies: one cannot be understood without the other. One of the key points of connection is gender, in particular the construction of masculinities. In *Foundations of Violence* I showed how the construction of virile manliness in the Roman Empire was the glue that connected the spectacles of death in the amphitheatres with the ideology and enactment of war (or violent peace) at its frontiers. Later in this book I shall discuss the close relationship between the cult of animal sacrifice and the holy wars of ancient Israel as represented in the Hebrew Bible; neither are thinkable without the idea of the covenant enacted in circumcision which inscribed a construction of masculinity on the body of every Israelite male. In later volumes I shall show how gender constructions were again involved in European colonization of the 'new world', which was routinely feminized against the masculinity of the conquerors, a mastering masculinity all too often expressed in violence at home as well as abroad. The links between the violence inside a group – not least its gender violence – and its conduct of warfare are easy to demonstrate.

It is therefore not without significance that just as Girard is silent on the subject of war, so he has very little to say about gender. One exception is his discussion of Dionysus in *Violence and the Sacred*; he notes the 'minor importance' of the 'role played by women in the religious and cultural structure of a society', and asserts that:

> Like the animal and the infant but to a lesser degree, the woman qualifies for sacrificial status by reason of her weakness and relatively marginal social status. That is why she can be viewed as a quasi-sacred figure, both desired and disdained, alternately elevated and abused.
>
> (Girard 1977:140–2)

However, Girard never questions this marginal status, never investigates the violence that keeps women 'in their place'. Gender violence, actual or threatened, is a major dimension of many societies (including all the societies of Western modernity); it is obviously related to the construction of masculinities and thus to ideologies of mastery and warfare; and it is often given religious justification. But none of this falls discernibly into Girard's category of the victimage mechanism. If Girard is attempting to provide an explanation of violence in relation to religion, and yet has nothing to say about war, gender violence, and their religious justifications, then at the very least the gaps in his theory must be of enormous concern.[2]

This brings me to my most fundamental difficulty with Girard. According to his theory, peace, hominization, and all the goods of civilization ultimately have their foundation in the victimage mechanism and thus are a result of violence. This is to say the least counterintuitive. Violence breeds violence. At an international level the result of violence is a spiralling escalation of war, conflict and terror; within a group, too, violence reproduces itself either immediately or in festering hatred. Violence does not bring peace. Of course the weaker party can be bombed or bludgeoned into submission, but that is not peace. Only justice brings peace. Girard argues that escalating reciprocal violence, as in a blood feud, can only be resolved by both sides venting their violence on a surrogate victim and thus coming to peace between themselves. But is this true? If, for example, there is a major violation of one party by another – if a powerful nation appropriates the land or resources of a weaker nation, subordinating or killing much of its population, then it is highly likely that the weaker nation would fester in anger until it could retaliate; but it is hardly plausible that the two would together join forces against a third nation (or that anything would be resolved if they did). Or again at an individual level, if two people who are feuding were to deal with their grievances by attacking a third – say, arguing parents venting their violence on a child – this would hardly count as a resolution of the problem but a wholly inappropriate displacement of it.

Girard is of course aware that violence breeds violence, and never pretends that the achievement of peace is quick or easy. Nevertheless, he holds that the very escalation of violence pushes the community to a point where the chain reaction has to stop; and at that point the surrogate victim will appear. 'The sheer escalation of the crisis, linked to progressively accumulating mimetic effects, will make the designation of such a victim automatic' and thus will lead to the resolution of the conflict (Girard 1987:25). But what evidence could Girard bring to support this claim? It is hard to see what his justification for it could possibly be. Even in situations of conflict in which both sides realize that the violence has gone on far too long and must stop, peace is only finally achieved through negotiations which both sides feel to be fair and which results in justice that although perhaps imperfect is nonetheless recognized by both sides as a new start. Think for example of the collapse of apartheid in South Africa, or the movement towards peace in Northern Ireland. In both cases there was all too much violence and both sides could see that it had to stop; but in neither case was there a turn to a surrogate victim. Nor can I imagine anyone involved in conflict resolution ever advocating that there should be such a turn or that anything would be improved if there were. More sadly, the spiralling violence between Israel and the Palestinians seems out of control and in urgent need of change; but here again it is absurd to think that the situation would be helped if only the two sides could unite against a common target. Examples could be multiplied; I can think of none in which the victimage mechanism could possibly be the foundation of peace. All the evidence points the other way: violence begets more violence. Sometimes Girard writes as though this victimage mechanism should be read back into prehistory as the origin of religion, not as an account of violence today. If that is how he means to be read, then my objections drawn from contemporary events would not stand. But then Girard faces two questions. First, given the difference between his view of violence in prehistory and what we see today, what evidence could he possibly adduce for his theory that it was the victimage mechanism that brought peace? Second, if his theory is not an account of how violence functions today, then is it of any but historical interest? Surely the whole point of his theory is that it claims to gives insight into *present* violence?

Desire and newness

And yet sometimes peace does come; slowly and imperfectly, but nevertheless it comes. If it does not come out of violence, if Girard's theory of the victimage mechanism cannot be supported by the evidence, then how *does* peace come? How does newness enter the world? These questions bring me back to the starting point of this chapter, on the relationship between violence and creativity. They also bring me back to Girard's starting point: the centrality of desire. Girard argues, as we have seen, that desire is mimetic, that mimetic desire turns into rivalry, and that rivalry turns into violence. I want to argue, by contrast, that not all desire is mimetic; and that even mimetic desire need not turn to rivalry.

Girard holds that mimetic desire leads to rivalry which degenerates to violence. Even in his later work, where he talks about 'good mimesis' as the 'imitation of Christ', this 'active, positive desire for the other' cannot be part of human nature but can only occur if 'there is some kind of divine grace present' 'whether or not it is recognized as such' (Girard 1996:65): it is not true of normal human beings for whom desire is mimetic and rivalrous. But need this be the case? Why need desire lead to rivalry rather than to co-operation or sharing? Girard notes that children with equivalent toys still sometimes quarrel; he does not note that sometimes they play together quite happily. But if desire *need* not lead to rivalry and violence, then we require some other explanation or account of how and why violence arises: how is it that sometimes desire – even mimetic desire – can express itself in cooperation and generosity whereas at other times it leads to resentment and hostility? Unless that question can be answered we will be no further forward in understanding the relationship between desire and violence, let alone how violence can be resolved.

I suggest that within Girard's work on rivalry as the inevitable result of mimesis lurk some unacknowledged (but still very common) gender assumptions quite similar to those I identified in the thinking of Levinas: first, that the human is normatively male, and second, that masculinity involves mastery and therefore rivalry. Girard's ideas of mimetic rivalry seem plausible if we think, perhaps, about the way in which businessmen operate, or about football, or about all the many ways in which men strive competitively for mastery. But what sense do they make if we think instead, for example, about the relationship between a mother and her child? Here the child learns by imitation, but if the imitation turns to rivalry and aggression then this is a sign that something has gone wrong, not that the relationship is progressing appropriately. Similarly, a teacher delights in the learning of a pupil, and recognizes that her chief work is to make herself dispensable, to teach the pupil so well that the pupil can go forward without further assistance, perhaps beyond the skill or knowledge of the teacher herself. An insecure teacher can of course feel resentment when a student surpasses her; but a teacher secure in her own contribution can rejoice and take pleasure in her student's progress. Girard leaves no room for generosity of spirit rather than rivalry and incessant struggle.

This leads to the deeper question of whether desire itself is mimetic. Girard's description is of course true of many desires, which arise out of a wish to have what someone else has, to value what they value. Moreover, Girard is right to say that much of our education and enculturation would be impossible without imitation. In everything from learning to play a musical instrument to building character, we make progress by trying to copy those whom we admire, as Aristotle said.[3] But I would argue that while much desire is mimetic, there is also an immensely important and under-theorized aspect of desire for which mimesis cannot be an adequate expla-nation. The crucial point here is that mimetic desire is desire that is premised upon a lack; it is desire for what we do not have, or desire that what we have now shall not be taken from us in the future. But what about creative desire: the desire to make something beautiful, something new? The desire to create cannot, I suggest, be reduced to lack. Rather, creativity bespeaks fullness that overflows, that wants to give of its resources, express itself.

The paradigm case is once again creation; as God is portrayed in the Hebrew Bible and Christian theology, God does not lack. The divine is in need of nothing. Yet God desires to create the world; and desires to make it beautiful. God desires to make a new heaven and a new earth, where peace and beauty will be restored. This creative desire is traditionally represented theologically as springing from infinite divine resources, not out of lack; it is not mimetic. Similarly, it can be argued that there is more to human crea-tivity than mimesis; it, too, comes out of an abundance of resources, not simply out of lack. Of course imitation plays a great part in learning the skills without which human creativity cannot be expressed; but ultimately that which is genuinely creative is original, not imitative. It must arise out of the resources of the creator and their desire to create. The desire to create, to make something new, must arise out of fullness, not lack. I cannot produce good music or paint a picture or write a book solely out of lack or mimetic desire, just because someone I envy or admire has written one and I would like to do the same. I can do so only if I have something new or fresh in me to express, something that is not reducible to imitation. This is even more obviously true when that which is new is a new life. Much as a child owes to its parents, the newness that enters the world with the birth of a child goes far beyond imitation; and we would rightly worry about a family in which the prospective parents desired to produce and nurture a child only out of mimetic rivalry.

I suggest that the same considerations apply to conflict resolution. It is not a surrogate victim who can bring peace; rather it is creative thinking, new ways of looking at old problems, that can find a way forward. Of course creativity does not come out of the blue; of course it requires skills built up by long imitation and practice, but unless there are inner resources, not just lack, we could not hope for newness to enter the world. In contrast to Girard, therefore, I suggest that it is not violence and the victimage mechanism but creativity, desire springing from fullness rather than premised upon a lack, which is the root of hominization and the foundation of culture; and that its paradigm is the newness of natality. This does not mean that creativity will necessarily produce good; it is possible to be inventive about evil. Without creativity, however, newness cannot emerge.

Beauty and natality

But how can that creativity be understood and its potential for good fostered? Here I want to turn back to the biblical accounts of creation and beauty. For all the complex ambiguities and the tensions with violence which is ever ready to erupt, the themes of creativity and beauty cannot be dismissed from the text. In later chapters I will look at the tensions that arise between beauty (often marginalized) and specific aspects of violence; here I want to focus more broadly on the poetics of beauty as it presents itself in the biblical text, and how creativity and beauty stand against violence and offer newness to the world.

Chapter 2

Imagining natality

Narrative and Utopia

In the previous chapter I argued that the attempts of recent scholars to define an essence of violence have failed. I also argued that violence cannot be overcome by more violence, but only by finding creative alternatives, new possibilities that emerge not out of mimetic rivalry or lack but out of generous desire whose resources are like a well springing up ever and again with newness of life and beauty, and I showed how this is illustrated in biblical representations of divine cruelty. But I did not develop any account of violence in place of the definitions I rejected. Neither did I offer more than hints about how the resources of creative alternatives could be identified and encouraged, or how human creativity could be directed to flourishing rather than to ever more elaborate technologies of violence. Without some way of tapping in to creative resources, the mere theoretical recognition of them is at best a pious affirmation, at worst tantalizing cruelty. In this final introductory chapter I propose therefore to take the idea of narrative and to show how narrative works to remedy both these deficiencies. Using narrative it becomes possible to give an account of violence in terms of function rather than of essence, and also to indicate where resources for creative alternatives are to be found. Having developed these ideas at a theoretical level in this chapter, I shall then proceed in the rest of the book to trace the genealogy of violence and creativity in Western religious thought and practice.

Function and narrative

Each of the theorists whose accounts of violence I considered in Chapter 1 tried to define or explain violence by identifying its essence: the exertion of force, or the making of boundaries, or mimetic rivalry. I argued against each of these definitions in turn. There is, however, a more fundamental objection that undercuts all such definitions together, an objection drawn from the work of Michel Foucault. One of the most significant aspects of Foucault's intellectual legacy is his persistent questioning of the very idea of essence. He never tired of showing that in all the cases where Western thought has attempted to identify an essence or a universal definition, reality is in fact much more complex. Foucault's strategy was to develop 'a systematic scepticism with respect to all anthropological universals', a scepticism that was fostered by 'interrogating them in their historical constitution' (Foucault 1994:317). In his own work he applied this strategy to rationality, discipline, sexuality, etc., to undermine the idea of a universal fixed essence for each of these categories. What was needed instead, as he showed, was an account of how each of these functioned through time, changing in different historical and cultural contexts. Although Foucault did not apply his strategy to the idea of death and violence, it is not difficult to see that these ideas, too, have varied; they have a history, a narrative which underlies and frames our present conception.[1] What are the forms which violence – in particular religious violence – have taken in the West? How has it functioned? And where are the resources for alternatives?

Foucault used the terminology of genealogy or archaeology of a concept, excavating its layers to show how its sediments continue to underlie present thought. I shall in addition use the idea of narrative, especially as it has been developed in the work of Hannah Arendt and Adriana Cavarero. Narrative is a particularly useful concept here for three reasons. First, while maintaining the idea of genealogy, it widens the approach so that the changing function of violence is seen within the broader historical trajectory. Second, narrative as I shall use it cries out for attention to its gendered dimensions, an aspect which Foucault's genealogies much too readily ignored. Third, Judaism and Christianity, the religions that have shaped the West, are themselves explicitly rooted in narratives and emphasize to their adherents the importance of remembering and retelling these narratives, as I shall show more fully in a moment. Therefore using narrative to come to understand violence and its alternatives in Western religious thought is not imposing an alien category upon it, but rather seeing it through a lens of its own making.

The idea of narrative, especially the idea of such a long and over-arching narrative as I am telling in these volumes, has not been uncontested in contemporary thought. Jean-François Lyotard famously defined the '*postmodern* as incredulity toward metanarratives', whether metaphysical, political, or economic (Lyotard 1984:xxiv). Any totalizing discourse, any narrative that subsumes everything within its grand scheme, must be suspect, since by its very nature it allows nothing to stand against it. What we need is not a grand theory of everything, but rather an alertness to those things which would call our metanarratives into question: our search must be for instabilities, the alien, the marginal and the foreign, which discomfort us in our too-easily unchallenged scheme of things.

Whether the sort of narrative I am telling of the functions of death and death-dealing in the West would count as a metanarrative in Lyotard's terms is doubtful, however. This is not a grand scheme of things; neither is it uncontested. On the contrary, what I wish to show is that ever and again the choice of violence can be seen as precisely that: a choice, which could have been made otherwise. There are resources of resistance; and they come, often, from the marginal and the foreign to destabilize received certainties just as Lyotard hoped. In any case, whatever Lyotard would say about this project, our identities are forged, as individuals and as societies, by our memories, the narratives we assume about ourselves. We can be more or less explicitly aware of these narratives; we can all too easily bury unwelcome aspects of it in our unconscious. Yet the stories are there all the same, framing our sense of ourselves and one another and shaping the ways in which we act. We have stories whether we like them or not. Our choice is not about whether we have stories but about whether we become conscious of them and choose how they shall shape our future.

Narrative identity

Who are you? Who am I? Who are we – as a group, a society, a nation? To answer any of those questions requires a story, a story that at an individual level involves a name, parents, a place and time of birth, and an account of the trajectory of the life of the individual from then until now. Adriana Cavarero, in her important book *Relating Narratives* (2000), has shown how significant our personal narratives are to our identity. Our selfhood is inextricable from the story that can be told of that self.

> Without effort or intention, every time and in every circumstance, we perceive ourselves and others as unique beings whose identity is narratable in a life-story. Each one of us knows that who we meet always has a unique story. And this is true even if we meet them for the first time without knowing their story at all.
>
> (Cavarero 2000:33)

Ever since Plato, philosophy has been immersed in the question of *what* 'man' is – and has seldom bothered much about woman. In our actual lives, however, we are far more concerned with *who* we are, ourselves, and also the people we meet: the unique, unrepeatable and always gendered selfhood of each of us. As Hannah Arendt was fond of insisting, it is not 'Man' – not the universal – who inhabits the earth, but individual, unique, fragile men and women[2] (Arendt 1958:7). Although philosophy has concerned itself with the universal 'Man', and sought to provide an ontology or define the essence of this 'featherless biped', Arendt argues that human reality, whether individual or social, cannot be understood by appeal to such universals. Take for example Oedipus, when faced with the riddle of the Sphinx. Which animal is it, the Sphinx asked, who goes first on four legs, then two, and at last three? 'Man!', Oedipus triumphantly replied, remembering infancy, maturity, and crippled old age. But clever as he was, this solution, this idea of Man, did not tell him what he needed to know about himself as an individual man, and thus did not save him from the disaster of murdering his father and marrying his mother. For him to 'know himself', as Greek philosophers were fond of exhorting, he needed to know more than universals. He needed to know his own story: crucially, he needed to know the story beginning with his birth. It is the narratable life story, beginning with birth and continuing with all the specificity and irreplacability of the individual life, which provides meaning and locates an individual in the understanding of herself and others. Nor is this an optional extra. As is vividly illustrated in the case of Oedipus, one's actions flow out of the life story one tells about oneself – with disastrous consequences if that story is mistaken at crucial points.[3]

Oedipus's need for a story shows, as well, the centrality of memory for personal identity, and the importance that the memory be accurate. As Cavarero says,

> We are all familiar with the narrative work of memory, which, in a totally involuntary way, continues to tell us our own personal story. Every human being, without even wanting to know it, is aware of being a *narratable self* – immersed in the spontaneous auto-narration of memory.
>
> (Cavarero 2000:33)

This is the case even when, as in the story of Oedipus, the auto-narration is in fact false. How we live, what we choose to do, depends on the memory we have of ourselves; and it now becomes clear that for some of these memories we are dependent upon others. This is paradigmatically true in relation to birth, as the story of Oedipus again shows. We cannot remember our own birth, and yet who we are, the story we tell about ourselves in the 'auto-narration of memory', cannot start without it.

Philosophers in modernity have been acutely aware of the significance of memory in relation to personal identity, but they have seldom paid attention either to birth or to the need for the memories of others to intersect with and contribute to one's own. John Locke, in his famous tale of the prince and the cobbler, suggested that if the 'soul' of each were to inhabit the body of the other – if, that is, the cobbler woke up one morning with all the prince's memories, and vice versa – then the prince and the cobbler would actually have turned into each other. The cobbler would live in the prince's body and in the prince's palace; and although he would look like the prince he would be the cobbler and know himself as such, remembering the cobbler's life story as his own. The same would be true for the prince. Though now he would be greeted by the neighbours of the hovel in which he found himself living – since he now had the cobbler's body and appearance – he would be gravely affronted by his circumstances and their coarse familiarity as altogether unbefitting to the prince which he knew himself to be.

Locke's story has been subjected to many sorts of scrutiny, especially in relation to the importance of the body for personal identity. Most often, however, it has been the isolated individual who has been in focus, the prince and/or the cobbler, not the wider community with which each of their lives intersect. But what if Locke's tale were told not from the perspective of the prince or the cobbler but from the point of view of their parents, spouse, and children? Who would the cobbler's mother consider to be her son: the man whose body she had known since his infancy or the man who remembered the bedtime stories she used to tell? Which man would the children call 'Daddy': the one they now lived with and who looked like their father, even though he now seemed not to know them, or the one who knew all about them but whose body they had never seen before? Which man would the princess royal be willing to sleep with, the man whose body she knew intimately but who seemed to have gone off his head with silly ideas about shoe making, or the man who looked like a cobbler, but who, like Odysseus, could remember the bed they had shared? Who would be chosen to sire the royal line?

Whichever way we answer these questions, it is obvious that Locke's story is vastly more complicated than he himself saw: indeed it is perhaps ultimately incoherent. What they also make clear, however, is the way in which our identity, our narratable self, is interlocked not only with our gendered body and its history (think of the additional complexities if one of Locke's protagonists had been female) but also with the memories and narratable selves of others. Ultimately, it is the collection of intersecting narratives that forms the history of a group or society or nation. As Hannah Arendt says,

> That every individual life between birth and death can eventually be told as a story with beginning and end is the prepolitical and prehistorical condition of history, the great story without beginning and end ... History ultimately becomes the storybook of mankind.
>
> (Arendt 1958:184)

Just as philosophers have sought to define an essence of 'Man', so also they have tried to ascertain the 'Meaning of History'. But if Arendt is right that history is 'the storybook of mankind', then the philosophical understanding of history cannot properly be detached from the intersecting stories of those selves.

Cavarero goes so far as to say that 'since it results from the interweaving of individual stories, the great History of humanity is nothing but the book of single stories' (Cavarero 2000:124). This I think overstates the case: history involves not just the accumulation of stories but also includes attempts at interpreting them and making sense of their interaction. Nevertheless, Cavarero is certainly right to insist that it is ultimately upon the stories of narratable selves that historical accounts must stand or fall. Philosophers can generate universals in abstraction, but insofar as we hope to understand the world and the society which we inhabit, let alone offer constructive interventions, we cannot dispense with actual life stories, the narratives of individuals and their intersections.

Moreover, since we act, individually and collectively, out of our sense of identity, giving continuity and coherence to our only partly conscious auto-narrative, it is obvious that the stories we tell of ourselves have an afterlife. Our stories shape our futures as they tell about our past. They frame for us what is thinkable and thus what are our options for action. This is as true at a social and political level as it is of the individual. As Zillah Eisenstein has written,

> History is never just simply the 'past' … History resonates in the present, even if unconsciously. So the present is also always rooted in its earlier forms. And people continue these beginnings in and through daily life. History is made while old histories are simultaneously reproduced, without most of us ever owning the story told.
>
> (Eisenstein 2004:25)

As Pierre Bourdieu put it in his development of the idea of the *habitus*, history reproduces itself on the basis of history (Bourdieu 1990:56; cf. Jantzen 2004:9). Therefore if the story we tell, individually and collectively, is a story of death-dealing, a narrative in which violence is valorized, then it is all too likely that violence and the attitudes and ideas that legitimate it will reproduce itself.

Stories can be told in more than one way, of course. Each of us chooses not only what aspects of our individual stories we share with others but also at least to some extent what aspects of our own stories we remember and what we forget or even repress. No auto-narrative is a complete recital of all the events of a life. A story is not a chronology. A story shapes events, giving prominence to some and omitting others, so that it has structure and meaning. Narratives that construct or represent identity, whether individual or social, are not necessarily accurate representations of objective fact (which may never be ascertainable). In spite of that, they are the framework of self-understanding and the source from which subsequent action flows.

While this is true, however, if there is anything that we have learned from psychoanalysis it is that things are always more complicated. Along with the stories we tell of ourselves and the action that flows from our self-under-standing, there is always also the action that flows from what has been repressed, the repeated patterns of unresolved trauma. There are deliberate falsifications and fabrications as well as sincere but misguided interpretations and selections of events. A narrative is not 'true' in the sense of being a complete recital of facts nor in the sense of being the only possible inter-pretation (or even the best possible interpretation) of those facts; it is never-theless the story which is continued or modified as its trajectory moves onwards. Narrative is therefore as much about the future as it is about the past. The history we (rightly or wrongly) claim as our own has an afterlife; its patterns repeat themselves.

In the final section of this chapter I shall discuss the significance of this repetitive nature of narrative in relation to the violence of Western religion, and also the possibility and urgency of counternarrative as a resource for change. Before I do so, however, I wish to delineate briefly the extent to which narrative is built into the religious self-understanding of the West, with roots deep in the Hebrew Bible. My argument (for which the rest of this volume provides the evidence) will be that the violence deeply embedded in this narrative has shaped Western identity and been acted out in repeated patterns of escalating force; but also that within the narrative itself there are suggestions for a counternarrative which need to be lifted up so that we may be empowered for change.

Narrative and Western religious identity

To begin with the obvious, the Bible itself is a book of stories, a sequence of narratives large and small which together make up the larger narrative of the early Israelites. Most children in the West learn Bible stories: the creation of the world, Noah's flood, Abraham and Isaac, Jonah and the whale. There are longer accounts, too, such as the chronicles of the lives and reigns of kings. To what extent any of these stories are (or even purport to be) accurate history is a matter of continuing dispute, but they have been taken as the auto-narrative of the Israelites. There are of course also other ingredients in the Hebrew Bible – psalms, proverbs, legal codes – yet even these fall within the context of the narrative and would make little sense without it (Alter 1981; Gunn and Fewell 1993).

Basic to the identity of the Israelites as represented in the Hebrew Bible is the narrative of their liberation from Egypt and the protection of God as he led them through the wilderness to the promised land. Time after time this story is rehearsed in prose and psalm and ritual. The writer of Deuteronomy particularly exhorts the people not to forget the narrative of their origin and trajectory, how

> God ... brought you out of the land of Egypt, out of the house of bondage, who led you through the great and terrible wilderness, with its fiery serpents and scorpions and thirsty ground where there was no water, who brought you water out of the flinty rock, who fed you in the wilderness with manna which your fathers did not know ...
>
> (Deuteronomy 8.14–16)

Shortly before the Israelites are to cross the Jordan River and claim Canaan for themselves as the land promised to them by divine covenant, Moses rehearses at length the history of their wilderness wanderings and reminds them of the laws of God which had been given to them. All these things they are to remember. Above all, they are not to forget God, lest they perish.

> Take heed … lest, when you have eaten and are full, and have built goodly houses and live in them … and all that you have is multiplied, then your heart be lifted up, and you forget the Lord your God, who brought you out of the house of Egypt, out of the house of bondage … You shall remember the Lord your God … And if you forget the Lord your God and go after other gods and serve them and worship them, I solemnly warn you this day that you shall surely perish …
>
> (Deuteronomy 8.11–20)

The same insistence on the importance of memory is repeated at various places in the Hebrew Bible, and the dire consequences of forgetting God are emphasized. The prophet Jeremiah writes in his account of the calamities that are coming upon his people:

> Therefore thus says the Lord:
> my people have forgotten me,
> they burn incense to false gods …
> Like the east wind I will scatter them before the enemy.
> I will show them my back, not my face,
> in the day of their calamity.
>
> (Jeremiah 18.13–17)

It is obvious in these passages that forgetting or remembering God is not the same as ordinary forgetting or remembering. Forgetting God is not like forgetting to buy milk at the corner shop or forgetting the name of our next door neighbour. Neither would the failure of memory in old age cause a person to forget God. In the terms of these passages, forgetting God is tantamount to the Israelites forgetting themselves, forgetting their own narrative and the ways in which God was involved in it. If that narrative is not remembered, then there is the likelihood that the Israelites will turn to other gods. But this would in effect be forging a new narrative, giving themselves a different identity. Repeatedly they are reminded of events in their history which have made them what they are: a people with a special relationship to God. But that relationship can only be sustained by repeatedly rehearsing the stories within which it is constituted. It is through their narrative that their identity is structured and preserved.

Moreover, it is because the narrative structures the Israelites' identity that their active remembrance of that narrative sets the parameters for action. Remembering God, remembering the stories of how he liberated them from Egypt and succoured them in the wilderness, is not a matter of detached recollection of names or facts, as though the Israelites were being asked to hold themselves in readiness as contestants for *Mastermind.* Rather, remembering God and their own narrative identity was meant to ensure that the Israelites would not become worshippers of other gods but would instead continue to follow the laws of God enshrined in the story of their past. Their history has an afterlife. The stories they tell themselves about their past construct the framework of their future. It is when they forget – or refuse – to rehearse those stories that they turn to other stories of other people's gods, with disastrous results. It was their memory of their own story that would ensure their continued faithfulness. The collective life story would provide a meaningful account of their society, would give them an identity, a sense of who they are. That sense of themselves, continually reinforced by rehearsal of their narrative, would make faithfulness more likely, since to 'go after other gods' would be a betrayal of who they were and a fracturing of their identity. But positively, behaving in accordance with their narrated lives would be acting in a way that continued rather than disrupted the meaning of their story.

But then how was it that they turned to other gods after all? The Israelites had a great deal more in their story than continuous faithfulness. Time and again we are told of their 'turning aside', forgetting God, worshipping the gods of the people who lived in the land before them, or their neighbours. Indeed the book of Judges is a book where a single pattern is repeatedly enacted: the Israelites worship other gods, God punishes them by allowing them to be defeated by their enemies, they repent, God delivers them from their enemy by raising up a leader or 'judge' under whose command they are victorious. Taken at face value the stories show a people who are very slow indeed to learn faithfulness. They also show a god whose primary tactic for instilling faithfulness is violence, though this is perhaps not the lesson the writers intend us to draw.

But can the story be taken as a literal account? Memory, as we have seen, is at best multi-faceted and can be treacherous; and narrative can be fiction as easily as history. In a later chapter I shall examine the argument that very much of the narrative of ancient Israel was written hundreds of years after the events they purport to recount, and that they were in fact a deliberate attempt to give beleaguered Israelites of the sixth to fourth century BCE an ideology and national identity by giving them a 'history' of their origins and development. My present point is that the Bible stories, whether fiction or history, give a narrative which allow the Israelites to think of themselves as the special people of God, a self-representation in which they were bonded to God in a covenant relationship repeatedly re-enacted through the violence of blood sacrifice and holy war. Not only did their narrative give them their self-identity, but that identity was embedded in layers of religiously sanctioned violence, as we will see more fully in later chapters.

The detail of the narrative can be omitted for now, but even a cursory glance shows how that narrative had a profound afterlife that has profoundly shaped Western consciousness. The idea of being the chosen people was taken up by the Christian Church, basing itself on the violent 'sacrifice' of Christ. Here again, narrative is central. The four Gospels of the Christian New Testament consist of stories of Jesus: his birth, his ministry of healing and teaching, his encounter with prostitutes and Pharisees, and finally his death and resurrection. The book of Acts tells stories of the early Christian community and its gradual spread around the Roman Empire through the efforts of early apostles. Like the Hebrew Bible, these stories of the New Testament are selective not exhaustive, and their historicity is open to continuing debate. What cannot be doubted, however, is that the self-identity of Christendom is grounded in the narratives of the New Testament and the doctrinal teaching which bases itself upon them. Again, this is not an argument for the veracity of either the stories or the dogmas but an observation of the centrality of narrative to the self-identity of Christendom and a recognition of the way narrative lives on and frames subsequent belief and practice.

Nowhere is this more important than in the story of Jesus' last supper with his disciples. Here, according to the biblical account, they were explicitly enjoined to remember and repeat the ritual; and the words are still said, as they have been for millennia, at each celebration of the communion/ eucharist/mass – even the terminology reveals both the unity and the dispute to which the 'memory' and narrative identity has given rise.

> The Lord Jesus on the night when he was betrayed took bread, and when he had given thanks, he broke it, and said, 'This is my body which is for you. Do this in remembrance of me'. In the same way also the cup, after supper, saying, 'This cup is the new covenant in my blood. Do this, as often as you drink it, in remembrance of me'. For as often as you eat this bread and drink the cup, you proclaim the Lord's death until he comes.
>
> (1 Corinthians 11:23–26)

It is a perfect example of how one narrative is embedded in another, but also extends it. The idea of 'new covenant' could not be understood were it not for the story of the original covenant which shaped the identity of the Israelites. Similarly the notion of Jesus as 'sacrifice' or 'Lamb of God' is part of the afterlife of the narratives of Abraham's sacrifice of Isaac and the rituals of blood sacrifice in the history attributed to ancient Israel. Without these prior narratives of sacrifice, Jesus's death could not have been interpreted in the terms that have become familiar; yet that very interpretation also reshapes the narrative and extends its afterlife into Christendom and beyond.

The narratives of Christendom and of the Hebrew Bible are different in important respects from the narratives of classical civilization, but they combined with them to form the self-identity of the West. In the first volume of this project I showed how the Romans appropriated for themselves the Greek narratives of heroism, especially the Homeric epics, so that for example Vergil portrayed Augustus Caesar as descended from the gods through the heroic Trojan line. This narrative became part of the ideology of Roman greatness, and served as justification for empire. Romans – at least upper class Romans – saw themselves as superior to barbarians, a superiority massively reinforced when it was combined with the idea held by Christendom of being the specially chosen people of God, the Church as the ark of salvation which would bear its adherents to heaven while the rest of the world was damned. Whatever cruelties or injustices Christians visited upon the peoples they conquered or colonized, they could represent themselves as bringing a generous mission to people less fortunate than themselves, civilizing them in this world and saving them from damnation in the next. The Roman Empire, duly Christianized, became a crucial part of the narrative of the West. It lived on in repeated patterns of the Holy Roman Empire, the Spanish and Napoleonic and British Empires, and now the American Empire. All of these styled themselves at least in part on Christianized narratives of Rome.

Since that narrative was deeply invested in gendered violence, it is not surprising that its afterlife is a history of violent repetitions. As I discussed in Volume 1, masculinity was represented in Roman thought as paradigmatically active killing – penetration by penis or by sword. In Christendom this combined in sometimes uneasy patterns with ideas of violent martyrdom and sacrifice, real and rhetorical, and the practices of holy war on heretics and infidels. I shall explore this further in later chapters; my point here is that the gendered violence of the narratives has an afterlife which continues to structure the West until this day. As Regina Schwartz has argued, 'The Bible encodes Western culture's central myth of collective identity' (Schwartz 1997:6), an identity forged in terms of the specialness of the 'chosen people' and the exclusion of anyone designated as *not* chosen.

> It has been the biblical narratives, for better and for worse, that have wielded so much influence, even more than the classics, with the result that the Bible could be deployed against whatever 'Canaanites' people wanted to loathe, conquer, or exile.
>
> Through the dissemination of the Bible in Western culture, its narratives have become the foundation of a prevailing understanding of ethnic, religious and national identity as defined negatively, over against others. We are 'us' because we are not 'them'.
>
> (Schwartz 1997:x)

Now, it might be thought that the power of this violent narrative of identity would lose its grip in secular modernity. With the deliberate separation of church and state in the American Constitution, and the sharp decline of the churches of Europe, surely biblical narratives of covenant, chosenness and holy war can no longer be used to justify political or military action? I would argue, however, that discounting the role of biblical narratives is misguided for two reasons. In the first place, as already argued, it has become apparent that religion plays a much larger role in Western political thinking in the twenty-first century than had previously been acknowledged, especially in the USA where no politician can afford to ignore the power of the religious right and where every presidential address ends with 'God bless America'. In American interventions from Nicaragua to Iraq it is obvious in both action and rhetoric that America considers herself to be superior, not only militarily, which she obviously is, but also morally and politically, which is much less obvious. Any means may be used to preserve her way of life and impose 'democracy' and 'freedom' (to say nothing of global capitalism) on others: indeed it is her vocation to do so. The vocabulary of 'vocation' or 'calling' comes easily to presidential lips, a vocabulary that implies a divine call to a chosen people. Although British and European political leaders would use such overtly religious language less glibly, they too appeal to notions of trust and moral obligation, and easily assume the superiority of western democracy and culture over that of others.

This points us to the second reason why it is important to take biblical stories and ideas as fundamental even to the ostensibly secular identity of the West. As John Gray has argued, modernity itself is founded upon the religious idea of salvation.

> The prevailing idea of what it means to be modern is a post-Christian myth. Christians have always held that there is only one path to salvation, that it is disclosed in history and that it is open to all … Worshipping one God, Christians have always believed that only one way of life can be right.
>
> (Gray 2003:103)

Gray points out that eastern religions such as Hinduism or Buddhism do not seek for a meaning in history: salvation does not occur *in* time or history but rather is liberation *from* it. In the modern West, however, history itself is construed as 'progress', the secular variant of 'salvation history'; and the West considers itself farthest along that road of modernity, which should come to all nations as they continue to 'develop'. There is therefore in Western nations a secular faith, inherited from the Christian idea of salvation, that 'as the rest of the world absorbs science and becomes modern, it is bound to become secular, enlightened and peaceful – as, contrary to all evidence, they imagine themselves to be' (Gray 2003:118). Moreover, the West has a moral or missionary duty to assist in every way possible the advance of this secular salvation, not only in the 'developing' world but within itself as well.

Here is a truly Faustian ambition – to transform by physical action not merely the earth, but the qualities of the creatures who dwell upon it, an ambition related to the modern quest for the breaking down of mountains, the escape from the bounds of the earth, the control and reform of human genetics, the manipulation of life itself ...

(Stillman and Pfaff 1964:29, quoted in Gray 2003:118)

I shall argue later in this volume that the Christian idea of salvation from *sin* was transformed, partly through its absorption of Greek philosophical concepts, into the idea of salvation from *finitude.* Once release from finitude was envisaged, then scientists, politicians and economists could rely on the religious mythology that informs the half unconscious auto-narrative of the West to support their drive for progress and development. To suppose that because the modern West is secular it is no longer influenced by biblical narratives is therefore to misunderstand the character and basis of secular modernity.

Narrative and resources for change

The auto-narrative of the West, steeped as it is in biblical stories and the classical world, is an auto-narrative deeply invested in gendered death-dealing. War and killing are marks of masculinity: men follow the Lord of Hosts to battle, literal or spiritual, while women are passive and accept suffering and sacrifice. Mimetic desire as analysed by René Girard is a powerful account of the spiral of violence of the West and its fixation on death; far too much of the history of the West can be told in terms of necrophilic longings premised upon a lack which is filled by violence and mastery on the part of men, and the sacrifice and submission of women.

As I argued in the previous chapter, however, not all desire is mimetic or premised upon a lack. The desire to be creative, to bring something new into the world out of the overflowing fullness of resources, is at least as important as mimetic desire, though it has received far less scholarly attention. But how is this creative desire to be understood, and how can it be channelled to generate resources for change?

I suggest that it is once again to narrative that we can look as a place to begin the investigation. In any story of a self, we assume that it has a beginning and has (or will have) an end: birth and death. Our auto-narratives begin with our parents and our birth, even though the story of our birth (and ultimately also our death) can only be told in the first instance by somebody else. Moreover although it is inevitable that each of us will die, it would be perverse – or sick – to tell the story of our lives as though death were its whole focus or meaning. The lives that we live and the narratives we tell of those lives are full of actions and events that are done and experienced with the resources that we have from birth and have developed since then. It is paradigmatically with the birth of a child that newness comes into the world: new possibilities of choice and action and creativity.

Birth and death are the events that begin and end each human life; natality and mortality are the philosophical categories that take their bearings from these events. As I have argued elsewhere, Western philosophy has been much preoccupied with mortality, defining the meaning of life by reference to its temporal finitude, the fact that it must end. This is as true at the level of society as it is for the meaning of individual lives. In the first volume of this project I showed how Western consciousness from Homer to the Roman Empire has been shaped by a preoccupation with mortality, a preoccupation which expressed itself in gendered violence. In this volume I shall show how the same dread and love of mortality – 'necrophilia' as I have labelled the obsession – characterizes the religious symbolic of the West in its auto-narration of covenant, sacrifice and holy war. In each case, however, this investment in mortality and violence is not inevitable. It is a choice; and it could have been – could still be – made otherwise.

Even the narrative can be told in more than one way. Full of wars and violence as the West has been, it has also been full of love and beauty and creativity. A history that concentrates on violence and war is like a life story that places the focus of meaning upon death. Death is significant, to be sure, and not to be ignored; but birth, too, is part of the story; and it is with birth, with creativity, that newness can enter the world. Natality is that which offers the possibility of fresh starts, new and creative approaches that can subvert violence and destruction. It is therefore crucial, in developing resources for change, that we look not only at the narratives of mortality, war and violence, where mimetic desire as lack spirals into destruction, but also at narratives of natality and creativity, expressions of beauty and newness.

Moreover, natality cannot be thought of without body and gender: the body of the mother and the sexed newcomer to whom she gives birth and whose life story begins in the web of relationships anchored in the mother. A focus on mortality can ignore gender. It can look away from the body, as it has through centuries of Christendom, and concentrate instead on an immortal soul. It can treat the self as an atomistic individual, unconnected with others, since it is after all possible to die alone. But no one can be born alone: a focus on natality must recognize the narratable self in interconnection with other selves, each of whom is as unique and irreplaceable as itself.

Once we begin to tell stories of the self and stories of culture in a way that takes natality seriously, another shift occurs. It becomes obvious that the metaphor of salvation which has dominated Western history (both sacred and secular) is indeed a metaphor, and one that fits snugly with a focus on mortality. Salvation connotes rescue from an intolerable situation, not a change in the situation itself, a rescue that is effected by someone outside, not brought about by the one in peril. It bespeaks atomistic individualism, just as does mortality: one individual can be miraculously 'saved' while everyone else is destroyed. Christendom is full of such stories, from Noah's flood to the book of Revelation, where hand-picked individuals rejoice in heavenly bliss while the rest of the world is swallowed up in damnation. The body, and especially its unruly sexuality, has often been seen as a hindrance to salvation: it is the soul that is saved, on some accounts by escaping the body, on others by effecting the body's transformation. It is hardly surprising that in a religious rhetoric that focuses on mortality and salvation, the woman – sexually attractive, embodied, birth-giving – would be represented as inferior to the male, conceptually linked to the immortal soul and to God.

If, however, we begin with birth and use the category of natality as a frame of reference, then we can see how the metaphor of flourishing as a garden or a plant flourishes and flowers, comes to mind, as I shall discuss more fully in Chapter 8. Unlike salvation, which could be granted to one individual alone, flourishing (like natality) implies interconnection in a web of life, a web in which each contributes to the wellbeing of the other in a circle of interdependence (as plants, bees, birds, rain and the earth itself need one another to flourish). If there is something amiss, it must be put right: a single individual cannot flourish while leaving an intolerable situation as it is. Nor does flourishing require miraculous rescue from the outside. Provided that conditions are right, flourishing is natural, it comes from within, from the resources of life growing into fullness. It is therefore vitally reliant upon the body, and upon nourishment and reproduction. Working from the metaphor of flourishing one would never minimize the importance of the body, gender, or the maternal; and the misogyny which has plagued Christendom would have no place. The metaphor of flourishing has an important place for death as the natural end of life, but it does not allow the idea that it is death which gives life its meaning and significance.

The metaphor of flourishing has a place in biblical writings, as I shall show in detail later, but it is very largely displaced in Christendom by the metaphor of salvation, to such an extent that flourishing may now seem like a novel concept and salvation as literal doctrine, not a metaphor at all. In the development and transmission of biblical narratives (as of any narratives) certain elements are given prominence while others are marginalized or displaced from consciousness. In the narrative of the West, the focus on mortality and the metaphor of salvation have given rise to an ideology of dominance and the technologies and practices of violence, while natality, creativity, beauty and flourishing have been suppressed or ignored.

But this does not mean that they do not exist. Just as the narratives we tell of our individual lives select some things and omit others, depending on the purposes for which we tell them, so also the religious narratives of the Bible and of Christendom select and omit, depending on the story-teller and the context in which they were written. The Bible is after all not a single book, even though the Christendom of the West has chosen to present it as if it were, by enclosing it in a single set of covers, with uniform typeface and consecutive pagination. It is a whole collection of literature written by authors with conflicting agendas and to audiences with varying needs. Hence 'the biblical canon should not be understood as the product of a peaceful consensus, but as the result of protracted struggles for authority between competing communities' (Schwartz 1997:146).

I shall discuss theories of how, when and by whom the Bible was written later. The present point is that it is not a monolithic narrative. Within the Bible there are counter-narratives which qualify or subvert the narrative of violence that achieved dominance in the West, voices in the margins which lift up themes of natality and beauty. If this is so within the Bible itself, it is equally true of the narratives of Christendom which base themselves upon it.

> If historical events give rise to narratives in complex ways, the historical afterlife of a given narrative is equally convoluted ... Narratives rewrite one another, altering emphases, changing contexts, shifting focus, sub-stituting characters, times and places. If from one perspective biblical typology opens its vast maw to ingest all the events of history, from another the ancient text is dismembered, rewritten, rethought, and relieved ...
>
> (Schwartz 1997:156)

A process that continues through its whole afterlife until the present.

Michel Foucault made a significant distinction between traditional history, which tells a single continuous story in which all elements are made to fit into a developing theme, and a much more complex and ambiguous notion of history which he calls 'effective' history. In his words,

> History becomes 'effective' to the degree that it introduces discontinuity into our very being – as it divides our emotions, dramatizes our instincts, multiplies our body and sets it against itself. 'Effective' history deprives the self of the reassuring stability of life and nature, and it will not allow itself to be transported by a voiceless obstinacy toward a mil-lennial ending. It will uproot its traditional foundations and relentlessly disrupt its pretended continuity.
>
> (Foucault 1977:154)

It is within the fissures and ambiguities of narrative, I suggest, that 'effective' history is found, a history that renounces the complacency of ideology and looks instead for the resources that can help to bring about change. As long as our auto-narratives, individual or collective, turn away from ambiguities and reject the disruptions inherent in them and the invitations to think and act otherwise, we will repeat the patterns established in that narrative, as Pierre Bourdieu showed, and may well be unconscious that we are doing so. If in the West history reproduces itself on the basis of history then we can expect escalation of violence with more or less explicit religious under-pinnings. On the other hand, if we accept the invitation to destabilize this auto-narrative, then I suggest that we can discover openings which lead to resources for change. It is my task in these volumes to probe the narrative of the West precisely to discern these ambiguities and openings.

The resources for change emerge in two ways. First, awareness of the counternarratives, ambiguities, and voices in the margin disrupts the notion that the West is really progressive and peaceful and that development along its trajectory benefits everyone. When we ask who gains and who loses, listen to their voices, the negative values of the religious ideology and classical heritage of our auto-narrative disrupt the complacent traditional history which we otherwise largely assume. Second, these voices can also point towards alternatives, ways of thinking and being that too often have not been chosen but are still available to bring newness and flourishing into the world.

Before proceeding in the rest of this book to illustrate this methodology in relation to the Bible and early Christendom, I wish to discuss each of these two ways in turn in a little more detail.

The power of the negative for change

A philosopher who expended much effort in theorizing the significance of the negative and its role in bringing about change was G.W.F. Hegel. Hegel is often caricatured as a philosopher of totality: one form of life or con-sciousness meets its opposite, and in the conflict a new third form emerges, only to meet its opposite in turn in a stately waltz of the Absolute through time. There is something in this caricature; certainly in the *Phenomenology* Hegel appears to be charting the advance of (human? German?) spirit in terms of such encounters. The detail has been endlessly discussed.

However, it is much more interesting for my purposes to ask about how Hegel understood the role of opposition or the negative in such encounters, the dynamism of the negative which makes it a resource for change. Here we return to the idea of desire as lack. In Hegel's terms, consciousness sees itself over against what it is *not*, what it does not have. This gives rise to desire, a desire which works to fill the lack. Although I have already argued that not all desire should be seen in terms of lack, there is no denying that much of it is, and that by working through this lack toward fulfilment desire acts as a powerful dynamic of change. Judith Butler, in her analysis of the role of desire in Hegel's thought, says:

> Conceived as a lack, a being-without, desire initially signifies negativity; as the pursuit of substance, desire thus implicitly raises the question of whether human negativity, that which constitutes its ontological differ-ence, can be resolved into an encompassing network of being. Human

desire articulates the subject's relationship to that which is *not* itself, that which is different, strange, novel, awaited, absent, lost.

(Butler 1999:9)

Desire as negativity is thus vital as the dynamic of change. Both Hegel and Butler write in abstract terms; it is easiest to conceive of their 'subject' as an individual human consciousness. But it is not hard to see how this theory is concretely instantiated in relation to the ambiguities of narrative and effective history. As the individual or collective subject becomes conscious of the fissures and disruptions, comes to recognize the complacent ideology of traditional history for what it is, and hears the voices from the margins of what might have been but is not, the subject comes to desire this negative.

Desire for what one is not can of course be destructive and violent, as Girard showed in his account of mimetic rivalry. The example that springs most readily to mind in relation to Hegel is his account of lordship and bondage, where two subjects desire recognition from one another and engage in a struggle to the death in order to achieve it. While the importance of this aspect of desire as lack could hardly be overstated, however, it is not the whole account. Desire can also, after all, be for what is good, what is creative, that is experienced as a lack or a negative by the desiring subject. Thus negation is not merely a principle of destruction but also a principle of creativity. Judith Butler says,

> The negative is also human freedom, human desire, the possibility to create anew; the nothingness to which human life had been consigned was thus at once the possibility of its renewal. The nonactual is at once the entire realm of possibility. The negative showed itself in Hegelian terms not merely as death, but as a sustained possibility of *becoming.*
>
> (Butler 1999:62)

Neither Butler nor Hegel write in terms of narrative, but it is clear that the account of the creative role of the negative can be applied. When the ambiguities and fissures of effective history disrupt the traditional story, glimpses appear of what it is not, its negative; and these begin to show themselves as possibilities of what might be. I shall argue in a moment that unless there is also desire that overflows, desire *not* premised upon a lack, then these negatives on their own can lead at best to partial transformation, at worst to mere reversal: the old slave becomes the new master but the system of slavery is not overcome. Nevertheless, the negative, and desire for what is not, is of enormous importance in the development of narrative identity. Yearning for peace instead of violence, generosity rather than greed, flourishing rather than dereliction is indispensable for the creation of a better future, even though this yearning, so long as it is based on a negative, is as yet yearning only for the mirror image of what is undesirable. Sometimes, indeed, confronting the negative *as* negative is all that is possible in a concrete situation. Jean-Paul Sartre famously recognized that there are times when the only freedom left to an individual or a group is the freedom to say no. The power to refuse an intolerable state of affairs is a terrible final freedom in a situation where such resistance comes at the price of one's life; but nevertheless it remains open, and in the context of Nazi occupation and the resistance movement within which Sartre wrote, this freedom of resistance, the ultimate negative, was embraced often with great heroism. If it was not within their power to bring about a better world, they could at least refuse to be party to the evils of the regime that was being imposed upon them. They could say no.

The negative is thus crucial as part of the dynamic for change, and should not be passed over too quickly. Hegel writes of '*tarrying* with the negative', 'looking the negative in the face' (Hegel 1977:19, emphasis mine), not treating it merely as nothing or false or of no importance. It is important to confront the violence and death-dealing of Western self-identity in all its dimensions if we are to develop resources for change. Only by facing up to and tarrying with the negative in our individual and collective auto-narratives will the yearning for change grow. If we turn too quickly away from it, do not come to terms with it as that which has made us what we are, then our efforts at change are likely to be mere repetitions.

Confronting our auto-narrative with all its dissonances and ambiguities is, of course, central to individual psychotherapy; I am arguing that the same is true for our collective identity. In both cases it is tempting to hurry over the negative and try to move quickly to a solution, a prescription that will make things better. But as Paul Ricoeur once said, 'If we want to be instructed by events, then we must not be in a hurry to solve them' (Ricoeur 1965:247). To jump quickly from an immediate crisis to a 'solution' without confronting the ambiguities of the history which forms the context in which the crisis occurs is to risk repetition and escalation, history reproducing itself on the basis of history.

Thus if in our present context we hope to offer constructive suggestions for non-violent alternatives to the conflicts that are tearing the world apart in the name of God, we must take the time to study the genealogy of religious violence in the West. The goal of this study is threefold. First, it will make us aware of the complex ways in which religion, gender and violence have been interlocked in the history of the West. Second, it will increase yearning for an alternative, desire for the 'negative' of this destructive pattern. Third, by raising up the counternarratives and dissonances, listening to the voices from the margins, we will find clues for how it could have been different, how we might learn to think otherwise and bring about change for the better.

Thinking Utopia

This third goal, however, already indicates that though it is essential to tarry with the negative and not pass over it too quickly, ultimately the negative is not good enough. Though the negative is dynamic, fostering desire for change, the desire that is premised on lack will still always be desire for the polar opposite of the situation perceived as negative: master and slave will reverse positions. If change is to be truly transformative rather than simply the antithesis of the present (like the negative of a photograph), then the negative is not enough. It is at this point that creativity enters, the desire to bring about something new, out of overflowing abundance, not out of lack, and aiming towards flourishing rather than destruction.

In political terms, the vision for positive change has been presented as Utopia. Utopia literally means 'no place': it does not exist (or does not exist yet) and perhaps never could. It is the place outside the auto-narrative of the community, extraterritorial, that calls traditional history into question and reveals other possibilities.

> From this 'no place' an exterior glance is cast on our reality, which suddenly looks strange, nothing more being taken for granted. The field of the possible is now open beyond that of the actual; it is a field, therefore, for alternative ways of living.
>
> (Ricoeur 1986:16)

Paul Ricoeur, who wrote these words, contrasts Utopia with ideology. Ideology can (with qualifications) be seen as the auto-narrative of traditional history, the complacent story (in the West) of progress, freedom and democracy. The exterior, the outside, the place on the margins problematizes this complacency; but it is also the place from which real alternatives can be imagined.

> May we not say then that the imagination itself – through its utopian function – has a *constitutive* role in helping us *rethink* the nature of our social life? Is not utopia – this leap outside – the way in which we radically rethink what is family, what is consumption, what is authority, what is religion, and so on? Does not the fantasy of an alternative society and its exteriorization 'nowhere' work as one of the most formidable contestations of what is?
>
> (Ricoeur 1986:16)

Any theoretical account of how this 'leap outside' is to be achieved is about as useful as a theoretical account of any sort of leap, or indeed any sport or skill. One does not learn to run or jump or play an instrument by reading books about it, but by practice; and if that practice is guided by a skilled coach or teacher it is all the more likely to produce good results. In the effort to find an 'exterior' place from which the 'contestation of what is' can get a purchase, we need not work in a vacuum: there are excellent guides among many groups who have been marginalized whether because of gender, race, colonization, disability, or any of the other ways of not being the normative white heterosexual affluent male. Teresa de Lauretis, discussing how feminism has learned to represent gender otherwise, writes of the 'exterior' place like this (using 'Utopia' here in a negative sense):

> That 'elsewhere' is not some mythic distant past or some utopian future history: it is the elsewhere of history here and now, the blind spots, the space-off, of its representations. I think of it as spaces in the margins of hegemonic discourses, social spaces carved in the interstices of institutions and in the chinks and cracks of the power-knowledge apparati.
>
> (de Lauretis 1987:25)

There are, de Lauretis says, spaces that exist and that can be discerned in 'counter-practices and new forms of community' (26). By attending to these 'chinks and cracks', listening to the voices from the margins of the biblical texts and the history of religion in the West (and being aware that many voices have been silenced altogether), there are resources for imagining and working towards newness.

The creativity of imagination empowered by desire for newness is inspired by the counter-narratives and alternative perspectives of exteriority, and guided by values of natality and flourishing. It is this imagination that is set free by attentiveness to the life and beauty that emerges ever and again as contrast with the sordid violence that structures the narrative of the West, and develops a poetics of transformation. In concrete terms, what is required is a painstaking genealogy not only of the religious violence that has formed the West but also of the voices of resistance, beauty and hope. It is that task to which I turn in the rest of this book.

Part Two

Judaism and the ancient near east

Chapter 3

The finger of God

In the biblical book of Isaiah, the writer tells how 'the Spirit of the Lord God is upon' him to preach and heal and bring comfort and liberty to those who have been oppressed.

> To give unto them beauty for ashes, the oil of joy for mourning, the garment of praise for the spirit of heaviness; that they might be called the trees of righteousness, the planting of the Lord ...
>
> (Isaiah 61.3 AV)

It is a passage part of which the Gospel writer puts also into the mouth of Jesus (Luke 4.18–19): the one who comes from God brings liberty, gladness and beauty. Like trees flourishing in a garden of the Lord, life and delight are promised by the one upon whom the Spirit of God rests.

In the narrative of Western religion, however, there has been little focus on beauty and flourishing. Much more attention has been paid to 'ashes', the violence and destruction which is to be replaced by beauty. History itself, in the auto-narrative of the West, has constituted itself on the premise of violence. History is about politics and war, about 'what happens'. Beauty does not 'happen', is not construed as an event, is therefore not a part of 'history'. As Mieke Bal has written, there is an eagerness to define 'history as primarily military and political history' which 'prevents scholars from seeing other issues and continuous structures' (Bal 1988:13). Since that eagerness is rooted in an androcentric perspective it is hardly surprising that beauty has often been construed not only as not having to do with history but also primarily of concern to women. In the focus on death, violence and war, beauty is displaced to the future, to Utopia, to women, to the unhistorical.

There are complex interconnected issues here, of historiography, gender, aesthetics and religion. What counts as history? Who does the counting? – and from what perspectives of gender and power? How do 'continuous structures' like beauty figure in or frame history and how are they displaced? There is ongoing debate about these issues among historians and historiographers, and it is not my intention to bring theoretical resolution to them here. Instead, I want to show how the Hebrew Bible itself, one of the germ-inal texts of the auto-narrative of the West, trains the gaze on ashes: the ashes of sacrifice, of burned cities, of holocaust and holy war, all based in an originary covenant with God. These are themes which have shaped and continue to shape Western self-understanding and action in their afterlife in our habitus, structuring the gendered symbolic of death and violence which I am tracing in these volumes.

Yet always in the margins are the counter-memories which disrupt and destabilize this violent symbolic and suggest alternatives of natality and flourishing, of beauty for ashes. There are voices which protest at injustice, women and men whose understanding of the divine is not constricted by self-protective boundaries defended by aggression and violence, songs and stories which lift up beauty and flourishing. And it is upon these, according to both the writer of Isaiah and the Gospel, that the spirit of the Lord rests.

The inspiration of scripture

> All scripture is inspired by God and profitable for teaching, for reproof, for correction, and for training in righteousness, that the man of God may be complete, equipped for every good work.
>
> (2 Timothy 3.16–17)

This view of scripture, as inspired by God and thus as the divinely author-ized basis for thought and action, has been at the heart of Jewish and Christian theology. There have of course been many debates about how that 'inspiration' should be understood; but underlying all of them is the idea that the Bible is a special book, not in its literary merits but in the sense that it is or contains a revelation of the divine in a way that no other book can, and especially equipping the 'man of God' for life and for death.

Thus although there are many parallels between this volume and Volume 1 (*Foundations of Violence*), there is also a dissimilarity, the importance of which defies calculation. It is from the Hebrew Bible and the Christian New Testament that the religions of the West take their origins, thus giving these books a status in Western consciousness quite different from that of even the most beloved texts of the classical world. The cultural capital derived from the biblical writings has for centuries been accorded nothing less than divine authority.

Even though there has been endless dispute about the religious meanings and interpretations of the biblical texts, these disputes have resonances quite different from those surrounding the texts of Homer, Plato or Seneca. Few people think that their standing before God is determined by how they respond to Sophocles or Euripides, even if these dramatists are acknowl-edged to be representing issues of great moral weight. Many people, by contrast, have thought and still think that their standing before God is indeed determined by how they read Moses or Paul. Again, although Plato and Plotinus look for immortality while Lucretius denies life after death, not even their most ardent supporters would argue that those authors were able to confer the immortality or extinction which they or their protagonists discuss. Yet over the centuries it has been held that the gift of eternal life or damnation to hell is meted out by the Christ of the Gospels. The preoccupation with death and mortality in the founding documents of Judaism and Christianity, and the sediments of that preoccupation in Western culture, are therefore on a different scale of moral and religious seriousness from that of the classical civilizations which I discussed in Volume 1. The Greek and Latin authors have formed the backbone of Western education, and have structured the thought patterns of the men who marched to war or built empires or wrote documents of Western culture; but the literature of the Bible, read and heard throughout the liturgical year and from cradle to grave, formed the religious sensibilities of the West, and these run most deeply of all.

But if the special status of the Bible which makes it different from classical literature is because the Bible is scripture, what exactly is 'scripture'? Technically, the word 'scripture' simply means 'writings'. As the term has come to be used, however, it carries connotations of special authority. The scriptures are the written documents that are revelatory of God and God's dealings with humankind that form the basis of religion. The Bible is called a 'holy' book, a book set apart from all others. Jews and Christians are sometimes called 'people of the book': the same is true of Muslims in relation to the Qur'an.

Because of this special status accorded to the Bible, and the effects it has had upon the violent habitus of the West, it is useful to pause to ask how the Bible actually came to be written. Who wrote it, and when, and in what circumstances? Whole libraries have been written about these questions, and aspects of the replies are still heavily contested; I shall do no more here than indicate some lines of current scholarship, and shall do so only to show something of the grip that the Bible has had on Western consciousness, the afterlife of its narrative.

The Bible was for many centuries taken as the 'word of God': its contents somehow communicated by God himself. The prototype was the 'tables of stone, written with the finger of God' which God gave to Moses on Mount Sinai (Exodus 31.18): the tables are usually taken to have contained the Ten Commandments.

> And Moses turned, and went down from the mountain with the two tables of the testimony in his hands, tables that were written on both sides; on the one side and on the other were they written. And the tables were the work of God, and the writing was the writing of God, graven upon the tables.
>
> (Exodus 32.15–16)

Other parts of the Pentateuch (the first five books of the Bible as we now have it) are said to be, if not written with the finger of God, at least spoken with the voice of God. Repeatedly, sets of instructions are prefaced with the words, 'and the Lord said to Moses' (e.g. Exodus 20.22; Leviticus 8.1; Numbers 9.1); the book of Deuteronomy represents Moses as repeating to the Israelites the words which God had said to him. Sometimes, indeed, they too had heard God speak. As Moses reminds the Israelites:

> These words the Lord spoke to all your assembly at the mountain out of the midst of the fire, the cloud, and the thick darkness, with a loud voice; and he added no more.
>
> (Deuteronomy 5.22)

The same sort of language is used in the books of the prophets in the Hebrew Bible. Jeremiah repeatedly states that 'the word of the Lord came to me, saying ... ', and his book then reports what God has said to him. Isaiah, Ezekiel, Amos and others similarly represent themselves as mouthpieces of God, speaking the words that God has spoken to them.

David Clines, commenting on the account of God speaking to the Israelites, ponders what to make of this.

> Taking these words seriously, and not brushing them aside as some strange Hebrew idiom, I find myself asking: Did God (if there is a God) actually speak audible words out of the sky over a mountain in the Arabian peninsula in the late second millennium BCE?
>
> (Clines 1995:27)

In similar vein we could ask about God actually writing on a stone tablet: is the divine finger so hot or so sharp that it can engrave stone? Or did God use some kind of stylus? What did divine calligraphy look like? Could a tape recorder (or a video camera) have recorded the words of God when he spoke to the prophets?

Questions like these seem somehow improper, irreverent. Very few biblical scholars even in medieval times let alone in modernity would aver that God literally shouts down a mountainside or writes words on stones. But then what? If these descriptions are metaphorical rather than literal, what do they mean? Clines points out that commentators regularly pass over this question, while still using language that implies that the words were somehow never-theless received from God, that they were 'direct, unmediated communication of Yahweh himself' as Brevard Childs asserts (Childs 1974:397). Or again Moshe Weinfeld says,

> In their role as the fundamental demands made by the God of Israel on the Community of Israel, the Ten Commandments were familiar to

every Israelite loyal to his heritage. They became the crowning point of his religious and ethical tradition ... It was only the Ten Commandments that Israel was privileged to hear directly spoken by the Deity.

(Weinfeld 1990:21)

Comments like this sound as though they are meant to be taken literally. Yet a literal meaning could hardly be entertained: apart from anything else, it has usually been assumed that God is not embodied as humans are, and therefore has neither fingers nor mouth. Rather, as James Barr says,

Israelite law was not, as a superficial reading of the Old Testament might suggest, dropped complete from heaven, but grew and developed through various phases of the life of the Hebrew people.

(Barr in Nielsen 1968:vii)

But if that is the case, then has the connection with God been lost? In what sense, if any, can the Ten Commandments (and with them the rest of the Bible) be taken as expressing divine directives or revelation?

Once those sorts of questions are raised, various possibilities present themselves. One possibility, frequently taken up by biblical commentators or theologians, is just to ignore stories about God's fingers writing on stone tablets or his voice calling commands down a mountain in bad weather. While passing over such physical details in silence, they nevertheless seem to assume that we know quite well what they must really mean: thus Childs's and Weinfeld's remarks, cited above, of direct and unmediated communication from God, without further discussion of how that communication might have taken place. Again, in their *Introduction to the Hebrew Bible*, standardly used as a teaching resource and now in its fourth edition, the authors assert in the opening pages,

Both Israel's conception of God and its awareness of its own destiny can be traced to that time when God delivered it from bondage in Egypt and made it God's own people by entering into covenant with it at Sinai.

(Flanders *et al.* 1996:5)

The import of their book is that God is known through his deeds: his deliverance of the Israelites from Egypt, his dealings with them in the wilderness, and so on. In this respect they are in agreement with Barr. But of course the same old problems arise: just as the idea of a literal voice or finger of God strikes a modern reader as impossible, so also the idea that one could identify divine action within or behind historical events is unclear. If God did not literally speak at Sinai, then what does it mean to say that he entered into a covenant with the Israelites? How did they know he did? According to the text of the Bible, they knew it because God said so to Moses; but then we are back where we began, with questions about what it might mean to assert that God spoke.

Many theologians dismiss such questions as crass literalism, inappropriate to the genre(s) of the Bible, and offer varying accounts of how the Bible is revelatory, in what sense it is the 'word of God'. Some appeal to an inward or mystical awareness of God, an 'inner voice' rather than a voice whose words could be captured on a tape recorder. Others, following Karl Barth, reject such experiences as subjective, and appeal to a divine Word that speaks through preaching and through the Bible, cutting through all human difficulties and preconceptions and calling forth a response of faith (Barth 1968; 1957f; see also Lindbeck 1984). Others again discuss biblical narrative, seeing in the myths and stories of the Bible glimpses of the divine, discerning through the letter of the text the spirit of God (Frei 1974; Stroup 1981).

There is a vast literature on the whole question of the nature and authority of the Bible, and whether and in what sense it can be said to be (a means of) divine revelation. It is fair to say, however, that these questions are of interest largely to professional theologians, much less so to ordinary Christians, and simply a nonissue to the vast majority of people in western Europe who do not read the Bible at all and do not consider themselves 'believers' in any conventional sense. In secular modernity the whole idea of divine revelation or of the Bible as having any special authority has come to seem irrelevant at least to public concerns (Reventlow 1984). If individuals wish to profess religious belief they are of course free to do so, but this is their own private matter. Business, education, politics and public policy are firmly secular.

Or are they? As I have already argued, the violence which marks the beginning of the twenty-first century is charged with religious meaning, not least in the USA. Although there is a separation between church and state written into the American constitution, the USA affirms its status as 'One nation under God', every Presidential address concludes with 'God bless America', and it would be the end of any candidate's chance for election to public office if they underestimated the huge voting power of the religious right or failed to take their interests into account when shaping public policy. The public importance of religion has been heightened in the so-called 'war on terror', when 'terrorists' are routinely represented not as freedom fighters or as political or social extremists but as *religious* extremists, whose specifically religious stance is what motivates their action. Even though western politicians repeat monotonously that Islam as such is not violent or a problem for the West, the very fact that 'terrorists' are regularly linked with Islam (rather than with, say, political or economic desperation) makes the underlying assumption of Western consciousness obvious. It is also obvious, in the political rhetoric especially of the USA but also of Britain, and other European countries, that if Islam is the Other, 'we' are Christians. Even though there is less and less overt religious commitment in western Europe, at least as measured by such things as regular church attendance, there is nevertheless increased rhetoric about our 'Christian heritage' as part of the basis of Western values and even of democracy itself.

Thus it is clear that underneath the secular veneer of modernity, the cultural symbolic of the West is saturated with religion, drawn largely from the Bible. The Bible, even when people no longer read it, is assumed to be in some sense a 'holy' book, a book having religious authority. It is special, different from other books. It is assumed to be self-consistent and unified, and what religious people believe. It is often shown to be set apart from other books even in the way it is presented: often it is beautifully and expensively bound in leather and given as a special gift on a religious occasion like a confirmation or a marriage. In addition, as John Barton points out,

> The Bible in any of the forms it is encountered in the modern world gives out the strongest possible signals of unity, coherence and closure. All the books [that make up the Bible] have the same typography, the same style of translation, a consistent pagination, and a fixed order: features that arouse strong expectation that the contents will be a single 'work'.
>
> (Barton 1997:151)

They also, of course, give the expectation that that work carries religious authority. Although at a conscious level hardly anyone would accept that the Bible was written by the finger of God or was literally spoken by God, there is still an underlying sense not only that it has historically shaped the cultural symbolic of the West but that it is still 'our' holy book, no matter how secular we have become. In any instance where issues of public morality arise – whether the justification of war or the legitimacy of gay marriage – it is not unusual for a politician or the media to appeal to the Bible as the authority that trumps all other appeals. Sedimented in the habitus of the West is the notion of the finger of God, divine authority inscribed in the Bible.

But this brings us back to the starting point. If when we think about it we cannot believe in literal notions of divine fingers writing on stone, do we then just ignore or deny biblical authority at a conscious level while all the while it structures our responses in the form of unacknowledged assumptions and presuppositions? There is another possibility; namely to investigate when and by whom and in what context the various parts of the Bible were actually written, and how they came to assert the status which they have. After all, even those who are strongest in their affirmation of divine revelation in or through the Bible affirm that its books were written by a human being: Moses, perhaps, or Jeremiah, or Ezra, or others whose names are not known to us. But human beings are always historically and socially located, and their writings necessarily express their perspectives from that location. If we wish to understand how biblical writings came to assert their authority over western consciousness, I suggest that it is helpful not so much to develop a theological theory of divine revelation but rather to look at the human perspectives and interests that shaped their writing and transmission. When a human writer asserted that what he wrote was inscribed by the finger of God or uttered by the voice of God, what did he mean and why did he say it? Who believed him, and why? Who did it leave out? What was the social function of the text? And if, as we may assume, the text is normally an expression of dominant interests (or it would not have been preserved and transmitted, much less made canonical), are there nevertheless traces of suppressed voices, hints in the margins that point to dissent or alterities?

As I shall argue in relation to specific instances later in this volume, many of the biblical writers assume and reinscribe patriarchy and sometimes outright misogyny. They are ethnocentric and xenophobic. Above all, they are, as I shall show, obsessed with violence and death. There are many passages in the Bible which celebrate killing as enthusiastically as the Homeric writings; the difference is that they do so in the name of God. In consequence, insofar as biblical writings continue to exert authority over the western cultural symbolic, even – or especially – when that authority is unconscious or unacknowledged, its violent preoccupation will be part of the cultural mind set, waiting to be reasserted ever and again in gendered violence from witch hunts to wars, undertaken and justified in the name of God or 'Western values' which are assumed to reflect divine authority.

But that is not the whole story. As we saw in Volume 1, texts that carry one message at an overt level often carry within them seeds of a quite different message which, when pursued, qualifies or subverts the first: Penelope in the *Odyssey*, Parmenides' goddess, Sappho in Plato's *Phaedrus*. In the Bible, these destabilizing voices are more easily discerned because (in spite of its unified binding and pagination in modern leather-covered editions) the Bible is in fact a compilation of many books, by a whole range of authors who wrote at different times and places and reflect different interests and perspectives.

> Because of its multivocal nature, the Bible, despite its biases of gender, race/ethnicity, and class, makes provision for its own critique. It points to its own incongruity ... The Bible shows us not merely patriarchy, élitism and nationalism; it shows us the fragility of these ideologies through irony and counter-voices ... Voices from the margins, voices from the fissures and cracks in the text, assure us that male sovereignty is contrived and precarious, that racial/ethnic chauvinism is ultimately insupportable, that social élitism is self-deluding, that religious rectitude is self-serving.
>
> (Gunn and Fewell 1993:204)

In the chapters that follow, I shall show how beauty asserts itself against destruction, creativity against violence. Within the biblical writings themselves, there are resources available to challenge the hegemony of violence, that insist that killing is anything but godly, that offer beauty for ashes. If the deeply sedimented violence of the Western cultural symbolic is to be dismantled and transformed, then its roots in the biblical writings must be uncovered. In doing so, we will find in those same writings resources for newness and hope.

Who wrote the Bible? And when? And why?

For readers in the Middle Ages, for Luther, Calvin and their Catholic counterparts, for readers up to the eighteenth century and beyond, the Bible was taken as 'an exact historical manual going right back to Methusalah, to Adam, and to the seven days of creation' (Barr 2000:62; Scholder 1990:68). If the Pentateuch was said to be the 'Books of Moses' then so it was. The small difficulty that the death of Moses was described in the Book of Deuteronomy was easily overcome, either by saying that the last chapter of that book was written by Joshua, who then carried on the narrative in his own book, or else by the simple expedient of God giving Moses an account of his own death so that he could record it before it happened. Many of the Psalms were attributed to David, the Proverbs to Solomon, and so on. Moreover the historicity of the Bible was taken for granted, so that for example by adding the ages of the patriarchs from Adam to Methusalah one could calculate the date on which God created the world: 4004 BCE, according to James Ussher, Bishop of Armagh in the seventeenth century. The Bible, including its history, was taken as the framework within which life and experience should be understood and by which it should be evaluated. As Erich Auerbach has famously put it,

> Far from seeking, like Homer, merely to make us forget our own reality for a few hours, [Old Testament narrative] seeks to overcome our reality: we are to fit our own life into its world, feel ourselves to be elements in its structure of universal history ... Everything else that happens in the world can only be conceived as an element in this sequence; into it everything that is known about the world ... must be fitted as an ingredient of the divine plan.
>
> (Auerbach 1968:15)

Gradually this idea that the Bible was a unified volume written if not by the finger of God at least by direct divine inspiration and therefore factually correct and religiously authoritative, gave way before scientific and historical investigation. By the time Martin Noth wrote his *History of Israel* (1960, but first published in 1950), it was widely accepted by biblical scholars that the material from the early chapters of Genesis to Abraham could not be taken literally, and the stories of the 'Twelve Tribe Confederation' of Israel were not actually historical, though they might contain historical material. Noth argues that not until 926–925 BCE do we have accurate dating of biblical events: that is, from the end of the reign of Solomon. 'His death is the earliest event in the history of Israel which it is possible to date precisely, with the possible error of merely a few years', and from this date forward there is an 'uninterrupted chronological sequence' of kings that forms the backbone of subsequent biblical history (Noth 1960:225).

Now, one of the events of that alleged history is the discovery, during the reign of King Josiah (about 622 BCE), of a 'book of the law', usually taken to be the book of Deuteronomy, which precipitated a religious reform. However, recent scholars of Deuteronomy have argued that that book must be dated much later, after the beginning of a period of exile of Israelites when the land was captured by Babylon (cf. Blenkinsopp 1998). If this is so, then it follows that the whole chronology that Noth thought he could establish is in question. Virtually the whole story of Israel would be a narrative written much later, to serve the purposes and interests of the writers or their paymasters. Thus for example Philip Davies argues that most of the material of the Hebrew Bible was literature (not history) written in the fifth century BCE, as an attempt to provide an identity and ideology for the 'post exilic' Israelites. It is of course not the case that the books were 'commissioned and written to order'.

> But it is conceivable that the task of constructing a history of the society in which the cult, laws and ethos of the ruling caste would be authorized would be undertaken deliberately and conscientiously by scribes serving the ruling caste, partly at their behest, partly from self-interest, and partly from sheer creative enjoyment.
>
> (Davies 1992:115)

The rulers of Israel, including the priests and the officials of the court, were trying to forge the post-exilic immigrant people into a nation with political and religious self-consciousness, different from those who already lived in the land. They therefore constructed and imposed a 'history' and a religious system which in effect created an idealized Israel. Davies argues that:

> The immigrants, like the Pilgrim Fathers, had their minority experience come to determine the identity of the majority whose real history was different. However, this central paradox, by which the immigrants displaced the indigenous, manifested itself in other narratives too, celebrating an original 'Israel' that was brought into the 'promised land' from the outside, and distinguished itself radically and polemically from the indigenous population. There are in the biblical literature several

such stories of origin, including the stories of Abraham, the Exodus and the conquest.

(Davies 1992:115)

Thus the Hebrew Bible is not a history of Israel and its religious literature, accurately portraying real events, but a set of stories, poems, hymns and wise sayings put together from the fifth century onwards to consolidate national identity in part by giving them an imagined idealized past complete with religious rituals and stories of origin that enabled the weak and emergent nation to reconceive themselves as the special people of God.

The amazing thing, according to Davies, is that it worked. Not only at the time, but even up to the present, the literature written in the fifth century and onwards has been taken to be from a much earlier period and as representing actual history.

> The ideological triumph of the biblical story is to convince that what is new is actually old. It has been successful to the point of establishing a virtually unchallenged premise of biblical scholarship.
>
> (Davies 1992:114)

As we have seen, not only in popular perception but also in the opinion of leading scholars until recently, biblical literature has been taken as based in history and written much nearer the times which they represent than is true on Davies's account.

His suggestions are hotly contested. William Dever, for example, characterizes Davies's position as 'postmodern piffle' (2001:254) that, if taken seriously, would undermine the historical truth of the Bible and would thus be a danger to Christian belief. Dever appeals to archaeology to show that there is objective evidence confirming statements made in the Bible, as Albright had done half a century before. However, setting aside his vindictive tone, there are two problems with Dever's argument. One is that the archaeological finds and their interpretation are in considerable doubt (Finkelstein 1994). The second is that even if it were granted that archaeological discoveries confirm the historicity of some Biblical claims, the most that this could show would be that the books that were allegedly composed during the Persian period were not invented *ex nihilo* but used earlier material, oral or written, some of which had a historical basis.

This much Davies grants; though other scholars (e.g. Barr 2000; Provan 1998) argue that greater weight than Davies allows should be placed on the earlier material and (at least for the period of the kings) its historical references. Even on this assumption, however, it remains the case that the material selected for inclusion in the fifth century would have been selected in accordance with the religious and political needs that were obtained at that time. Other oral or written material inconsistent with forging a national religious identity would have been suppressed, though as we shall see, traces of it remain. Thus although debate continues regarding whether particular stories or passages are new compositions in the Persian period or date back to earlier times, it remains the case that the biblical books as we have them, reflect the thoughts and intentions of their sixth- to fourth-century author-editors. With regard to the first five books in particular (the Pentateuch) it can be said that:

> Few doubt that the Pentateuch in its completed form is a product of the Persian period ... The narrative from creation to the death of Moses, in which the laws are embedded, responded to the need for a national and ethnic founding myth urgently felt after the hiatus of the Babylonian conquest and subsequent deportations. Older narrative material in both written and oral form which survived the disasters of the late sixth century BC would presumably have been incorporated into this story of founding events.
>
> (Blenkinsopp 1998:184)

The same can be said with varying degrees of contention for the 'historical' books (Joshua to Chronicles) (Provan 1998), the prophets (Wilson 1998), and the wisdom literature (Alter 1998), all of which were gathered together (in yet another selection process betokening further needs and intentions) in the third- to second-century BCE in what became known as the 'Septuagint', a Greek translation of the Hebrew books. It was this Septuagint which effectively became the 'Old Testament' for early Christians. According to one Jewish tradition, the Hebrew canon was closed in the fourth century BCE in a 'Great Synagogue' initiated by the Jewish priest and statesman Ezra; others argue for a somewhat later date. Whatever the detail, from this period onward, if not before, the books were treated by Jews and later by Christians as a unit, a bible, and as having their source in divine revelation, whatever the human channels of reception (Childs 1979, 1985). They were thus formative of the communities and thought patterns of Jews and Christians from that time forward, carrying the authority of God himself, even though they were read and interpreted in very different ways by different groups.

As I have already indicated, the pages of the Bible – both the Hebrew Bible and the Christian New Testament – are soaked in blood, preoccupied with death and violence. Assuming that the above sketch of the provenance of the biblical writings is correct at least in broad outline, it becomes possible to investigate more fully some of the themes of that violence and its place in the formative ideology of those who wrote these books and those who read them and took them as scripture. In order to do this I will of course draw upon the work of mainstream contemporary biblical scholars and theologians. My concern, however, is not theology but genealogy: how was necrophilia inscribed in the consciousness and habitus of the West in relation to the writing and reading of these books and exacerbated because these books were attributed to a divine source? I shall also draw on feminist and womanist scholars who are alert to the silences and voices in the margins which, if attended to, produce a counter-narrative, ways of thinking otherwise. What were the ways in which these books were read that correlate with killing in God's name, and what are the fault lines or strategies of resistance which can also be found in the texts and the reading of them?

Chapter 4

The chosen ones

Death and the covenant

Central to the auto-narrative of the 'Israelites' as represented in the Bible, and to both Judaism and Christianity which appropriated it, is the ideology of covenant. The Israelites of the Bible, or the Jews, or the Christian Church, are the 'chosen people', specially selected and favoured by God in contrast to all other nations and peoples. If the intention of the writers-editors of the Pentateuch was to help forge national identity, then the religious ideology of the covenant can be seen as key to their project. The story of a unique covenant between God and Israel, projected into the distant past, gave the Israelites a narrative, central to which was the idea that they were special to God, chosen above all other nations even if those nations had, like the Babylonians, the Greeks and the Romans, proved themselves militarily superior. Whatever oppression they might suffer, Israel could be secure in the knowledge that they were God's 'own possession among all peoples', a 'holy nation' set apart to God (Exodus 19.6).

It is a commonplace of biblical scholarship that in ancient Jewish thought there seems not to have been a preoccupation with death or with life after death, let alone a geography of other worlds. It is this world, this life, which is the space of the divine covenant which continues with the blessing or chastisement of God; and it is this life, not death and an afterlife in some other world, which is desired and emphasized. As Giza Vermès summarized it,

> The general hope was for a long and prosperous life, many children, a peaceful death in the midst of one's family, and burial in the tomb of one's fathers. Needless to say, with this simple outlook went a most sensitive appreciation of the present time as being the only moment in which a man can be with God.
>
> (Vermès 1987:55)

Vermès seems unaware of the sexism of these sentences. What I wish to show in this chapter, however, is that although overt preoccupation with one's own death is much less pronounced in the Hebrew Bible than in, say, late medieval spiritual writing, it is displaced into preoccupation with a patriarchal and violent ideology of covenant.

Central to the ideology of being a people especially chosen by God was the notion that the land of Israel was given to them by God: it was the 'promised land'. Narratives like that of the escape from Egypt through miraculous divine intervention on behalf of 'his people' strongly reinforced both the sense of chosenness and the significance of the land as a secure place in which Israel could live in peace without interference. These ideas would of course have been particularly reassuring to Israelites struggling to forge a nation-state in the Persian and Hellenistic eras under the eye of powerful neighbours and overlords.

Covenants, typically, are between two parties; and if God's part of the covenant was the land of Israel, the people's part also reinforced the idea of being set apart. The 'holiness code' with its purity laws and its sacrificial system rewrote the covenant in blood; and every male child had the covenant inscribed on his body in the rite of circumcision. Moreover, the covenant required utter rejection of any alternative religious perspectives: the 'gods of the land' must be utterly destroyed and the people who worshipped them exterminated without pity.

As will become clear in this chapter, these ideas form a constellation of gendered violence legitimated by religion. Even though it can be argued that individual death was not a major preoccupation, the covenant itself was deathly. It is a classic case in which identity is constructed in relation to difference, and difference is perceived as dangerous. Because Israel is seen as unique, Israelite males must bear the bodily sign of uniqueness; and the blood of circumcision and divine acceptance must be spilled by surrogate victims, animals slaughtered daily in rituals of blood sacrifice. Because other nations and their religious systems are different from Israel they are perceived as a threat and must be ruthlessly exterminated. In the context of Persian and Hellenistic power it is hardly mysterious that Israel felt under threat and that those who wrote or compiled a narrative 'history' of Israel should have found the idea of covenant particularly apt not only to assert the specialness of Israel but to signal the violent fear represented by the dangerous other. Difference could lead to death. That fear of death, translated into positive ideology, constitutes the basis and legitimation of violence: necrophobia leads to killing. It is therefore my contention that contrary to what might be thought, although the obsession with death took a very different form than it took in classical civilizations, it was if anything more acute. Gender and killing were linked together in the name of the Father God, the Lord of Hosts.

The afterlife of this narrative of violence and difference has shaped Western civilization. Taken at face value, the biblical stories of the covenant present a divine mandate for religious intolerance and ethnic cleansing. If the endless ritual slaughter of the sacrificial system is the preoccupation with death turned inwards, the holy warfare against the indigenous people of the land turns the violence outwards. The religious violence of the West has repeatedly been legitimated by appeal to the constellation of ideas linked in this narrative: the idea of covenant and chosen people, a promised land, purity and sacrifice, adherence to one god and warfare against those who worship differently. Whether or not a closer reading of the biblical texts supports such a reading is of course another matter; indeed I shall argue that when we attend to voices in the margins and ambiguities in the text, a dissenting counter-narrative emerges. But that the violent reading has shaped the autonarrative of the West can hardly be in doubt. From the Crusades to the Pilgrim Fathers, from the Vortrekkers in South Africa to European appropriation of the Americas and the southern hemisphere, and continuing in the present displacement of Palestinians, these ideas have been used to legitimate violence in the name of God. What Mieke Bal has written about the book of Judges could be said of much of the Hebrew Bible:

> The book ... is about death. It is one of those numerous monuments of antiquity that celebrate death and that we celebrate, because of their respectable old age, without realizing that we celebrate death in the same move ... The book is full of murder: public and private murder, war and individual murder. It openly celebrates murder. And murder, in this text, is related to gender.
>
> (Bal 1988:1)

But its counter-narrative, as Mieke Bal recognizes, is also about the prohibition of murder, about reconciliation, about alternatives to violence; and these ideas, too, are related to gender, to creativity and beauty, to the possibility of 'beauty for ashes'.

In what follows I wish to explore various aspects of this narrative and its alternatives in more detail. I shall begin by looking more closely at attitudes to death in the Hebrew Bible, attitudes which on the face of it run counter to the claim that the book celebrates death or is even much preoccupied with death. Next I shall consider the covenant in some of its biblical representations, followed by more detailed discussion of inward-looking and outward-looking violence, sacrifice and holy war, and the ways in which they are saturated with patriarchal assumptions. Throughout, I shall indicate fissures and cracks in the fabric of the narrative, and in the final section of this chapter I shall attend to these more closely to see how they may give rise to a counter-narrative of natality and flourishing.

Attitudes to death in the Hebrew Bible

Death, sin and gender

The first mention of death in the Hebrew Bible comes from the lips of God to the human pair in the Garden of Eden:

You may freely eat of every tree of the garden; but of the tree of the knowledge of good and evil you shall not eat, for in the day that you eat of it you shall die.

(Genesis 2.17)

The man and woman had never experienced death, so it is hard to see how they could have understood the warning. Nevertheless, they seem to have taken it to heart, because when the serpent comes to tempt Eve, she repeats God's warning.

But the serpent said to the woman, 'You will not die. For God knows that when you eat of it your eyes will be opened, and you will be like God, knowing good and evil'.

(Genesis 3.4–5)

Eve ate, of course; and thus began the long association of the ideas of death, sin and gender that have shaped the Western world. Yet at first it might have seemed that the serpent was right. According to the text their eyes were indeed opened, and although God punished them by driving them out of paradise, they continued to live.

Nevertheless, in due time death came, not only to Adam and Eve but to their descendents as well. All through the book of Genesis the consequence of sin is reinforced: the patriarchs one by one lived, produced children, 'and he died'. Whether through acts of violence, as in the murder of Abel or the genocide of the flood, or at the end of a long life, death became the inevitable destiny of every person. Would there have been death if there had been no sin? Taking the Genesis story at face value it would seem that if humankind had obeyed God they would have lived forever in Paradise, gradually filling the earth as they complied with the divine command to 'be fruitful and multiply'. The story does not encourage speculation about such obvious questions as what would happen when the earth was full, or whether animals also live forever. Its point is simply that death is a consequence of disobedience to God. It could have been avoided.

But only by Adam and Eve. Once they had eaten the forbidden fruit and incurred the divine death sentence, then that sentence was passed on to all their descendents. In the Genesis story there is no explanation of why that should be so. It is simply treated as inevitable that all will eventually die, even if the patriarchs live prodigiously long lives. Moreover, there is no mention of any further punishment for sin after death. It is death itself that *is* the punishment. Thus there is no indication of a judgement *after* death, let alone any notion of hell or torment, or of a heaven from which sinners are barred. Physical death carries with it a ring of finality. No state after death is suggested, nor any sort of other world, whether of bliss or of suffering. Within the contours of the myth one might speculate that if

Adam and Eve had not sinned they might have lived forever on this earth, but there is no suggestion of a heaven to which they might have gone, any more than a hint of hell or a place of torment in consequence of their sin.

Indeed, there is much less speculation in the Hebrew Bible about the connection between sin, death and gender than might have been expected from the first chapters of Genesis. It is only with later writers, like the author of 2 Esdras (also known as 4 Ezra) in about 100 CE that the link is explicitly stated:

> You [God] gave him [Adam] your one commandment to obey; he dis-
> obeyed it, and thereupon you made him subject to death, him and his
> descendents …
>
> For the first man, Adam, was burdened with a wicked heart; he sinned
> and he was overcome, and not only he but all his descendents. So the
> weakness became inveterate. Although your law was in your people's
> hearts, a rooted wickedness was there too; so that what was good came
> to nothing and what was bad persisted.
>
> (2 Esdras 3.7, 21–22 *NEB*)

Why was Adam, who had been created by the hand of God, 'burdened with a wicked heart'? This question is left unasked by the writer of Esdras; what is important to him is the connection between sin and death, and its transmission to subsequent generations.

It was this idea of 'original sin' and its consequence of death that was given prominence in Christian teaching through the writings of Paul:

> Sin came into the world through one man and death through sin, and so
> death spread to all men because all men sinned.
>
> (Romans 5.12)

Again there is no discussion of why or how sin caused death, let alone how one man's sin meant that all others would also sin: all this is taken as given, and is made the basis of a theological discussion of Christ as a new, sinless Adam who brings life rather than death through his sacrifice of himself. Later Christian writers like Augustine came to hold that the act of procreation itself was sinful (or at least infected with sin), and thus that every human being is born with 'original' sin, inherited through his or her conception and therefore heirs also of the punishment of death. This, however, was not early Jewish teaching. Nevertheless, although they did not specify the means of transmission in the same way, it was commonplace that all sinned, and that death was the divinely appointed consequence.

Neither is the idea that women were somehow responsible for sin, though prominent in later writings, much of a theme in the Hebrew Bible. As John

Collins points out, 'The story of Genesis 2–3 has remarkably little influence in the world of the Hebrew Bible' (Collins 2002:359). One of the first to explicitly blame women for sin and death was Ben Sira, writing in about 180 BCE. In a long passage of misogynist sentiments, Ben Sira includes this observation as though it could be taken for granted:

> Woman is the origin of sin,
> and it is through her that we all die.
> Do not leave a leaky cistern to drip
> or allow a bad wife to say what she likes.
> If she does not accept your control,
> divorce her and send her away.
>
> (Ecclesiasticus 25.24–26, *NEB*)

The theme of Eve as the type of all women, as Adam was the type of all men, is introduced here as though it were as obvious as the need to mend a leaky cistern; it echoes the Genesis story in which Eve is described as 'the mother of all living' (3.20) who was the first to eat the proscribed fruit.

In Christian literature, beginning with Paul (or writings attributed to him), such misogyny becomes part of received theology.

> Let a woman learn silence with all submissiveness ... For Adam was formed first, then Eve; and Adam was not deceived, but the woman was deceived and became a transgressor.
>
> (1 Timothy 2.11, 13–14)

From here it is only a short step to the infamous vituperations of Tertullian, writing to Christian women:

> And do you not know that you are (each) an Eve? The sentence of God on this sex of yours lives in this age: the guilt must of necessity live too. *You* are the devil's gateway: *you* are the unsealer of that (forbidden) tree: *you* are the first deserter of the divine law: *you* are she who persuaded him whom the devil was not valiant enough to attack. *You* destroyed so easily God's image, man. On account of *your* desert – that is, death – even the Son of God had to die.
>
> (Tertullian in MacHaffie 1992:27)

Thus death, sin and gender were intertwined. Women were identified with Eve, Eve with sin, and sin with death. Moreover, since woman was also conceptually linked with beauty and especially with sexual attractiveness, the configuration of beauty, death and woman had endless permutations in Western culture, shaping its symbolic complement to the auto-narrative of man the warrior.

Death as natural

As already intimated, however, this triangulation of sin, death and gender was not taken for granted by writers of the Hebrew Bible as later Christian thought might lead us to assume. For many Jewish writers, death was a natural end to human life. God simply had not created humans to live forever. The writer of the Psalms, for instance, meditates on the return of people to the dust from which they were created, and says,

> For all our days pass away under thy wrath,
> our years come to an end like a sigh.
> The years of our life are threescore and ten,
> or even by reason of strength fourscore;
> yet their span is but toil and trouble;
> they are soon gone, and we fly away ...
> So teach us to number our days
> that we may get a heart of wisdom.
>
> (Psalm 90.9–12)

It may be that, with the mention of divine wrath, the Psalmist is indicating an underlying connection with sin; but in the so-called Wisdom writings of the Bible, as well as the apocryphal writings of Ben Sira (also known as Ecclesiasticus) there are passages which seem to present death not as punishment but simply as part of the original divine intention for human beings. On the other hand, in the biblical book of Ecclesiastes, the brevity of life and the certainty of death give rise to meditations of futility. What is the point of all the labour, wisdom, or possessions earth can offer, seeing that God has decreed that the rich man dies as surely as the poor, the wise man as surely as the fool? (Ecclesiastes 2). All of this is 'vanity and striving after the wind'. Sometimes the writer draws from the brevity of life the moral that one should enjoy it to the full while it lasts, for it will soon be gone. At other times he seems simply to despair. The day of death is better than the day of birth, he says (7.1), and striving for pleasure or power or even goodness is pointless.

> For the living know that they will die, but the dead know nothing, and they have no more reward; but the memory of them is lost. Their love and their hate and their envy have already perished, and they have no more forever any share in all that is done under the sun.
>
> (Ecclesiastes 9.5–6)

Later writers have often commented on the bitterness and the paradox of Ecclesiastes: 'on the one hand, we must live spontaneously in the here and now, forgetful of future oblivion; on the other, to live fully in the here and now we must remember impending oblivion' (Dollimore 1998:42). But there is also a strain of compassion in the Wisdom writings, and an acceptance of death as the natural end of life, fixed by the Creator. Thus for example, Ben Sira writes:

> The Lord created man from the earth
> and sent him back to it again.
> He set a fixed span of life for men
> and granted them authority over everything on earth.
> He clothed them with strength like his own,
> forming them in his own image.
>
> (Ecclesiasticus 17.1–3, *NEB*)

The only one who 'lives forever is the Creator of the whole universe' (18.1); human beings, in comparison, 'are like one drop of sea-water or a single grain of sand' (18.10). Even though human life is finite and comes to an end, its finitude renders it no less precious or significant.

And after death?

Although for many biblical writers death seems to be a full stop, there also appears in the Hebrew Bible the idea of Sheol, a shadowy place to which people go after death. In this respect it seems to share with most peoples of the ancient Near East an idea of a netherworld inhabited by the spirits of the dead (Spronk 1986:234). Although there is no suggestion of torment or divine punishment, as in later Christian ideas, Sheol is definitely not attractive (see Tromp 1969; Collins 2002). In the book of Job for example, Job asks God to desist from sending sufferings upon him so that he could live in peace for awhile,

> before I go whence I shall not return,
> to the land of gloom and deep darkness,
> the land of gloom and chaos,
> where light is as darkness.
>
> (Job 10.21–22)

In other passages Sheol is described as a miserable place of ignorance and silence.

> For the living know that they will die; but the dead know nothing, and they have no more reward; but the memory of them is lost. Their love and their hate and their envy have already perished, and they have no more forever any share in all that is done under the sun ... There is no work or thought or knowledge or wisdom in Sheol, to which you are going.
>
> (Ecclesiasticus 9.5–6, 10)

Worst of all, Sheol is sometimes portrayed as a place of isolation even from God. In Psalm 88, the poet laments,

> My soul is full of troubles,
> and my life draws near to Sheol ...
> Dost thou [God] work wonders for the dead?
> Do the shades rise up to praise thee?
> Is thy steadfast love declared in the grave,
> or thy faithfulness in Abaddon?
> Are thy wonders known in the land of darkness,
> or thy saving help in the land of forgetfulness?
>
> (Psalms 88.3, 10–12)

These grim depictions of Sheol are in many respects reminiscent of the idea of Hades in the Homeric writings, or of the Netherworld described by Enkidu in the *Epic of Gilgamesh*. There is no joy or beauty; and though it is the common lot of humankind there seems to be no community or human fellowship. The Bible does speak of death as an individual being 'gathered to his people' (e.g. Genesis 25.8); but this seems to refer to burial customs (Collins 2002:359), not to any suggestion of a grand reunion after death. On the other hand, neither is there any mention of divine judgement after death, such as we find in the complicated thought and practice of ancient Egypt, where eternal destiny was decided when the god Osiris weighed the heart of the deceased in a scale, balanced against the Feather of Truth. Sheol is cheerless, but not a place of torment.

There are in fact some passages in the Hebrew Bible which may suggest that not even Sheol is removed from the presence of God. Perhaps most striking is Psalm 139:

> Whither shall I go from thy Spirit?
> Or whither shall I flee from thy presence?
> If I ascend to heaven, thou art there!
> If I make my bed in Sheol, thou art there!
>
> (Psalm 139.7–8)

These are, however, poetic writings, and scholars debate whether this does in fact indicate an afterlife in God's presence or is rather a hyperbolic insistence on the impossibility of evading God (Rowley 1956:160; Curtis 1994:7–10). In any event it would be mistaken to read into 'Sheol' or 'heaven' the overtones of the 'heaven' and 'hell' of Christendom. At most what could be said is that the depth of trust in God generates an unresolved problem in the Hebrew Bible. In the words of Hans Wolff,

> Death is on the one hand described as a sphere of pitiless alienation from God – an area where Yahweh can no longer exert any influence ...

But on the other hand death is denied any independent power of its own over against Yahweh; it is unthinkable that an independent sovereign should rule the world of the dead.

(Wolff 1974:107)

There is no separate god of the underworld, as there is in Greek or Near Eastern mythology. As monotheism is emphasized, so death itself comes within Yahweh's reach, even if in other respects Sheol seems much like Achilles' Hades or Enkidu's Netherworld.

There are even isolated hints in the Hebrew Bible of some hope of immortality or resurrection in which the righteous are vindicated or rewarded for their suffering. One famous example is the exclamation of Job, made in the context of severe suffering in which he had often wished for the release that death would bring.

I know that my Redeemer lives,
and at last he will stand upon the earth;
and after my skin has been thus destroyed,
then from my flesh I shall see God,
whom I shall see on my side,
and my eyes shall behold.

(Job 19.25–27)

In the literature of the Apocrypha the idea of immortality emerges more clearly, especially in the Wisdom of Solomon. There, the writer insists that 'Death is not king on earth, for justice is immortal' (Wisdom 1.14). In words still regularly quoted at funeral services, the writer says of those who have died:

The souls of the just are in God's hand, and torment shall not touch them ... They are at peace ... they have a sure hope of immortality ... They will be judges and rulers over the nations of the world, and the Lord shall be their king for ever and ever.

(Wisdom 3.1–8)

The Essenes, a Jewish sect who lived at Qumran near the Dead Sea from about 150 BCE to 70 CE, write not only of eternal life for the just but damnation for the wicked.

As for the visitation of all who walk in this spirit, it shall be healing, great peace in a long life, and fruitfulness, together with every everlasting blessing and eternal joy in life without end, a crown of glory and a garment of majesty in unending light.

(1 QS IV, Vermès 1987:65)

The wicked, by contrast, can expect 'everlasting damnation by the avenging wrath of the fury of God, eternal torment and endless disgrace together with shameful extinction in the fire of the dark regions' (Ibid p.66). Ideas such as these would make their way into Christendom and would be the basis of many a threatening or consoling homily and painting; we shall return to them later in this book. During the period of the Hebrew Bible, however, a resigned acceptance of mortality together with a consciousness of standing before God in this life is much more typical.

> Who can endure Thy glory,
> and what is the son of man
> in the midst of Thy wonderful deeds?
> What shall one born of woman
> be accounted before Thee?
> Kneaded from the dust,
> his abode is the nourishment of worms.
> He is but a shape, but moulded clay,
> and inclines towards dust.
> What shall hand-moulded clay reply?
> What counsel shall it understand?
>
> (1 QS XI, Vermès 1987:80)

Narrative and counter-narrative

Writers of the Hebrew Bible meditate on death from time to time, as every thinking person must do, but it could not be said that in the Bible as we have it death and its aftermath constitute a central preoccupation. Far more prominent is the idea of covenant; the special relationship with God formed the dominant ideology from at least the sixth century BCE onwards. Yet the variety of attitudes towards death and its aftermath, ideas that are sometimes in tension with each other, offer glimpses of a counter-narrative that destabilizes the optimistic ideology of covenant.

At the sunny end of the spectrum is the assurance that not even death can remove a person from the loving watchfulness of God. Death is not seen as desirable in itself (unless as a release from unbearable illness or pain); there is no longing for death as we find in Plato, no notion that the body is a prison-house from which the soul can escape to an eternal realm of truth and beauty. On the contrary, truth, beauty and goodness are part of this life, this world. They must be sought and experienced here and now, not in some other world beyond the grave. Nevertheless, when death does come, as it must finally come to all who live, God's loving care is not removed. Has he not made a covenant with his people? Scholars who focus on the dominant strand of the biblical writings and the centrality of the covenant argue that trust in God's faithfulness removed from the early Israelites much of the obsession with death which characterized other peoples of the ancient Near East. For the Israelites the dead were in the hand of God, and 'the grave has little significance' (Wolff 1974:100).

However, another look at the texts, coupled with archaeological discoveries of burial practices, suggests a gloomier view, and with it a reappraisal of the covenant itself. The archaeologist Elizabeth Bloch-Smith studied the findings of 850 burials from sixty sites of Iron Age (1200–1586 BCE) Palestine. In common with many other areas around the Mediterranean, including the Aegean of the same period, many articles of dress, jewellery, combs, mirrors and other personal items were found in the graves; also human and deity figurines, male, female and indeterminate, animal figurines like horse, and in some cases items of furniture such as thrones, beds or even shrines. While there is nothing to rival the scale of the tombs of Egyptian kings like Tutankhamen, it would seem that ordinary people were being provided with what they might need for their journey to Sheol. The regular feature of pottery, especially a jar and bowl, 'indicate that food and liquids were provided for the dead' (Bloch-Smith 1992:108; see also Spronk 1986:238–57).

Bloch-Smith argues that there is evidence also for widespread belief that the dead could foretell the future, and that they had both benevolent and malevolent powers towards the living (121). Though the extent of this belief is disputed by other scholars (Schmidt 1994:275–93), all are agreed:

> That kinship, family and religion were closely intertwined. The care, feeding, and commemoration of the dead attested in the sources verifies the centrality of kinship and family in religious and social life.
>
> (Schmidt 1994:275)

Moreover, the place of the ancestral tomb was related to claims to land. Bloch-Smith therefore argues that:

> In Judahite culture [i.e. Iron Age Palestine] the dead were an integral part of social organization. Individuals believed that their descendents would nourish and care for them following death, just as they had provided for their predecessors. Moreover, the legitimacy of land-holdings was validated by the ancestral tomb, and the prosperity of the land may have been thought to be blessed or insured by benevolent ancestors.
>
> (Bloch-Smith 1992:132)

A closer reading of the texts shows an undercurrent which supports the view that there was much more preoccupation with death than at first appears, a preoccupation which the sixth-century writers/editors of the covenant ideology tried in vain to suppress. In the Hebrew Bible there are plenty of indications that the dead were consulted about the future, as King Saul is said to have consulted the ghost of Samuel (1 Samuel 28). Those who assist in such consultations are called mediums (1 Samuel 28.7), necromancers (Deuteronomy 18.11), or 'wizards who chirp and mutter' (Isaiah 8.19). The biblical terms are highly pejorative, but the very fact that the biblical writers found it necessary to insist so strongly on the evils of consulting the dead indicates that the practice was probably widespread.

Everything to do with such a cult of the dead was vigorously opposed by the biblical writers of the Persian-Hellenistic period who projected their writings into a distant past, as I discussed in the previous chapter. The Holiness Law Codes of the Hebrew Bible in its present form, and such books as Deuteronomy and Isaiah, left no room for competitors in the cult of Yahweh which they were trying to establish for the people of Israel. According to this Code, the dead and everything to do with the corpse is designated as ritually impure.

> He who touches the dead body of any person shall be unclean seven days ... Whoever touches a dead person, the body of any man who has died, and does not cleanse himself, defiles the tabernacle of the Lord, and that person shall be cut off from Israel.
>
> (Numbers 19.11–13)

Not only a newly dead corpse, but even a grave or a bone renders one who touches it ritually unclean (Numbers 19.16), and anything that comes into contact with a dead body, whether of human or animal, is rendered impure, even pots or jugs, items of clothing, and ovens or stoves (Leviticus 11.32–35). Excessive mourning is also forbidden, especially to priests, who are not to render themselves ritually impure except for the death of very close kin:

> They shall not make tonsures upon their heads, nor shave off the edges of their beards, not make any cuttings in their flesh. They shall be holy to their God.
>
> (Leviticus 21.5–6)

These features of mourning were common practice in the Near East in which the dead were believed to have power: as Wolff argues,

> they are designed to make the mourners unrecognizable and hence undiscoverable. Such respect for death is impossible in Yahweh's presence.
>
> (Wolff 1974:105)

Wolff takes this dominant narrative at face value in his analysis of Israelite attitudes to death. I am suggesting, however, that the repeated stringent prohibitions and strong penalties indicate that the cult of the dead was a major threat to those who were promoting the Yahwist ideology. As the religion of Yahweh increased its grip, such apotropaic practices were condemned, along with all practices of necromancy or consultation of the dead. Inquiring of the dead was forbidden to priests (Deuteronomy 18.10–11) and to people (Leviticus 19.31); and the harshest of penalties was reserved for mediums:

> If a person turns to mediums and wizards ... I [Yahweh] will set my face against that person, and will cut him off from among his people.
>   A man or a woman who is a medium or a wizard shall be put to death; they shall be stoned with stones.
>
> (Leviticus 20.6, 27)

Opposition to such consultation is vehement in the prophetic writings as well as in the books of the law. Isaiah, for example, writes in disgust and exasperation:

> And when they say to you, 'Consult the mediums and the wizards who chirp and mutter', should not a people consult their God? Should they consult the dead on behalf of the living?
>
> (Isaiah 8.19; cf. Jeremiah 16.5–7)

And in Deuteronomy it is again made very clear that a true prophet, and indeed a true people of the covenant and the land, will have no truck with the 'abominable practices of the nations' which they are represented as supplanting.

> There shall not be found among you any one who burns his son or daughter as an offering, any one who practices divination, a soothsayer, or an augur, or a sorcerer, or a charmer, or a medium, or a wizard, or a necromancer. For whoever does these things is an abomination to the Lord ... For these nations, which you are about to dispossess, give heed to soothsayers and to diviners; but as for you, the Lord your God has not allowed you so to do.
>
> (Deuteronomy 18.9–14)

Instead of consulting the dead through mediums and necromancers, the people were encouraged to consult 'true prophets', that is, the prophets of Yahweh. Only they were to be believed and honoured.

When we read these commands and prohibitions from the perspective of a counter-narrative, it is easy to see power politics at work in the religious rhetoric. Elizabeth Bloch-Smith argues that:

> Jerusalem priests and prophets hoped to purify and centralize the Temple cult, resanctify the people of Israel and assert their status as

faithful servants of Yahweh. In this way they would ensure their livelihood as the only acceptable intermediaries of Yahweh and as beneficiaries of the tithe.

(Bloch-Smith 1992:131)

Anyone who consulted a medium or a prophet would of course be expected to bring a fee or a 'gift'; so if the cult of the dead could be banished then the money, power and prestige would all accrue to the prophets of Yahweh and the Temple cult. Therefore,

> the promulgators of the Deuteronomic and Holiness Law Codes, together with prophets (notably Isaiah), adopted societal regulations and taboos regarding the dead, devised sanctions, and denounced mortuary activities in order to strengthen their own positions. The views which they advocated were designed to preserve the functions and holiness of prophecy and priesthood, and to protect the holiness and current practice in the Temple.

(Bloch-Smith 1992:132)

Along with the prophets and priests of the Temple cult, the central government with whom they worked would also be strengthened. Mortuary cults would keep attention fixed on the clan and the ancestors. If these could be curtailed and attention directed instead towards the king and the national god, the power base of the national structures of monarchy and religion would be increased at the expense of tribal loyalties. The denunciation of the cult of the dead can therefore be seen to be of a piece with the nationalist-religious project of the Persian-Hellenistic period, correlating with attempts to develop a narrative of a covenant people and to suppress alternative religious practices represented by the gods and goddesses of the land.

How effective this denunciation was in curtailing the cult of the dead and promoting an ideology of covenant with Yahweh is of course open to debate. What matters for this book is that in the fissures of the dominant narrative of covenant there are clear traces of a counter-narrative which gives a quite different estimate of the preoccupation with death from the life-affirming stance which has often been assumed to be characteristic of early Israelite thought and practice. But if this is so, then what about the covenant itself? Was it as life-affirming as has usually been thought? Although the cult of Yahweh insisted that there was nothing to celebrate about death, the narrative of the early Israelites is a narrative of continuous violence and killing. The practices of animal slaughter for sacrifice and of holy war are central, and are represented as divine requirements. How was it that in an ideology where overt necrophilia was severely repressed, the infliction of violent death held such an important place? It is to these questions that I now turn, beginning with a closer examination of the idea of covenant.

Covenant

> The word covenant ... is so to speak a convenient symbol for an assur-
> ance much wider in scope and controlling the formation of the national
> faith at its deepest level, without which Israel would not be Israel. As an
> epitome of the dealings of God in history, the covenant is not a doc-
> trinal concept ... but the characteristic *description of a living process*
> which was begun at a particular time and at a particular place.
>
> (Eichrodt 1961:14)

Walter Eichrodt, a German theologian writing in the 1930s, believed that the
place was Mount Sinai and the time was the time of Moses. In his view, as in
that of many other biblical scholars both Christian and Jewish of the twentieth century, covenant was constitutive not only of the theology of Israel but
also of their existence as a people.[1]

In the case of Eichrodt and many other Christian scholars, their reading of
the Hebrew Bible was intended simultaneously as a historical exercise and as
a service to Christian theology and Christian churches. With the Nazi
ideology in the ascendant, Eichrodt was at pains to distinguish the theology
of covenant from that of a popular Nature religion based on blood and soil.
He wrote:

> The covenant agreement excluded the idea, which prevailed widely and
> was disseminated among Israel's neighbours as well, that between the
> national God and his worshippers there existed a bond inherent in the
> order of Nature, whether this were a kind of blood relationship, or a link
> between the God and the country which created an indissoluble asso-
> ciation between himself and the inhabitants ... Israel's religion is thus
> stamped as a 'religion of election', using this phrase to mean that it is
> divine election which makes it the exact opposite of the nature religions.
>
> (Eichrodt 1961:42–3)

As an example of the way in which biblical scholarship could be used
polemically against a National Socialist ideology of blood, land and nation,
Eichrodt's theology is impressive; and it has been enormously influential
upon subsequent biblical scholars.[2] What Eichrodt does not do, however, is
recognize the historical difficulties of ascribing covenant theology to an
entity called 'ancient Israel'; he takes the biblical narrative as sufficiently
historically accurate to accept the account of the Mosaic covenant, draw
contrasts between ancient Israel and her neighbours, and so on. Accordingly,
he does not investigate the technologies of power implicit in the ideology of
covenant, nor its multiple investment in violence and saturation in blood.

In the Hebrew Bible as we have it today, the first mention of covenant
comes in the story of the flood. When God informs Noah that a genocidal

flood is coming, and instructs him to build an ark, God says, 'I will establish my covenant with you' so that the lives of Noah and his family would be preserved. (Genesis 6.18). When the flood is over and the people and animals who have been preserved emerge from the ark, God sends a rainbow as a sign of the covenant, which is now extended to all living creatures.

> When I bring clouds over the earth and the bow is seen in the clouds, I will remember my covenant which is between me and you and every living creature of all flesh; and the waters shall never again become a flood to destroy all flesh.
>
> (Genesis 9.14–15)

The writer is emphatic that the covenant extends to all. He insists that this is indeed the covenant affirmed by God; the word 'covenant' occurs seven times in the space of ten verses (Genesis 9.8–17).

This generous characterization of covenant is soon replaced in the book of Genesis by a much more restrictive reading in the story of Abram/Abraham. According to this story, Abraham is the father of the people of Israel through his son Isaac who was born miraculously to Abraham and Sarah when they were in their old age. Abraham had obeyed the divine summons to leave his father's house in Ur and to travel to a new land at God's direction. On one occasion God told Abraham to sacrifice animals, laying out the carcasses in a row.

> When the sun had gone down and it was dark, behold, a smoking fire pot and a flaming torch passed between these pieces. On that day the Lord made a covenant with Abram, saying, 'To your descendents I give this land, from the river of Egypt to the great river, the river Euphrates, the land of the Kenites, the Kenizzites, the Kadmonites, the Hittites, the Perizzites, the Rephaim, the Amorites, the Canaanites, the Girgashites and the Jebusites'.
>
> (Genesis 15.17–21)

Just who all these people were or what was to happen to them is left unclear, but it is obvious that unlike the covenant after the flood in which all living things were included, the covenant with Abraham is made with him and his descendents at the expense of other people. The children of Abraham could consider themselves special to God in a way that all these 'others' were not.

In one of the accounts of the covenant between God and Abraham, Abraham was asked to perform a special action to signify and ratify the covenant from his side. He was to be circumcised, along with all the males of his household.

> You shall be circumcised in the flesh of your foreskins, and it shall be a
> sign of the covenant between me [God] and you ... So shall my covenant
> be in your flesh an everlasting covenant.
>
> (Genesis 17.11, 13)

On God's part, he will ensure that Abraham will have a multitude of descendents,
to whom God will give the land forever:

> And I will establish my covenant between me and you and your des-
> cendents after you throughout their generations for an everlasting cove-
> nant, to be God to you, and to your descendents after you. And I will
> give to you, and to your descendents after you, the land of your
> sojournings, all the land of Canaan, for an everlasting possession; and I
> will be their God.
>
> (Genesis 17.7–8)

In this story, therefore, the Jewish practice of circumcision is projected
back on to God's dealings with Abraham and made part of the covenant
itself. The covenant is inscribed in blood on the body of every male. But
what about women? Is there no covenant with them? I shall revisit the
gender structures of the covenant narratives below, and the violence implicit
in the requirement of circumcision in the next chapter; but it is already
apparent that in the dominant narrative the covenant ratifies masculinist
patriarchy.

Significant as are the stories of the covenant with Noah and with
Abraham, the account that is usually taken as definitive of the covenant
between God and Israel is that of the meeting at Mount Sinai. According to
the book of Exodus, God had miraculously liberated the Israelites from
Egypt where they had been oppressed, and led them through the desert until
they came to Mount Sinai. There, God spoke to them through Moses their
leader, making promises to them and giving them laws and regulations by
which they are to live. God tells Moses to say to them:

> You have seen what I did to the Egyptians, and how I bore you on
> eagles' wings and brought you to myself. Now therefore, if you will obey
> my voice and keep my covenant, you shall be my own possession among
> all peoples; for all the earth is mine, and you shall be to me a kingdom
> of priests and a holy nation.
>
> (Exodus 19.4–6)

Moses duly 'wrote all the words of the Lord' (24.4). He then transmitted
them to the people in a gory ceremony. First he offered sacrifices of oxen,
whose blood he put into two basins. Half the blood he threw against an altar
which he had built.

> Then he took the book of the covenant, and read it in the hearing of the people; and they said, 'All that the Lord has spoken we will do, and we will be obedient'. And Moses took the blood and threw it upon the people, and said, 'Behold the blood of the covenant which the Lord has made with you in accordance with all these words.'
>
> (24.6–8)

From the outset, the Sinaitic covenant is soaked in blood and linked with violent death. The oxen whose blood spatters the altar and the people have been ritually slaughtered; the Egyptian army which had tried to prevent the escape of the Israelites was drowned; all the first-born sons of Egypt had died by a direct act of God in order to 'persuade' the Pharaoh to let the people go. Like the story of the flood, the only way to read this story with any sort of equanimity is to situate oneself firmly among the beneficiaries of the covenant and think as little as possible about the victims. Yet this covenant between God and Israel, in which he takes them as his special chosen people, has regularly been taken (as by Eichrodt) as key to the whole of the Hebrew Bible and definitive of the people of Israel both religiously and politically.

In the Exodus story, moreover, the covenant promises more violence in the future. God promises Moses that he will give the land of Canaan to the Israelites as theirs forever. But that land is already occupied by others, who worship other gods. These people and their gods must never be allowed to distract the Israelites from their covenant with Yahweh; above all, they are not to enter into any competing covenants with them. God says,

> Behold, I will drive out before you the Amorites, the Canaanites, the Hittites, the Perizzites, the Hivites, and the Jebusites. Take heed to yourself, lest you make a covenant with the inhabitants of the land whither you go, lest it become a snare in the midst of you. You shall tear down their altars, and break their pillars, and cut down their Asherim (for you shall worship no other god, for the Lord, whose name is Jealous, is a jealous God), lest you make a covenant with the inhabitants of the land ...
>
> (Exodus 34.11–15)

The covenant with God excludes all other covenants, and violent pre-emptive action is to be taken to ensure that there will be no competing loyalties.

I shall return to the Sinaitic covenant below; but first I want to note briefly how the stories of the covenant became part of Israel's auto-narrative as expressed in their Psalms. For example, the Israelites sang of the covenant with Abraham and his descendents, made good through their miraculous escape from Egypt and acquisition of the 'promised land', in a Psalm which represents all of this in terms of God honouring his promise.

Remember the wonderful works that he has done ...
O offspring of Abraham his servant,
sons of Jacob, his chosen ones!
... He is mindful of his covenant forever,
of the word that he commanded, for a thousand
generations, the covenant which he made with Abraham,
his sworn promise to Isaac,
which he confirmed to Jacob as a statute,
to Israel as an everlasting covenant,
saying, 'To you I will give the land of Canaan
as your portion for an inheritance'.

(Psalm 105.5–11)

Hymns and prayers deepen and reinforce conviction in a way that goes beyond intellectual assent. Therefore, to the extent that Psalms were used in Israelite worship (Mowinckel 1962; Alter 1998), a Psalm such as this one would be yet another powerful factor solidifying the ideas of covenant, promised land, and chosen people.

It is in the Psalms, also, that there is explicit reference to a covenant with David, echoing and reinforcing the covenant with Abraham and with Israel at Mount Sinai. If these latter two accounts are projections back into the mists of prehistory, the stories of David and Solomon are presented in a narration that reads like sober chronology. Assuming, as suggested in Chapter 4, that these narratives too were written or compiled in the Persian-Hellenistic period, they would have given a sense of continuous history to their readers (as indeed they have to modern interpreters e.g. Noth 1960). If, therefore, the 'ancient' covenant was repeated to David, at the beginning of the period of the putative kings of Israel and Judah, then it could be taken as reaffirmed by God and enduring in its validity, even when events seemed contrary. This, indeed, is precisely what the Psalm proclaims.

I have found David, my servant;
with my holy oil I have anointed him ...
I will not violate my covenant,
or alter the word that went forth from my lips.
Once for all I have sworn by my holiness;
I will not lie to David.
His line shall endure forever,
his throne as long as the sun before me.
Like the moon it shall be established forever;
it shall stand firm while the skies endure.

(Psalm 89.20, 34–37)

The Psalm goes on to complain that God has cast off his chosen people and 'renounced the covenant' that he had made: how long would God continue to hide himself? It was of course an appropriate lament during the Persian period when the fortunes of Israel were subject to the interests of their powerful neighbours. Strengthening the ideology of the covenant, the chosen nature of the people and the land, would help to consolidate the national identity and the monarchy perpetuated by the royal court and the temple.

The covenant, thus, was crucial to the auto-narrative of the Israelites. It is a staple of biblical scholarship that the covenant was made and remade between God and his people; and in Protestant theology 'his people' is regularly deemed also to signify the Christian Church, which is therefore held to be in some sense the inheritor of the divine promises. Because of the attention to the covenant, moreover, it is sometimes alleged, as we have seen, that there was (or at least need not be) great preoccupation with death. The covenant is with the living people of God; and the focus is on their obedience, their descendents, and their possession of the land, not on death and certainly not on some life beyond the grave.

But we have already had indications that things are not that simple. Although in one sense it is true that the covenant is focused on life, in another sense it is structured in violence and steeped in blood, from the blood of circumcision and endless animal slaughter to brutal extermination of the 'people of the land'. In the genealogy of death and violence in Western civilization, the ideology of the covenant plays a major part, not least in its insistence that 'others' are excluded. It is to these 'others' that I now turn, in part to show more clearly the gendered violence of the covenant and in part to begin a counter-narrative from their perspective.

Whose covenant?

In the stories of the Sinaitic covenant, Moses gathered all the people of Israel at Mount Sinai. They were to prepare themselves to meet God by 'consecrating themselves' and washing their garments. Then, as a final word of advice, Moses says to 'the people' – as though all of the people were intended – 'Be ready by the third day; do not go near a woman' (Exodus 19.15). It becomes clear, therefore, that 'the people' is actually shorthand for 'the men'; Moses's advice could only apply to men. Judith Plaskow, a modern Jewish biblical scholar, points out in her book *Standing Again at Sinai* (1990) that 'entry into the covenant at Sinai is the root experience of Judaism, the central event that established the Jewish people' (1990:25). Yet when 'the people' of Israel were summoned to that event, in fact it was only the men who were addressed.

> At the critical moment of Jewish history, women are invisible. Whether they too stood there trembling in fear and expectation, what they heard when the men heard these words of Moses, we do not know.
>
> (Plaskow 1990:25)

In the book of Deuteronomy, whose narrative setting places it at the end of forty years of wilderness wanderings and just before the Israelites were to enter the land of Canaan, the covenant is repeated and celebrated. On this occasion women are explicitly included:

> You stand this day all of you before the Lord your God; the heads of your tribes, your elders, and your officers, all the men of Israel, your little ones, your wives, and the sojourner who is in your camp ...
>
> (Deuteronomy 29:10–11)

Women were also participants in festivals and sacrifices, the religious rituals of the Israelites (see Deuteronomy 12.12 and 18; cf. Emmerson 1989). In textual terms, the difference between the Exodus and Deuteronomy accounts of the covenant may reflect moves towards better treatment of women in the post-exilic period, as Grace Emmerson (1989) suggests, since Deuteronomy is by common consent of later date than the book of Exodus. Even in the Deuteronimic text, however, it is clear that women participate in the religious observances not as individual members of the community in their own right but as the wives or daughters of men. It defies imagination to suppose that Moses – or God – would ever address himself to 'women and their husbands' instead of to 'men and their wives'. The covenant was made between God and men. Women were included, if at all, only as part of a male-dominated household.

If the stories of the covenant were written or compiled in the Persian-Hellenistic period, the ideology which was being projected back into earlier times to form their narrative identity, was an ideology in which men communed with God while women, if present at all, were silent. 'The Hebrew laws regulating the relations of men and women are never complimentary to the latter', wrote Elizabeth Cady Stanton with characteristic forthrightness in *The Woman's Bible* in 1898, 'and every man was warned that the less he had to do with the "daughters of men" the more perfect might be his communion with the Creator' (Stanton 1974:80). Yet even the most masculinist text must recognize that women were indeed part of the community, and that the covenant could not exclude them if it was to be a covenant with all the people of Israel. What sort of counter-narrative might be produced if we were to begin from the perspective of these women, standing silent on the margins but nevertheless standing also at Sinai?

If male domination is obvious in relation to the Sinaitic covenant, it is perhaps even more striking in its narrative precursor, the covenant with Abraham; but in this instance the voices of women give stronger hints at how the stories could be told in a different way. According to the biblical story, Sarah had accompanied Abraham from the time he left Ur and began his wanderings in response to the divine command. Did she also hear God's voice, or did she simply have to do as her husband said?

> How far did Sarah's vision of the society extend? Did she feel that she had been transported to and isolated in a patriarchal future? Did she long for her non-patriarchal homeland? ... Did she, in fact, have a choice?
>
> (Teubal 1993:239–40)

Whatever the answer, the story tells of how God rewarded Abraham's obedience to the divine call by making the covenant with him and with his male descendents; again, Sarah is not mentioned. And when Abraham and all the males of his household were circumcised at the divine behest – ' so shall my covenant be in your flesh' (Genesis 17.13) – what did Sarah and the women of the household have to do with it? Even when God speaks to Abraham again, telling him that he will have a son by Sarah, she is not present. God says that he 'will bless her, and she shall be a mother of nations' (17.16), and God will re-establish his covenant with Isaac who Sarah will bear the following year. Sarah, it seems, is not consulted or even informed. She is represented as being ninety years of age; would she really want to bear a child? The biblical text leaves no room for such questions; it gives the impression that Isaac's birth is welcomed without qualification, celebrated as confirmation of the divine covenant. Yet when Sarah first heard the news that she was to have a child, she heard it not by being told properly, but by 'listening at the tent door' (18.10). She laughed. Was it a laugh of joy and pleasure? Was it a cynical laugh? As is the case with many biblical stories in which women are simultaneously crucial and marginal, 'we can do no more than speculate upon this possibility, but we can also do no less' (Ostriker 1993:47).

In the case of Sarah, the biblical text positively encourages speculation. Repeatedly, God treats Sarah better than Abraham does. When Abraham and Sarah journey to Egypt, he requires her to pass herself off as his sister, in case the Egyptians kill him in order to possess her; with the result that Pharaoh himself takes Sarah into his house and makes Abraham very rich for her sake.

> But the Lord afflicted Pharaoh and his house with great plagues because of Sarai, Abram's wife. So Pharaoh called Abram, and said, 'What is this that you have done to me? Why did you not tell me that she was your wife? Why did you say "She is my sister", so that I took her for my wife? Now then, here is your wife, take her, and be gone'.
>
> (Genesis 12.17–20)

A very similar story occurs a few chapters later. This time the king is Abimelech. When he takes Abraham's 'sister', God comes to him in a dream and tells him the truth. Abimelech confronts Abraham with what he has done, but Abraham has only lame excuses. So Sarah is again restored to Abraham because of divine intervention, in spite of his dishonest treatment of her; and again Abraham is given cattle and slaves and much silver for her sake.

What is striking in these stories, besides Abraham's appalling treatment of his wife and his willingness to use her for his own gain, is that God shows particular concern for her and intervenes on her behalf. Sarah matters to God. Indeed, it seems that she matters considerably more to God than she does to Abraham. True, we may still wonder why God rebukes Pharaoh and Abimelech rather than Abraham, since he was much more at fault than they were; and we may still find it outrageous that instead of being punished for his shabby schemes Abraham becomes rich by them. Nevertheless, according to these stories God watches over Sarah and does not permit the men to use her merely as an object of pleasure or exchange. Though patriarchy is unchallenged, there is more than a hint that Sarah is a person in her own right, a subject in the eyes of God.

The subjectivity emerges even more strongly in other parts of the text. Repeatedly when Abraham is in a difficult situation it is Sarah who speaks, Sarah who gives advice, and Abraham who does as she says. This is particularly true in relation to Hagar, a slave woman, who at Sarah's suggestion becomes Abraham's mistress and bears him a son, Ishmael. After Isaac is born, Sarah tells Abraham to remove Hagar and Ishmael from the household. Abraham is distressed; but God intervenes firmly on the side of Sarah, saying to Abraham, 'whatever Sarah says to you, do as she tells you' (Genesis 21.12). And he does. The story of Hagar is a disturbing one: neither Abraham nor Sarah come out of it well. But for all its injustice, what cannot be doubted is that Sarah has a voice. She is able to assert herself and claim a subject position. At times it seems that she may even be a participant in the covenant. The stories of Sarah provide material for a counter-narrative in which the covenant is made not only with the 'fathers', but with the wider community in which women take a full role.

In the end, patriarchy wins out in the text. When God asks Abraham to sacrifice Isaac (a story I shall consider more fully in Chapter 7), Sarah is nowhere consulted or even mentioned. There is no mark of the covenant on women's flesh, a constant reminder and reassurance as circumcision is for men. Even those who are most anxious to retain the biblical stories as in some sense divine revelation cannot ignore the patriarchal bias of the auto-narrative of Israel, or the afterlife of that patriarchal stance in Christendom. There are indications for a counter-narrative: women who listen in the tent door, women who give advice to men, women for whom God takes special care; but these are the exceptions, and patriarchy is firmly established. Thus, after Abraham and Isaac return from Mount Moriah where Isaac was (not) sacrificed, Sarah dies, and the divine promise is continued through the male line.

And yet, even in the story of the death and burial of Sarah there is something odd going on which suggests a different perspective. The narrative goes to great lengths to establish that Abraham wanted a tomb for Sarah, refuses to accept it as a gift from the man who owns the field on which it is situated, and insists on paying full price for the land; the passage where this is recounted is longer than the story of the sacrifice of Isaac. And yet twice in the story Abraham uses a very strange phrase: he asks that he may bury Sarah 'out of my sight' (Genesis 23.4, 8). Alicia Ostriker, in her analysis of the passage, points out that the Hebrew phrase means 'from before my face', or idiomatically 'away from my presence' or consciousness; it is used, for example, when God promises never to cast Israel away from his presence (Jeremiah 31:36–37). So Abraham is saying not only that he must bury Sarah: 'Sarah must not merely die and be buried but must be eliminated from presence, that is from consciousness' (Ostriker 1993:42). Indeed, one might think that his insistence on elaborate burial arrangements and ensuring that he paid all costs was a guilty compensation for his need to get Sarah out of his sight, out of his mind. Although he is weeping and mourning her loss, the story signals that at a deeper level something quite different may be going on.

Certainly Abraham had plenty to feel guilty about. He had repeatedly treated Sarah very badly, not least when he twice tried to pass her off as his sister.[3] In the first of these incidents, Sarah's great beauty is emphasized: both Abraham and the Egyptians say that she is 'a woman beautiful to behold', 'very beautiful' (Genesis 12:11, 14). In the terms of the narrative, that beauty has become a threat. Is it Sarah's beauty, or her strength of character when she gives him advice, or his bad treatment of her (or all of these together) which disturb Abraham so much that he needs to get her out of his sight, out of his mind? The question is unanswerable, of course, but that makes asking it all the more urgent. It is not clear how much of a counter-narrative is warranted by the text and how much must be imposed upon it. What is clear, however, is the triad of woman, beauty and death which is so familiar a theme in Western culture. Woman – beautiful, sexually disturbing woman – is left out of the covenant, or at best marginal to it. Men are circumcised; men are the ones who enter into the covenant and who pass on the law and the name of the fathers. Do they also, at some level, feel very guilty about it, so guilty that they soon erupt into violence?

Excluding the other

The biblical stories of the covenant not only marginalize women. They are also emphatic not only about those to whom the covenant applies and the land is promised, but also about those who are to be expelled. Again, the narrative begins with Abraham, and with Ishmael, his son by Hagar. Although Ishmael is Abraham's eldest son, and in spite of the fact that he has been circumcised, it is Isaac who is the son of the covenant. In the biblical stories, God connives in the shameful dismissal of Hagar and Ishmael from

Abraham's household, an episode which does neither Abraham nor Sarah (nor God) much credit. Although God promises Abraham (and later, Hagar) that he will make a nation also out of Ishmael's descendents, there is never a suggestion that that nation will be specially chosen by God as were Isaac's descendents. The land of promise is not for them. It is as though the narrative identity of the 'chosen people' can be maintained only if they can point to someone else who is not thus chosen; as though divine love and favour is limited and there is not enough to include everyone.

Not only are others not chosen, but the ones who are chosen are regularly exhorted to make very sure of the exclusion of those others. In the Sinaitic covenant, there is a long list of peoples who are considered evil, worthy only to be driven out of the land which had been their home but which God now reserves for his chosen ones: 'the Amorites, the Canaanites, the Hittites, the Perizzites, the Hivites, and the Jebusites' (Exodus 34.11). It is not obvious who all these people are; if the narratives of the covenant were written long after the events which they purport to relate, it may be that these names are not names of any actually existing peoples but stand for all others whose removal guarantees the Israelites' exclusive claim to the land. Whatever the case, the writers are making very plain that in the ideology of the covenant the chosenness of the Israelites precludes the possibility of including anyone else.

In the book of Deuteronomy, where the Sinaitic covenant is repeated and elaborated, all these 'nations' are again named and designated for extermination. Here, however, a special note is sounded, which would be taken up again in the Christian doctrine of election by such writers as Paul, Augustine and Calvin. The Israelites are told that it is not because they are greater in number than the peoples already in the land, or in any sense superior, but simply because 'the Lord set his love upon you and chose you' (Deuteronomy 7.7). Christian theologians, who regularly read narratives of the covenant implicitly identifying the Christian Church with Israel as the chosen people of God, explain such passages in terms of divine mercy and graciousness, saving and delivering his people not because of any special merit of their own but simply because of God's love. But as David Clines points out, such a reading is comfortable only if the reader implicitly situates herself or himself in the position of the chosen ones.

> If you adopt the point of view of the Egyptians or the Canaanites, God is not experienced as a saving God, and the only words you will hear addressed to you are words of reproach and threat. If you are not Israel, you do not know the presence of God, and the main reason is not some defect in you but the fact that you have not been chosen.
>
> (Clines 1995:208)

As the stories in the Bible unfold, the divine promise is repeatedly coupled with a license to violence. Indeed violence is commanded. Sometimes it is

God who will blot out all the inhabitants of the land; sometimes it is the chosen people who are called upon to do so in God's name. The land cannot be shared; neither is there enough love to go round to everybody. Regina Schwartz in her book *The Curse of Cain* (1997) has shown how the accounts of the covenant and the promised land are premised on an assumption of scarcity rather than abundance, exclusivity rather than generosity. If God makes a covenant with one nation, he does not make it with another; he cannot give gifts or land or love to everyone but only to a select few.

If these passages of the Bible which give stories of the covenant are read from the perspective of writers in the Persian-Hellenistic period who were trying to forge a theocratic ideology and sense of national identity to post-exilic Jews, and seen, therefore, as stories projected on to an imagined past, it is understandable that they would want to give Jews a sense of their special relationship with the land and with their god. But if they are read, as they have been read repeatedly in Western history, as a factual account, indeed as divine revelation, then it is open to anyone who puts themselves into the position of the chosen ones to do violence to those whom they deem to be excluded. I shall explore this more fully in the next chapter on holy war; it is an ideology which has had a long afterlife in the history of the West. I end this chapter with a meditation on the Sinaitic covenant in the style of a midrash by Jewish poet-scholar Alicia Ostriker:

> No other Gods. No images, no idols, no interbreeding, no whoring with the Others, whom the God of History has not chosen. What if the Others are great and we are little? Still they are the unclean, the not-us ... The doctrine of racial purity: this too, with its rhetoric, its simple appeal, is rooted in Sinai. For what is a Master Race if not the distorted mirror image of a Chosen People, at which all the devils in Gehenna laugh until their sides split?
>
> (Ostriker 1994:135)

Chapter 5

'I am a jealous god'

Monotheism and holy war

If the idea of covenant was of great significance to the consolidation of national identity, the key condition of that covenant was that the Israelites were to worship only one god. No rivals were permitted: the Lord is a 'jealous God' (Exodus 34.14). The very first commandment of the Decalogue was the prohibition against other gods: 'You shall have no other gods before/ besides me' (Exodus 20.3). Time after time in the stories of the wilderness wanderings, the people were warned against involvement with other gods, the gods worshipped by those who already lived in the land that God promised to the Israelites:

> When my angel goes before you, and brings you in to the Amorites, and the Hittites, and the Perizzites, and the Canaanites, the Hivites and the Jebusites, and I blot them out, you shall not bow down to their gods, nor serve them, nor do according to their works, but you shall utterly overthrow them and break their pillars into pieces.
>
> (Exodus 23.23–24)

The list of inhabitants is parallel to one we have already encountered; so is the exhortation. It is an exhortation repeated many times in the Bible.

In the previous chapter I showed how the auto-narrative of the covenant functioned to give Israelites an identity as a special people, chosen by God, and excluded everyone else. In this chapter I shall begin by showing how that exclusion also prohibited other gods: as the passage just quoted shows, these two exclusions were intertwined. Nor was all this merely a matter of rhetoric. It was to be enforced with war, holy war, in which all these 'Others' and their gods were to be exterminated without mercy. The covenant, which has been held by many scholars to be a positive and life-affirming antidote to any preoccupation with death, therefore turns into a covenant deeply embroiled in violence, a violence which has shaped the West as it took the narrative of covenant and chosen people to be its own.

Monotheism

As often as the biblical exhortation to worship only one God is repeated, it is transgressed. Many of the stories of the early Israelites are variations on the theme of idolatry, of worshipping gods other than the god to whom they are pledged in covenant. In the wilderness they make a golden calf and worship it. Once they get into the land of Canaan they get involved with the gods of the people of the land just as they had been warned not to do. The stories of the book of Judges are ever and again stories of Israel's apostasy and idolatry, divine punishment (often by allowing them to be defeated by an enemy nation), repentance and deliverance, upon which the sequence begins all over again. The kings and people of the 'monarchy period' repeatedly follow the gods Baal and Asherah until there is a dramatic show-down with the prophet Elijah. And so it goes on.

These stories have often been read by biblical scholars and theologians as though they represent the slow triumph of monotheism over idolatry and superstition, with the underlying assumption that monotheism is a 'higher' form of religion towards which humankind makes progress. Biblical scholars who operate on the presupposition that there is only one god and that the Bible is his revelation read monotheism into the distant past of Israel, at least to Sinai and possibly earlier (Albright 1957; Kaufman 1972; de Moor 1997).

However, there are major problems with such an account. First, the Hegelian or Darwinian assumption of progress or evolutionary development is highly problematic when applied to religion, not least in its treatment of many 'world religions' as species of a universal 'religion' of which there are higher and lower forms. Second, as I argued in Chapter 4, it is contentious (to say the least) to read the stories of Abraham and Sinai and even the judges and the kings as though they were history rather than literary constructions of the Persian-Hellenistic period.

It is, however, a third objection to the assumption of monotheism which I want to explore. It is simply that such a reading is inaccurate to the texts themselves. In many of the biblical stories it is not the existence of other gods that is denied. On the contrary: their existence is assumed; and Israel is forbidden to worship them. To do so is to break the terms of the covenant which binds Yahweh and his chosen people: it is unfaithfulness; sometimes represented is sexual terms as 'whoring after other gods' or 'playing the harlot' rather than being a faithful spouse of Yahweh (Exodus 34.16). As Mark Smith in his study of the origins of monotheism puts it:

> Within the Bible, monotheism is not a separate 'stage' of religion in ancient Israel, as it is customarily regarded. It was in fact a kind of ancient rhetoric reinforcing Israel's exclusive relationship with its deity. Monotheism is a kind of inner community discourse using the language of Yahweh's exceptional divine status over and in all reality ('there are

no other deities but me') in order to absolutize Yahweh's claim on Israel and to express Israel's ultimate fidelity to Yahweh in the face of a world where political boundaries or institutions no longer offered sufficiently intelligible lines of religious identity.

(Smith 2001:9)

In the biblical literature in which Israel is represented as one nation among many, the Near Eastern commonplace is often preserved of each nation having their own god or gods. Yahweh is the God of Israel, as Baal or Dagon are the gods of surrounding peoples. The warfare of Israel against these nations is then represented as also the warfare of Yahweh against their gods. Yahweh is of course represented as superior to all the others; they are to be defeated by him just as the nations who worship them are to be defeated by Israel. But this very rhetoric indicates that the writers assume polytheism, not monotheism. In the theologies informing the Pentateuch and conquest narratives, God's covenant with Israel promised them the land in return for their pledge of loyalty to him alone, among all the gods. In the literature of the monarchy, 'royal theology exalted Yahweh as the national god who sponsored the rule of the monarch' (Smith 2001:163); other nations had their own 'divine kings' sponsoring their earthly kings. Although there is continuous exhortation to the Israelites not to follow these 'gods of the nations' neither is there in much of the literature (until 'Second Isaiah', discussed below) reason to believe that the writers objected to these nations having their own gods just as Israel had Yahweh.

But Israelites must not follow them! The insistent repetition of the exhortation is as clear as possible an indication that other gods were in fact worshipped. And indeed archaeological finds reveal an abundance of images of gods and goddesses (Keel and Uehlinger 1998). There is no reason to suppose that these were worshipped singly, in the sense that each person would worship no more than one god. Rather, people worshipped many gods, of whom Yahweh was one. He may even have been seen as the most important. John Day has argued that 'those who worshipped other gods and goddesses surely still saw Yahweh as the chief god, with the other deities being regarded as subordinate members of his pantheon' (Day 2000:227).

The gender of monotheism

Whether or not it is the case that Yahweh was accepted as the chief god (scholars disagree about this), it is certainly true that many of the biblical writers seem to have assumed that these gods represented a threat to Yahweh, that he was in rivalry with them for the loyalty of Israel. This was particularly true of two of them: Baal and Asherah. Baal is the chief god of the Philistines, Israel's constant enemies in the literature of the monarchy. Yahweh and Baal are in continuous intense rivalry, and Israel receives divine blessing only when she (and especially her king) is loyal to Yahweh alone and does not build altars to Baal, sacrificing and burning incense 'on high places, and on the hills, and under every green tree' (2 Kings 16.4). Yahweh is to be worshipped only at the temple in Jerusalem. In Jerusalem, the royal court and the temple priests had a better grip on religious practices and could reinforce their control.

It has often been assumed that Asherah was a consort of Baal. They are coupled together in biblical writings; the story of Elijah, for example, places four hundred prophets of Asherah and four hundred and fifty prophets of Baal together 'at Jezebel's table' (1 Kings 18.19). In other Near Eastern sources it would seem that Baal and Asherah (or Ba-lu and Anatu) are similarly linked, for example in Ugaritic texts Anatu is represented as a violent goddess whose ritual blood-shedding is connected with Ba-lu's fertility and thus the fertility of the earth (Bowman 2003; see also Eaton 1969, Keel and Uehlinger 1998). However, the frequency with which reference is also made in the Bible to Asherah having altars in the Jerusalem temple or at least being worshipped alongside Yahweh, and the fierce intensity of the rivalry between Yahweh and Baal, has led some scholars to conjecture that in popular Israelite religion Asherah was the consort of Yahweh (Olyan 1988; Binger 1997). The writers of the sixth-century 'Deuteronimistic' literature which strongly promoted Yahwism as the centre of theocratic ideology, for example, nevertheless left references to Asherah in relation to Yahweh in the texts that they wrote or assembled. As Binger argues,

> Since we must assume that the Deuteronomists were in no way happy to pass on a tradition of a goddess having her natural place in the temple of Jerusalem, just as they must have felt very badly about any gods but their own being worshipped, the fact that they mentioned it at all can only be explained as one of two things: sloppy redaction of older materials – a not very feasible solution to my mind – or the fact that everyone knew Asherah to be a goddess whose natural place was alongside Yahweh in the central temple of Jerusalem; the deuteronomists would lose their credibility if they claimed otherwise.
>
> (Binger 1997:126)

Whether this was the case or not, the biblical writers who insisted on the supremacy of Yahweh and the covenant with him are emphatic in their rejection of Asherah, as though she represented a particular threat to the theocracy which they were trying to establish.

In this they are similar to writers in other ancient cultures: the male god is lifted up as the only true god, while the goddesses are denounced. There is, for example, a violent precursor in the Babylonian myth of creation, the *Enuma Elish*. In this story the goddess Tiamat is actually killed by Marduk the hero, who then makes the earth out of her brutally dismembered body.

He let fly an arrow, it split her belly,
cut through her inward parts
and gashed the heart.
He held her fast, extinguished her life.

(Jacobsen 1976:178)

He then split up her body, making heaven out of one half. From the other
half he used her breasts to make mountains and hills, pierced her eyes so
that the Tigris and the Euphrates flowed from them, and supported the sky
with her genitals. Tiamat is portrayed in the myth as evil, spawning monsters
and serpents full of venom; thus her murder is justified and the male god who
effects a rescue from such fearful evil is a hero. But the sexualized nature of
the account should not go unnoticed. In the first place there is the gendered
brutality of the murder itself: it is her 'inward parts', literally her womb, that is
the particular target of Marduk's violence. Then, it is specifically her breasts
and her genitals that he uses in his own creation, appropriating her creative
body for his own purposes even while she herself is vilified.

The accounts from ancient Greece are less gory; but as I showed in
Volume 1, here too the goddesses were supplanted by the calm voices of
(masculine) reason. The philosopher Parmenides, for example, appropriated
the goddess for his own purpose, ventriloquizing so that although it seemed
that she was being honoured, in fact she was being erased while his words
were taken forward. This pattern was followed by Plato in the *Symposium*,
as he stuffed his words into the mouth of Diotima and thereby silenced
whatever the goddess herself or her spokeswoman (Diotima/Sappho) might
say. From Babylonian thought to Greece, in the early Hebrew scriptures and
in Christianity, and even in modern scholarship on the history of religions,
there are aggressive efforts to obliterate goddess worship and even to erase its
memory (Eliade 1978; cf. Christ 1991). Indeed, one of the most striking
aspects of goddess worship is the vehemence with which it was put down. The
efforts at its obliteration in the West shows how threatening it is, especially in
connection with issues of gender and sexuality.

This portrayal of the goddess as evil or monstrous, especially sexually evil,
bringing forth from their wombs a brood of wickedness, is clear in the biblical references to Asherah. As we have seen, biblical writers repeatedly har-
angue the people of Israel about the 'graven images' which they continue to
worship, and the groves of trees on 'every high hill' where such illicit worship
occurs. With Asherah were connected sexual rituals of 'sacred marriage' to
renew the fertility of the earth (Long 1992:128–36). The violence with which
the writers of the royal court and the temple tried to destroy them is indication of the threat they were felt to pose to the patriarchal system. It also
suggests that worship of Asherah was far more prominent in popular religion than might be assumed if the exhortations to faithfulness to Yahweh
were read as indicating that Israel was in fact virtually monotheistic.

Thus for example, Josiah, represented in the text as a 'good' and reforming monarch who followed Yahweh, enacts his virtue by ruthlessly stamping out the images of Asherah that were in the Jerusalem temple.

> He brought out the Asherah from the house of the Lord, outside Jerusalem, to the brook Kidron, and beat it to dust and cast the dust of it upon the graves of the common people. And he broke down the houses of the male cult prostitutes which were in the house of the Lord, where the women wove hangings for the Asherah.
>
> (2 Kings 23.6–7)

He continued by desecrating the hill shrines that had been 'built for Ashtoreth the abomination of the Sidonians' (13). In place of 'abomination' the New English Bible translates the Hebrew as 'the loathsome goddess'. But to *whom* was Asherah/Ashtoreth an abomination or loathsome, and why? Obviously not to the people who worshipped her, and who seem to have rebuilt the shrines and reinstated the rituals on the 'high hills' as quickly as they could. Those, however, who were determined to establish a national identity in terms of a covenant with Yahweh the Father God could not afford to tolerate the goddess and her worship.

Of particular interest is the biblical treatment of Jezebel, the wicked wife of King Ahab. Her name to this day is symbolic of female sexual evil: seductress, vampire and witch all rolled into one. In the Bible, she is portrayed as a queen who fostered the cult of Asherah and supported her prophets (1 Kings 18.19), in consequence of which she was bitterly opposed by Elijah the prophet of Yahweh. He predicted that she would come to a terrible end and that 'dogs shall lick your blood' (1 Kings 21.19). When this actually occurred later in the story it is described as a punishment from Yahweh (2 Kings 9.30–37). Peter Ackroyd has pointed out that Jezebel was more than a detached patroness of the cult of Asherah; she may have actually symbolized the goddess and thus became a convenient target of the antagonism of followers of Yahweh.

> When she paints her eyes and dresses her hair and looks down from the window, she appears rather like the portrayal of the 'woman at the window', a familiar symbol of the Near Eastern art, and held to represent the Goddess as sacred prostitute. It is almost as if she is being presented, and rejected, as the Goddess herself.
>
> (Ackroyd 1983:259; cf. Beach 1997. The biblical reference is to 2 Kings 9.30)

In the ideology of the patriarchal and war-like 'Lord of hosts' a goddess who signified sexuality and fertility could not be tolerated. 'God the Father was quite distinct from the Mother Goddess' (Condren 1989:22). Jezebel, and the goddess she stood for, must be trampled in the dust.

There was considerable slippage, as the case of Jezebel shows, between the idea of foreign women and foreign gods. Time after time Israel is warned against intermarriage with foreign women, because this will lead to worship of foreign gods, and time after time in the stories of the kings they disobeyed the divine injunction with the predicted effect. Most famous was Solomon, who 'loved many foreign women'; and just as God had said would happen, 'his wives turned away his heart after other gods'. He built altars for these gods, and encouraged their worship, first for one, then another, and then 'for all his foreign wives, who burned incense and sacrificed to their gods' (1 Kings 11.1–8). The implication here and through many of the texts that follow this pattern is that the female, especially her sexual attractiveness, is a threat to men, just as female gods are a threat to the Father God. Religious fidelity and sexual fidelity are linked; and transgression of either leads to transgression of the other. Foreigners – especially foreign women – 'pollute' the land of the covenant, and their gods are 'filthy' or 'abominations'. When Joshua is about to die, for example, he gives a special final warning to the people, a warning that links monotheism, sexual fidelity, and the land of promise:

> Take good heed to yourselves, therefore, to love the Lord your God. For if you turn back, and join the remnant of these nations left here among you, and make marriages with them, so that you marry their women and they marry yours, know assuredly that the Lord your God will not continue to drive out these nations before you; but they shall be a snare and a trap for you, a scourge on your sides, and thorns in your eyes, till you perish from off this good land which the Lord your God has given you.
>
> (Joshua 23.11–13)

Monotheism (in the sense of strict fidelity to only one god) is thus the counterpart of the ideology of the covenant and the promised land for the chosen people, and both are intricately connected with gender. As Regina Schwartz has put it in her perceptive analysis,

> Monotheism/monogamy/land became a nexus in a system of ownership wherein Israel, women, and land are owned so they can be delimited, and delimited so that they can be owned. Women must be monogamous and Israel must worship Yahweh alone, or the land will be polluted. Furthermore, foreign marriages defile the land; alliances with other peoples defile the land; syncretistic worship practices defile the land; and the land must be held in perpetuity – with no pieces of it cultivated by foreigners – or it is defiled.
>
> (Schwartz 1997:64)

The sense of threat is palpable. There are so many ways of being polluted: how can anyone hope to remain clean? It is hard to resist the picture of

Israel like a person in the grip of a neurosis that drives them to wash their hands compulsively, over and over. And, indeed, there are complex laws of ritual purity, epitomized by the violence of sacrifice undertaken to avoid or rectify pollution: pollution from bodily fluids like menstruation or emission of semen, pollution from touching a corpse, or the pollution of transgressing a moral law. All of these seem to be on a continuum; and are connected with the covenant, with the land, and with a gendered monotheism. To quote Regina Schwartz again:

> Monotheism ... is not simply a myth of one-ness, but a doctrine of possession, of a people by God, of a land by a people, of women by men. The drive to own property issues in the deep homology between possessing a woman's body and possessing land. Both are conquerable territory, it would seem, connected not only by the familiar fertility imagery of ploughing and planting but also by the property images of boundaries and borders. In the Bible, this assumes the shape of a pre-occupation with physical wholeness, with not allowing borders to leak even though they are everywhere open. A host of bodily emissions, from blood to semen, are considered unclean.
>
> (Schwartz 1997:71)

The 'Holiness Code', which I shall discuss in a subsequent chapter, is a set of rules detailing the various forms of sin and impurity and what to do about them. Especially significant is the focus on death; ritual animal slaughter and a complex sacrificial system is given as a way of dealing with the pollution that, left undealt with, threatens to destroy the people and their connection with the land. It can be seen as a complex turning inward of violence.

But, as in any neurosis, violence can be turned outwards in anger and aggression instead of (or as well as) inwards. In the Bible, one way of dealing with pollution is by ritual sacrifice, but another way is by killing. If the enemy is slaughtered, then it can no longer be a threat. The Canaanites and their gods are to be utterly exterminated; God is portrayed as the Lord of Hosts, the God of Battles. The covenant and its demand for the worship of Yahweh alone becomes a license – indeed a summons – to violence in murder and warfare; and God himself will be the commander in chief. It is to this idea of holy war, deeply inscribed in the biblical text and thus in Western culture, that I now turn.

Holy war

When the people of Israel were at last about to cross the Jordan River to enter their 'promised land', God renewed his covenant with them. He says to Joshua (their leader after the death of Moses):

Now therefore arise, go over this Jordan ... Every place that the sole of your foot will tread upon I have given to you, as I promised Moses. From the wilderness and this Lebanon as far as the great river, the river Euphrates, all the land of the Hittites to the Great Sea toward the going down of the sun shall be your territory ... Only be strong and very courageous, being careful to do according to all the law which Moses my servant commanded you ...

(Joshua 1.2–7)

And so the people passed into the land of Canaan, with God parting the waters of the Jordan River to ease their passage as he had parted the waters of the Red Sea many years before. According to the story, God was keeping his part of the covenant with Israel. To indicate that Israel would also keep their part, Joshua reciprocated by circumcising all the males. It was the first act upon reaching the 'promised land'. It marked the possession of the land with blood and stamped it with masculinity; there is no mention of what the women did while the men were reaffirming their covenant with God.

If the first blood to flow was that of the Israelite males, this was soon followed by that of the Canaanites, who according to the narrative were killed in their thousands. God had commanded the extermination of all the inhabitants of the land, and the Israelites set about it with a will. They marched round and round the city of Jericho, and when, miraculously, the walls fell and they took the city, 'they utterly destroyed all in the city, both men and women, young and old, oxen, sheep, and asses, with the edge of the sword' (Joshua 6.21). They conquered the city of Ai, and 'slaughtered all the inhabitants of Ai in the open wilderness where they pursued them and all of them to the very last [fell] by the edge of the sword', about twelve thousand men and women (Joshua 8.24–25). In chapter after chapter there are stories of wars of conquest in which thousands of Canaanites are slaughtered as Yahweh gives the land and its cities to his chosen people as he had promised to do. Sometimes there are individual dramas; often there is a simple repetition of a pattern:

Then Joshua passed on from Makkedah [or Lachish, or Eglon, or Hebron or ...], and all Israel with him, to Libnah, and fought against Libnah; and the Lord gave it also and its king into the hand of Israel; and he smote it with the edge of the sword, and every person in it; he left none remaining in it; and he did to its king as he had done to the king of Jericho.

(Joshua 10.29–30)

Sometimes the Israelites were permitted to keep the spoil of the cities as booty, sometimes not; but in most cases they killed all the people 'with the edge of the sword, until they had destroyed them, and they did not leave any that breathed' (Joshua 11.14). Moreover the narrative makes a point of frequently repeating that all this slaughter was in obedience to the direct command of God, a command made first to Moses and then to Joshua. Indeed the continued martial success of the Israelites was in direct proportion to their obedience to the divine injunction to slaughter all the inhabitants of the land.

As the people of the land are exterminated, the land itself is parcelled out to the 'tribes of Israel' who 'possess it' as the land of promise, given to them by God himself. Shortly before his death, Joshua recounts the words of God to the Israelites:

> You went over the Jordan and came to Jericho, and the men of Jericho fought against you, and also the Amorites, the Perizzites, the Canaanites, the Hittites, the Girgashites, the Hivites, and the Jebusites; and I gave them into your hand ... it was not by your sword or by your bow. I gave you a land on which you had not laboured, and cities which you had not built, and you dwell therein; you eat the fruit of vineyards and oliveyards which you did not plant.
>
> (Joshua 24.11–13)

But what about the people who did plant them? The story as it is told in the Bible focuses exclusively on the Israelites and their relation to their god and the land which he gave to them. The fact that the land was already inhabited and belonged to somebody else was not a reason to respect their property rights but rather a reason to slaughter them. No compassion is shown for those who are dispossessed by Israel's possession, those who are made refugees or became homeless, let alone all those who were killed. The concern of the book, rather, is that Israel is to take every precaution to worship only Yahweh, and not the gods of the people of the land. Killing off these people is one way of ensuring that Israel will not be distracted from her loyalty.

If the book of Joshua thus paints a picture of God keeping his covenant with Israel, the book of Judges tells stories of what happens when Israel reneges on her part. The problems begin precisely when the Israelites are less aggressive and live peaceably with the inhabitants of the land.

> So the people of Israel dwelt among the Canaanites, the Hittites, the Amorites, the Perizzites, the Hivites, and the Jebusites; and they took their daughters to themselves for wives, and their own daughters they gave to their sons; and they served their gods ... serving the Baals and the Asheroth.
>
> (Judges 3.5–7)

It was exactly what they had been warned against. And when their fidelity to Yahweh alone was compromised, 'the anger of the Lord was kindled against

Israel' (8). God allowed them to be defeated by one or another king of the land, so that they had to serve him. Only when the people again cried out to God for help did he send them a 'judge' or leader to lead them into battle: Ehud, Deborah and Barak, Gideon, Samson and others. The pattern is constantly repeated: 'whenever the Lord raised up judges for them' who insisted that they serve only God, they are victorious; but

> whenever the judge died, they turned back and behaved worse than their fathers, going after other gods, serving them and bowing down to them ...
>
> (Judges 2.19)

and so the cycle repeats itself, time after time.

If the books of Joshua and Judges were written or compiled in the Persian-Hellenistic period, it is easy to see how they would function in the self-identity of the Israelites as promises and warnings, respectively. What I particularly wish to note, however, is the overwhelming preoccupation with violence and bloodshed. In the book of Joshua there is no indication that the inhabitants of Canaan do anything to provoke Israel's wrath beyond the simple fact of living on land and in cities which Israel would like to have for her own; yet the narrative treats their massacre as cause for celebration, indeed as divine blessing. The storyteller seems to delight in bloodshed; the greater number of people killed the better, and no account is taken of whether they are merely defending their homes and land, or even are non-combatants. 'The edge of the sword' is what God prescribes for them. The narratives are clearly meant to be read from the perspective of the Israelite; their lessons have to do with the importance of obedience to God and its consequences in the covenant relationship. But what sort of god is it who requires all this bloodshed, and whose blessings must be measured along a scale of violence? How would it change our understanding if we were to read the stories from the perspective of the dispossessed and slaughtered Canaanites, who were simply living in their land until the Israelites invaded?

If the books of Joshua and Judges are narratives of conquest, the books of Samuel and Kings are stories of the rise of monarchy. The wars are not wars to possess the 'promised land'; they are wars of expansion and empire. David and his son Solomon are represented as the high point of Israel's possession of the land; it is no accident that the stories include an account of the renewal of the divine covenant with David. Yet although in these books the tenure of the land is much more secure than in Joshua or Judges, the violence is no less intense.

Central to the narrative is the story of the rise of David, the shepherd boy chosen by God to become a great king. His career is violent in the extreme. Everyone knows the story of David and Goliath, the giant who was killed by a stone from the youngster's sling. The sequel to this story is a celebration of violence: the Israelites chase and kill the army of the Philistines whose champion Goliath was; and when they return the women of Israel sing of the victory:

> Saul [the king of Israel] has slain his thousands,
> and David his ten thousands.
>
> (1 Samuel 18.7)

In later chapters, after David becomes king he is said to have slaughtered huge numbers of people: twenty-two thousand Syrians (2 Samuel 8.5), eighteen thousand Edomites (13), another group of forty thousand Syrians (10.18), innumerable Philistines, and many others. All this killing is, as in Joshua and Judges, represented as cause for rejoicing and an indication of divine blessing. In the story, David writes a song of praise to God 'on the day when the Lord delivered him from the hands of all his enemies' (2 Samuel 22.1) – not only Saul, but all those who resisted the expansion of his empire:

> I pursued my enemies and destroyed them,
> and did not turn back until they were consumed.
> I consumed them; I thrust them through
> so that they did not rise ...
> They looked, but there was none to save;
> they cried to the Lord, but he did not answer them.
> I beat them fine as the dust of the earth,
> I crushed them and stamped them down like the mire of the streets.
>
> (2 Samuel 22.38–43)

David rejoices not only in his own victory but in the fact that when his enemies cried to God for help they were spurned. There is no sense of questioning in the hymn. David is triumphant, and triumphant because of God's favour. What did it feel like to those whom he crushed, when God refused to listen to their cry? What kind of a god is it who condones and even blesses such slaughter?

The Lord of hosts: Masculinity human and divine

Scholars of the Hebrew Bible have suggested that part of the point of these narratives of covenant and holy war is precisely to establish the nature of God as divine warrior. The wars of conquest under Joshua and of expansion under David are not so much wars of Israel as wars of Yahweh, God fighting against his enemies. Israel was his army; God was their leader. Julius Wellhausen, a famous nineteenth-century biblical scholar, stated that:

Israel means *El fights*, and Yahweh was the fighting El [god] after whom the people named itself. The war camp was the cradle of the nation, it was also the oldest sanctuary.

(Wellhausen 1884:10, cited in Jones 1989:299)

God is the 'Lord of hosts', the 'God of battles'; Israel is his army. Although we are prone to read the narratives as though they were human wars and God came to the aid of Israel, they actually represent the situation the other way around; these were God's wars, and the Israelites were his more or less worthy soldiers.

The warriors had to be acceptable to Yahweh in every respect and had to be bearers of Yahweh's intention even with regard to their inner disposition.

(Von Rad 1991:46)

Thus a warrior like David who slaughtered thousands of people was clearly one whom God favoured; he was obedient to God, 'a man after God's own heart' (1 Samuel 13.14).

It is worth looking a little more closely at what is involved in being such a 'man after God's own heart'; what is the construction of ideal masculinity that is being projected? David Clines, in a telling article on 'David the Man', gives an analysis of some of the main elements, pointing out that it is highly likely that the 'myth of masculinity inscribed in the David story was a very potent influence upon Israelite men' (Clines 1995:215). According to the biblical story, David is described as 'skilful in playing [the lyre], a man of valour, a man of war, prudent [or intelligent] of speech, and a man of good presence [beautiful]' (1 Samuel 16.18).

Although all these characteristics are important, chief among them is that David is a warrior. Clines counts up at least 140,000 enemy men for whose deaths in warfare David is given the credit; Israelite society was mobilized for war and was in effect a 'warrior society'. In a way that would later be true for masculinity in the Roman Empire, masculinity is represented as actively engaging in violence against other men.

It is essential for a man in the David story that he be strong – which means to say, capable of violence against other men and active in killing other men.

(Clines 1995:217)

Such active killing is the most overt form of mastery; but as Clines points out, David's intelligence or prudence of speech is another means to the same end. In the story David sometimes uses crafty speech to get himself out of trouble or to gain what he wants; this includes giving false advice (2 Samuel

15.33–35) and unscrupulous counsel (1 Kings 2.6–9) in a manner reminiscent of Odysseus in the Homeric writings.

Moreover, it is important to the biblical writer to say that David is 'beautiful' – handsome and attractive. To whom? As Clines shows, the story of David is one which strongly emphasizes homosocial bonding; in this respect it is similar to the *Iliad*. The most famous bond is that between David and Jonathan, for whom his love was 'surpassing the love of women' (2 Samuel 1.26); but there are also other significant friendships and alliances with men. By contrast,

> It is a striking feature of the David story that the males are so casual about women, and that women are so marginal to the lives of the pro-tagonists. There is in this story, on the whole, no sexual desire, no love stories, no romances, no wooing, no daring deeds for the sake of a beloved. This is not a world in which men long for women.
>
> (Clines 1995:225)

The exception is Bathsheba, a beautiful woman whom David saw bathing when he looked in voyeurist manner from the roof of his house. He 'sent messengers and took her' (2 Samuel 11.4); he then ensured that her husband Uriah was killed in battle, married her, and had several sons by her. The whole story of David and Bathsheba is a story of lust, abduction and murder, rather than a story of love; indeed there is no mention of love in the narrative. Once the episode of Uriah's murder is dealt with, Bathsheba appears in the story to be like David's other wives (at least 18, all told, counting concubines). They were functional; they served his sexual desire and produced children; but there is no depth to their relationships with him as there is with his male friends and companions. Indeed for all Odysseus' philanderings there is more loyalty and affection between Odysseus and Penelope in the Homeric writings than we find anywhere in the story of David. Insofar as David is represented as an ideal of masculinity, the focus is on his aptitude for mastery and violence; women are not significant. In the covenant with Yahweh, they produce the children that ensure his succession, but he and his armies conduct the holy war that keeps and extends the boundaries of the promised land.

If David the warrior king is a 'man after God's own heart', what does his character say about the Lord of Hosts, the Father God of the cove-nant? Biblical scholars have argued about whether it was 'holy war' that blended originally disparate peoples into a tribal confederation (Von Rad 1991) or the other way around (Smend 1970), and have pointed out par-allels and contrasts with other nations of the period who may have believed that wars on earth were a counterpart to wars in the heavens, with Yahweh intervening on Israel's behalf and overcoming the false gods of the sur-rounding nations (Miller 1973; cf. Jones 1989; Bolin 2002). The point that I wish to draw out, however, does not rest on the outcome of these disputes, but rather in the sheer 'brutality and glorification of violent conquest' (Bolin 2002:50) of the narratives, their preoccupation with violence and bloodshed. They portray a god who validates – indeed requires – the extermination of his 'enemies', and a covenant with Israel the terms of which require the Israelites to fight without mercy against other nations and utterly reject the idea that there could be anything good about them or their gods.

The significance of all this stands out vividly by comparison with the wars and conflicts of the Homeric writings which I discussed in Volume 1. There, too, was exultation in battle; in the Trojan War narrative no detail of blood and shredded bone is omitted. But there are very important differences. In the Homeric writings the focus is on individual heroes; their courage in battle will grant them immortality by making them the subject of glorious song. In the biblical narratives, by contrast, the stature of the main characters and their success in battle is in direct proportion to their obedience to God. Although Joshua, Jael, David and others become the subjects of biblical writings, they are not heroes in the way that Achilles, Hector or Odysseus are heroes. It is not simply in virtue of their valour that they are praised, but rather because they exerted their valour in relation to the covenant with Yahweh.

In the Homeric writings gods and goddesses help the Greeks and the Trojans; the goddess Thetis is Achilles' mother; Odysseus is a favourite of Athena; Hera favours the Trojans. At one level the outcome of the war is decided in the council of the gods on Mount Olympus and only then enacted on the battlefields of Troy. Yet one could never call the Trojan War a holy war in the way that the conquests under Joshua or David have been so characterized. There is no notion of the Greeks or the Trojans marching out at the command of Athena or under the direct leadership of Zeus, with Achilles or Hector merely the obedient servant of their god. The Trojan War is won ultimately by the ruse of the cunning Odysseus, who hatches the idea of the Trojan horse: how different this is from the conquest of Jericho, whose walls fall down by direct divine intervention after the Israelites march round and round it at the command of God.

Above all, there is no sense in which the conquest of Troy is undertaken as the human counterpart of a covenant with God, or that the extermination of all the Trojans would be pleasing to the gods of Mount Olympus. Neither is Troy a 'promised land' for the Greeks. When they are victorious they pack their ships full of booty and sail for home. But for the Israelites, warfare, conquest, and the complete extermination of all the inhabitants of the land is central to their identity as the covenant people of God, and the biblical writers valorize warfare in the name of the Lord of Hosts who will completely wipe out his enemies. The question of why they should be characterized as enemies in the first place, rather than as neighbours or as friends, is never asked. If they are different, they are ene-mies. And enemies are not to be tolerated or negotiated with, let alone made into friends. On the contrary, Israel is explicitly warned against any thaw in attitude towards them because they will then become a 'snare' to Israel, deflecting them from single-minded obedience to God; indeed when the Israelites do become more friendly with their neighbours God punishes them with great severity. Israel has nothing to learn from them, especially not from their gods or religious practices. They are to be wiped out, in loyalty to Yahweh the Lord of Hosts.

Narrative and identity

When we consider the probable circumstances of the composition of the conquest literature, we can see how its emphasis on covenant, monotheism and holy war could function. I have already discussed the idea, put forward by Philip Davies (1992) and others, that much of the Hebrew Bible was written or at least compiled during the Persian-Hellenistic period, and that its purpose was to help Israel develop a sense of identity by providing a narrative of her past. It served the purpose of the king and the court to promote a strong theocratic ideology; and the narratives of conquest and empire served that purpose admirably. Israel was struggling to reconstitute itself after a period of severe oppression under the Babylonians: 'the rhetoric of violence appropriated from the oppressor is turned by the oppressed into a vehicle of self-reconstitution' (Rowlett 1996:183).

Many scholars take the view that historically there was no conquest: the 'holy wars' never actually happened. Norman Gottwald, for example, argued that bands of nomads gradually and peacefully settled in the land of Palestine, and eventually formed a confederation that became known as Israel of the 'tribes of Yahweh' (Gottwald 1980; cf. Lemche 1988, 1990). Similarly, Lori Rowlett, in her study of the rhetoric of violence in the book of Joshua, concludes that although the narratives are narratives of the extermination of 'evil' Canaanites, in fact they are not the real targets. In the context of the theocracy, she argues, it is the Israelites themselves who are to take heed to comply with every aspect of the covenant; the rhetoric is direc-ted towards them, lest they think of resisting the hierarchy of court and temple which is being imposed upon them.

> The message is that the punishment of Otherness is death, and that insiders can easily become outsiders (Others) by failure to submit. The purpose of the rhetoric of violence in the conquest narrative is to serve as a warning to the people ... that the post-imperial power of the central government could and would be unleashed upon any who resisted its assertion of control.
>
> (Rowlett 1996:183)[1]

The stories of warfare and the extermination of others in the name of Yahweh who had chosen Israel as the special people of his covenant are therefore not to be read as real events. Rather, they are intended to help consolidate national identity by giving the people an imagined idealized past which enabled the weak and emergent nation to reconceive itself as the special people of God, in spite of her much more powerful neighbours and enemies (Perdue 1994).

What was being forged was a national identity that could maintain itself over against Babylon, Egypt, Greece and the developing power of Rome. To sustain that identity Israel constituted itself as different from them, not least in having a god who claimed total allegiance, indeed ultimately claimed to be the only god and the creator of the whole universe. With this god the people of Israel had a covenant relationship, projected back into their mythical past. In his eyes they were special, a chosen people; and the land was given to them by him in virtue of this covenant forever. Indeed, he would fight for them to retain it, provided only that they remain utterly and exclusively loyal to him. As the stories showed, he was their Lord of Hosts. But he was also their father, exerting his omnipotence and his mercy on behalf of those who were in his favour. The intensely patriarchal social structure and the valorization of aggressive masculinity mirrored and reinforced the picture of the relationship of Israel to their god. Women were to men as men were to God. The narratives, poetry and wise sayings of the Hebrew Bible, written or selected at this time, provided a body of literature that helped foster and perpetuate this theocratic identity, an identity bristling with defensiveness against their powerful neighbours and confidence towards their god who held it all together.

All of this, however, leaves many question unanswered. As Regina Schwartz asks in relation to the 'peaceful settlement' theory, 'if the process was so peaceful, how did the story of violent invasion come to be? Whom did it serve, when and why?' (Schwartz 1997:155). If the stories are not historically factual, who would benefit from constructing narratives of such a violent past and such a blood-thirsty God? Even if it was in the interests of the state to reinforce complicity with its rules and rituals by narratives warning that those who did not comply would meet the full force of the wrath of both the state and God, did it have to exult so strongly in violence and blood? Could there not be a relationship to others, even in a weak and struggling state, which emphasized negotiation and alternatives to violence? Would it not be possible for God to be represented as taking ethical initiative and leading his people to mutual flourishing with other nations (and maybe even their gods?) rather than to endless hostility? Or rather, since there are counter-narratives within the Bible itself which do advocate these more peaceable alternatives, why are the voices of peace so muted by the strident voices of violence and exclusion?

The afterlife of the narratives

Libraries have been written as biblical scholars ponder the history of the narratives; much less effort has gone into pondering their afterlife. Yet it is the case that whatever conclusions are reached with regard to their original composition, their effect upon the imaginary of the West has been incalculable. Those who have been able to construct their self-identity as heirs of the covenant, as divinely chosen, have had a ready-made set of linked ideas justifying war, extermination of 'others' in order to take their land. The biblical writings became scripture for the West in a way that the Homeric writings never did; the god of the Bible became the god of Western Christendom, and the stories of violence, covenant and conquest were accepted as historically true and an accurate representation of God and his relationship to his people. No matter how much scholars have warned that the narratives of the conquest should not be read as sober history, it even today remains the case that these passages form part of the popular understanding in the West of 'what the Bible says'. As Regina Schwartz has said, the violent stories of war and extermination 'are more widely known and read and hence they enjoy a broader political afterlife than any (albeit brilliant) biblical scholar's arcane theory, however politically palatable or historically plausible' (Schwartz 1997:158).

Thus for example, as we have seen, the biblical writings portray the Israelites as God's chosen people in a way that no other people are; and the land of Canaan intended for them by God himself; so the violence they inflicted in its conquest was mandated by God. The war was holy. Nor is this merely a view which can be attributed to ancient peoples but which has long since been left behind. Contemporary Jews, whether living in Israel or not, often consider themselves descendents of the ancient tribes of Israel (in a way that no one considers themselves descendents of Odysseus or Achilles or Agamemnon). Many Jews also believe that because of that descent they have a god-given right to the land of Palestine/Israel. In spite of significant dissent, the ideology of those who see themselves and the land as chosen by God is of sufficient strength to shape the contemporary Middle East. Moreover there is enough support in the West by Jews and non-Jews alike for the idea that Palestine/Israel is a homeland for Jewish people ever since biblical times to ensure that Jewish claim to the land at the expense of contemporary Palestinians is supported by the world's superpower and receives only muted challenge. As Stephen Zunes (among many others) has pointed out, the USA's policy towards contemporary Israel and Palestine is significantly shaped by the Christian Right and its support for the Republican Party:

> Based in part on a messianic theology that sees the ingathering of the Jews to the Holy Land as a precursor for the Second Coming of Christ,

the battle between Israelis and Palestinians is, in their eyes, simply a continuation of the Biblical battles between the Israelites and the Philistines. God is seen as a kind of cosmic real estate agent who has deemed that the land belongs to Israel alone – secular notions regarding international law and the right of self-determination notwithstanding.

(Zunes 2003:157–8)

The situation is even more complicated, because Christians as well as Jews claim the Bible as their own holy book. As early as the time of the New Testament, Christians have argued that they are now the true descendents of Israel, God's new chosen people, descended according to the spirit not according to the flesh. Paul writing to the Romans argued that:

he is not a real Jew who is one outwardly, nor is true circumcision [the ancient sign of the covenant] something external and physical. He is a Jew who is one inwardly, and real circumcision is a matter of the heart, spiritual and not literal.

(Romans 2.28–29)

In the light of teaching such as this, and especially the malicious teaching that Jews were responsible for killing Jesus the Son of God, Christians believed themselves not only to be the inheritors of divine promises and the new chosen people but also as having a right to violent anti-Semitism, a new form of holy war that erupted into pogroms, crusades, and attempts at gen-ocide. Even when such violence was deplored and Jews were considered elder brothers or allies of Christians, the Hebrew Bible was appropriated by Christians as the 'Old Testament'. It is now impossible for anyone brought up in the 'Christian' West to study the texts of the Hebrew Bible without having their perceptions of its meanings structured, consciously or unconsciously, by centuries of Christian interpretation.

Chapter 6

'When I see the blood'

Sacrifice ...

Closely connected with the ideology of covenant and holy war in the Hebrew Bible was the ritual of sacrifice. If holy war was intended to keep Israel pure from contamination by outsiders and their gods, sacrifice was to keep her pure from within, cleansed of sin and indicative of obedience to her god. The practice of sacrifice is of course not unique to Israelites: it has been part of a great many societies and cultures. Nevertheless, it is the ideology and practice of sacrifice as represented in the Bible that has had the greatest impact on the West, especially through Christendom's appropriation of its themes and application of them to Jesus, the 'Lamb of God' whose violent sacrificial death is held to take away the sins of the world.

But why is sacrifice necessary? Who can perform the sacrifice? Who can be sacrificed? What are the assumptions of gender and power implicit in biblical representations of sacrifice? How is the internally directed violence and purification of sacrifice related to the externally directed violence and purification of holy war? Above all, what sort of god is it who requires all this violence and delights in blood?

In this chapter I shall address these questions, and show the significance of sacrifice in the genealogy of violence in the West. I shall begin by tracing some of the central instances of sacrifice in the Hebrew Bible. While these instances cannot be presented without reference to the questions raised above, I shall reserve fuller discussion of them to later in the chapter, when I shall consider anthropological and theological theories of sacrifice. It will be my contention that the ideas of covenant, holy war and sacrifice form a constellation of gendered violence which has structured Western civilization, to its own detriment and to the detriment of all with whom it interacts. But where shall we find a counter-narrative from which to draw resources for change?

Sacrifice in the Hebrew Bible

Blood and the Father God

The theme of sacrifice and the importance of blood emerges very early in the biblical writings as we have them today. According to Genesis 4, the first pair of brothers, Cain and Abel, each brought an offering to God. Cain was a 'tiller of the ground', so he brought something that he had grown. Abel was a herdsman; he brought 'of the firstlings of his flock'. But the two offerings were not equally acceptable.

> The Lord had regard for Abel and his offering, but for Cain and his offering he had no regard.
>
> (Genesis 4.4–5)

Why not? Why would God want an offering in the first place, and why would one sort of offering be more acceptable than another?

The text gives no answer to these questions. Subsequent commentators in an attempt to make the story more plausible have sometimes suggested that the tragic sequel reveals the answer without stating it directly. Rather than accept God's verdict on the acceptability of their offerings, Cain became angry and jealous, and murdered his brother: clearly he must have had a bad attitude all along, and this is why God did not have regard for what he brought. This explanation, however, while making God appear less arbitrary, places far more emphasis on inward motivation (as contrasted with behaviour and action) than is typical of the book of Genesis, which is usually reticent about its protagonists' emotions or intentions.

Much more plausible, in the context of the book, is the idea that God preferred animal sacrifice to an offering of fruit or flowers. God wanted blood to flow. And flow it did: first from Abel's sacrifice and then from Abel himself, murdered by his brother. With this blood, however, God was *not* pleased. God rebuked Cain:

> What have you done? The voice of your brother's blood is crying to me from the ground. And now you are cursed from the ground, which has opened its mouth to receive your brother's blood from your hand.
>
> (Genesis 4.10–11)

Is the distinction between shedding human blood as contrasted with animal blood? Or is it between shedding blood (human or animal) as an offering to God as contrasted with doing so out of anger or jealousy? The story admits of either reading; and the rest of the book of Genesis carries forward the ambiguity.

A few chapters later, when Noah and his family have survived the flood in which God killed all other humans and all animals not with Noah in the ark, Noah took a selection of the animals he had preserved and offered them as burnt offerings on an altar which he had built; and God 'smelled the pleasing odour' and entered into his first covenant with humankind. Included in God's instructions at this point is his permission to Noah to eat animal flesh, so long as the blood has been carefully removed; and with it a prohibition against shedding human blood.

> For your lifeblood I will surely require a reckoning ... Whoever sheds
> the blood of man, by man shall his blood be shed; for God made man in
> his own image.
>
> (Genesis 9.5–6)

Since God had just finished exterminating virtually all human life, the
injunction reads as though God is reserving to himself the right to kill
people, while being pleased with Noah's killing of animals in sacrifice to
him. Some biblical scholars treat these verses as an ethical interpolation; be
that as it may, the story as it has been transmitted reads as though God has
a particular interest in blood and killing. It is an emphasis that continues
throughout the biblical writings, as we shall see.

Already the question begins to emerge: what sort of a god is it who takes
such an interest in blood? Scholars of the ancient Near East point to a contrast in this respect between Israel as represented in the Bible and neigh-
bouring cultures. A.L. Oppenheim, for example, argues that in
Mesopotamia, where there was also animal sacrifice, the emphasis was firmly
on feeding the god: the meat became 'the source of strength and power the
deity was thought to need for effective functioning' (Oppenheim 1977:191).
The actual slaughter of the animal and the shedding of its blood are not the
focus of attention as they are in the Bible.

> A difference that separates the sacrificial rituals in the two cultures is the
> 'blood consciousness' of the [early Israel], its awareness of the magic
> power of blood, which is not paralleled in Mesopotamia.
>
> (Oppenheim 1977:192)

I shall trace that 'blood consciousness' further in a moment. First, however, I
want to pause briefly to ask *why* there should be this difference of focus and
emphasis between the two cultures.

Here, two observations of anthropologists are pertinent. First, it has been
noted by those who have studied practices of sacrifice cross-culturally that
when there is an emphasis on blood in the ritual, there is usually also an
emphasis on the blood lines of the clan or group, organized along male lines
of kinship.

> Those systems of sacrifice that emphasize blood serve to maintain family
> groups, groups which are organized along common blood lines that are
> usually ... patrilinear. That is, blood sacrifice maintains a relationship of
> kinship between men by the emphasis on a tie of blood ...
>
> (Abusch 2002:46)

The preoccupation with blood in the biblical writings therefore indicate the
gendered dimensions of the ritual, even though gender is not explicitly

discussed in the passages in question. The significance of this gender connection will become more apparent in what follows.

Second, anthropologists have observed that it is not only the patrilineal blood lines of the clan or group that are reinforced through blood sacrifice, but also the gender of the deity.

> Fruit, cereals and the soil have often been associated with women and with devotion to female figures, whereas blood sacrifice is primarily associated with patriliny.
>
> (Delaney 1998:95)

If we place this observation alongside the story of Cain and Abel, it is hard to resist the implication that the story is insisting on a Father God rather than a goddess. The fruits of the earth that Cain brought would have been suitable gifts for a female deity. By rejecting them and accepting the blood sacrifice God shows himself to be masculine, a fitting Father for the patrilineal clan.

All of this is taken forward in the stories of blood sacrifice that follow. The next instance of bloodshed in the book of Genesis occurs in the bizarre story I recounted in Chapter 5, in which God requires Abraham to bring him a selection of animals – 'a heifer three years old, a she-goat three years old, a ram three years old' and so on –, slice them in half, and lay the halves facing each other in a line. 'When the sun had gone down and it was dark, behold, a smoking fire pot and a flaming torch passed between these pieces' (Genesis 15.17), and God makes his covenant with Abraham, to give the land to his descendents. Again, as with Noah, there is a connection between blood sacrifice and covenant, a connection reinforced in the story when Abraham and all males of his household are required by God to undergo circumcision so that God's covenant would be in their flesh. I have discussed this in a previous chapter; my point here is to indicate how the author/editor of Genesis repeatedly reverts to the theme of blood and sacrifice as particularly pleasing to God, and how routinely this theme reinforces patriarchy.

The Akedah

Only a few chapters later, God once again requires a sacrifice, and this time the demand has escalated to horrific proportions. Abraham is required by God to offer his son Isaac. God says,

> Take your son, your only son Isaac, whom you love, and go to the land of Moriah, and offer him there as a burnt offering upon one of the mountains of which I shall tell you.
>
> (Genesis 22.2)

Without protest, Abraham 'rose early in the morning', made his prepara-
tions, and set off, arriving three days later. He built an altar, bound his son
and laid him on it, and took up his knife to kill him. In the very nick of time
he was stopped by an angel. Isaac did not have to be killed after all, because
God had seen by Abraham's willingness to sacrifice him that Abraham
'feared' God. Instead he saw a ram caught by its horns in a thicket,

> and Abraham went and took the ram, and offered it up as a burnt
> offering instead of his son.
>
> (Genesis 22.13)

The *Akedah*, as this story is called, has had a central place in both Jewish
and Christian thought and ritual. Jews recite the passage each new year at
the services for Rosh Hashanah; indeed devout Jews use it daily in their
morning prayers. Christians include it in their Easter readings: the sacrifice
of Isaac is seen as prefiguring the crucifixion of Jesus, the 'beloved son of
God'. The story has become what Carol Delaney calls a 'foundational myth'
of Western culture, endlessly represented in painting, music and literature
(Delaney 1998:20, 139). It is therefore important to pause briefly on this
story which has had so major an impact on the narrative of the West.

As it stands, the story is disturbing. In the first place, all the worrying
themes of exclusion are reinstantiated without challenge. Although the narrative up to this point has made much of Sarah's miraculous pregnancy, she
is never consulted about Abraham's intention to kill their son: indeed in this
story she is never mentioned at all. It is as though the child is his alone to
sacrifice. Ishmael, Abraham's elder son by Hagar, an Egyptian woman, is
likewise erased from the story, the erasure coming from no less than the
voice of God, who refers to Isaac as Abraham's *only* son. The patriarch
becomes normative as a father of faith. Otherness of gender or of (Egyptian)
race is not invited to enter the consciousness of the reader.

Besides this silent violence against Sarah, Hagar and Ishmael, there is the
obvious violence against Isaac. Although in the biblical story Isaac was
saved at the last moment and a ram was slaughtered instead, the story is
uncomfortably near suggesting that God could demand child sacrifice.
Indeed in the afterlife of the narrative this was widely believed in both Jewish
and Christian interpretations, though often with the emphasis on the fact
that a child was *not* in fact killed. In such emphases we have an example of
what Carol Delaney terms 'evolutionary bias': the idea that the movement
from child sacrifice to animal sacrifice shows progress from a barbaric to a
more advanced society. Shalom Spiegel illustrates this view:

> The ancients can accept the rigors of sacrifice as they offer up their first
> born to the gods ... It is only inch by inch that laws were mellowed
> and humanized. [The sacrifice of the ram instead of Isaac is the]

remembrance of the transition from human to animal sacrifice – a religious and moral achievement which in folk memory was associated with Abraham's name, the father of the new faith.

(Spiegel 1969:63–4)

This defence of the story, however, has many problems. From the point of view of 'progress', the evidence is against Spiegel, since child sacrifice can be shown to have been practiced in societies more complex and sophisticated than the seminomadic organization in which Abraham is represented. More importantly, the literary and theological weight of the story points the other way. The story of Abraham's (non) sacrifice of Isaac is taken as foundational not because in the end Isaac was not killed but precisely because Abraham was willing to slay his son. '*That* is what establishes him as the father of faith' (Delaney 1998:6). Given that this is so, the questions become more insistent:

> Why is the willingness to sacrifice a child the model of faith? What is the function of obedience? Why so little attention to the betrayal of the child? Whose voice counts? Like another sacrificed by his father, did Abraham's son cry out at the critical moment: 'Father, father, why hast thou forsaken me?' Why have we eulogized their submission?
>
> (Delaney 1998:14)

Why indeed? And why have we constructed the willingness to slaughter others – even children – as something with which God might be pleased?

In their efforts to interpret this story, some strands of Jewish thought held that Abraham actually did kill Isaac, and that God later resurrected him (Spiegel 1969). Christians sometimes held a similar view, to make the parallels between Jesus and Isaac more exact. Most importantly of all, as Christians interpreted the death of Jesus they developed a theology in which God did in actual fact demand the death of his innocent son as a sacrifice to atone for the sins of the world: he became the 'Lamb of God', endlessly commemorated in Christian worship and in the music and painting of Western culture. Without the story of Abraham and Isaac, the Christian doctrine of atonement could hardly have developed as it did (Rosenberg 1965; Vermès 1973).[1]

The impact of the *Akedah* on the Western consciousness can be vividly illustrated by contrasting it with a story from classical literature with which on the face of it has certain structural similarities: Agamemnon's sacrifice of Iphigenia. In each case a father is willing to slaughter a beloved child; and in each case the sacrifice is portrayed as required by their god. In most Greek portrayals of the story, Agamemnon actually kills Iphigenia, though there is a variant in which the goddess Artemis miraculously substitutes a doe and spirits Iphigenia away (Euripides 1953).

In spite of apparent similarities, the implications of the two stories are vastly different. Whereas Abraham is honoured for his sacrifice and seen as a father of the faith, the Greek dramatists treated the myth with horror. In Aeschylus' treatment, Agamemnon's sacrifice of Iphigenia, ostensibly done so that the gods would send a fair wind to speed the Aegean ships on their way to Troy, is a sordid piece of violence which unleashes ever more destruction: the sack of Troy itself, with the slaughter of Greek and Trojan heroes and the killing or enslavement of Trojan women and children, and then the cycle of violence in Agamemnon's own household, as he is murdered by his wife Clytemnestra, and she, in turn, by her remaining children, Orestes and Electra. The Chorus sums up the way in which his 'reckless act' has had the effect of 'multiplying crime on crime', making violence breed ever more violence in vicious repetition (Aeschylus 1977:131). Both Sophocles and Euripides similarly emphasize the cycle of violence to which Agamemnon's act has given rise (Sophocles 1953; Euripides 1963, 1972). Euripides in particular stresses the madness of violence, its folly and cruelty, whether the sacrifice of Iphigenia, the Trojan War, or the vengeful retaliation of Electra and Orestes on their mother for her murder of Agamemnon, her daughter's killer. Indeed Euripides suggests that Agamemnon was out of his right mind to imagine that the gods could possibly be asking him to sacrifice his child; or, if that actually *is* what the gods require then they should be spurned, not obeyed (Euripides 1972:419; see Jantzen 2004:Chapters 5 and 6).

The treatment of the biblical story of Abraham and Isaac is in complete contrast to the Greek dramatists' representations of Agamemnon and Iphigenia. Nowhere is it suggested either that Abraham was mad or that God could never have asked such a thing of anyone (or should be disobeyed if he did). God is, throughout, represented as having the absolute right to demand anything without explanation, whether it goes against the grain of moral sensibilities or not. Moreover, as we have seen, not only is the concept of a god who demands the murder of an innocent child unquestioned in the story and by most later commentators, but the willingness of Abraham to commit the act of violence is held up not as a paradigm of sacrilege or as a crime, but as a paradigm of religious righteousness. This is true already in the Bible itself, as early Christian writers reflect on the story of Abraham.

> Was not Abraham our father justified by works, when he offered his son Isaac upon the altar? You see that faith was active along with his works, and faith was completed by his works, and the scripture was fulfilled which says, 'Abraham believed God, and it was reckoned to him as righteousness'.
>
> (James 2.21–23)

> By faith Abraham, when he was tested, offered up Isaac, and he who had received the promises was ready to offer up his only son, of whom it

was said, 'Through Isaac shall your descendents be named'. He considered that God was able to raise men even from the dead; hence, figuratively speaking, he did receive him back–

(Hebrews 11.17–19)

Just as God would raise Jesus from the dead after he had been crucified as a sacrifice to atone for the world's sins.

All these themes are brought together in Western modernity in the powerful meditation on Abraham and Isaac in Søren Kierkegaard's *Fear and Trembling* (1983). Kierkegaard explicitly contrasts Agamemnon and Abraham. The former, he says, is a 'tragic hero', a man who is willing to sacrifice his beloved daughter for the greater good of the whole community. His act, heart-rending as it is, nevertheless falls under the rubric of the ethical universal. As I have already suggested, Euripides can be interpreted as calling such a reading into question, representing Agamemnon not as an altruistic and tragic hero but as weak or even insane. Whatever the case, in Kierkegaard's view Abraham must be understood on a different plane altogether. He is not a 'tragic hero'; he is a 'knight of faith'. His willingness to sacrifice his son has nothing to do with the ethical; it will accomplish nothing for any community. Abraham is acting solely out of obedience to God, an obedience of faith 'that makes a murder into a holy and God-pleasing act' (Kierkegaard 1983:53). Abraham therefore exemplifies 'a teleological suspension of the ethical' (66) in which an individual does something which would otherwise call forth moral revulsion when he does it simply as a response of obedient faith to the absolute command of God. Again for Kierkegaard this is not merely a narrative with a moral message, which we can discuss and perhaps disagree about, as we could about Euripides' portrayal of Agamemnon. Rather, our response to Abraham and the story of his 'testing' is also a test for us, a trial of how we stand in faith and obedience before God. Through the story of Abraham, we too encounter God – or, if we fail to do so, it is because of our own shallowness and lack of faith.

> The point is to perceive the greatness of what Abraham did so that the person can judge for himself whether he has the vocation and the courage to be tried in something like this.
>
> (Kierkegaard 1983:52–3)

In our response will be an indication, Kierkegaard implies, of how we ourselves obey or fail to obey the divine summons.

Multitudes of biblical scholars and theologians have taken a similar view. To take only one example, the distinguished Old Testament scholar, Gerhard von Rad, interprets the story of Abraham and Isaac as one which ought to guide the sensibilities of the people of God when it seems to them that all the promises of God are being destroyed just as God seemed to require the destruction of Isaac, the child of God's promise to Abraham.

> The story of the offering up of Isaac goes beyond all the previous trials of Abraham and pushes forward into the realm of faith's extremest experience where God himself rises up as the enemy of his own work with men and hides himself so deeply that for the recipient of the promise only the way of utter forsakenness by God seems to stand open. Such forsakenness Israel had to experience in her history with Jahweh, and the result of such experience is made articulate in this story: Israel is to realize that in situations where God seems most unbearably to contradict himself, it is a matter of his testing her faith.
>
> (von Rad 1975.I.174)

It is this which 'now speaks to us in the story': von Rad, like centuries of biblical commentators, takes as his fundamental assumption that the god before whom Abraham stood is the same god before whom we who read the story must still stand. Even the most sympathetic interpreter of the story of Agamemnon's sacrifice of Iphigenia would never suggest that contemporary readers might find ourselves confronted by Artemis, or feel that if things go wrong in our lives it may be because she is offended or is testing us. The story of Abraham's sacrifice, by contrast, continues to be read as a profound indication of what God is like and what God might require. By such means the symbolism of sacrifice is sedimented into Western consciousness, its gendered violence valorized.

Ritual sacrifice in Israelite worship

If the *Akedah* as a foundation story inscribes gendered violence into Western religious consciousness, so too does the system of blood sacrifice that is represented in the Hebrew Bible as central to the people's worship and regular reaffirmation of the covenant. I have already referred to the story of Moses reading the book of the covenant to the Israelites, an event in which basins of blood of sacrificed oxen were thrown, half against an altar and the other half upon the listeners, with the words, 'Behold the blood of the covenant which the Lord has made with you' (Exodus 24.8). In the story, it is a solemn occasion but not a shocking one: the reader has come to expect that God will want blood. In subsequent chapters and books, detailed instructions are given for the construction of a 'tabernacle', with its central holiest place, and its consecrated priests, the main purpose of which was to be a sacrificial system in which animals were regularly slaughtered as offerings to God. Here there is no doubt that the animal's blood is a substitute for human death. For example, if a man brings an offering from his herd it is to be a perfect specimen, a male 'without blemish'.

He shall offer it at the door of the tent of meeting, that he may be accepted before the Lord; he shall lay his hand upon the head of the burnt offering, and it shall be accepted for him to make atonement for him. Then he shall kill the bull before the Lord; and Aaron's sons the priests shall present the blood, and throw the blood round about against the altar …

(Leviticus 1.3–5)

When all the details have been meticulously observed and the carcass is burnt whole on the altar, it is 'a pleasing odour to the Lord' (1.9): the phrase is repeated after the instructions for each of a range of sacrifices that the Israelites are expected to make.

Other offerings were to be made also, which did not require blood: there were offerings of baked loaves, flour, oil, wine and frankincense for example. But much the most attention is devoted in these books to the slaughter of animals for blood sacrifice. They were to be offered on a great many special occasions: the New Moon, each day of Passover (a festival commemorating Israel's escape from Egypt, when God killed the eldest son of every Egyptian family), every Sabbath, and many other times. In addition to all these, there was to be the 'continual burnt offering'. The instructions were precise:

Now this is what you shall offer upon the altar: two lambs a year old day by day continually. One lamb you shall offer in the morning, and the other lamb you shall offer in the evening … It shall be a continual burnt offering throughout your generations at the door of the tent of meeting before the Lord, where I will meet with you, to speak there to you.

(Exodus 29.38–42)

The impression is that God requires freshly shed blood at very frequent intervals, otherwise he will withdraw or be angry.

The most solemn of all the occasions of sacrifice is the annual 'day of atonement'. On that day the high priest is to bring a bull and two goats. The bull and one of the goats, chosen by lot, are to be slaughtered as 'sin offerings' for himself and the people. The priest is to bring the blood of the animals to the holiest place,

sprinkling it upon the mercy seat and before the mercy seat; thus he shall make atonement for the holy place, because of the uncleannesses of the people of Israel, and because of their transgressions, all their sins.

(Leviticus 16.15–16)

Having done that, he is then to take the other goat and perform a ritual which does not include slaughter but which may seem just as strange. The priest is to lay both his hands upon the head of the live goat, and confess over him all the iniquities of the people of Israel, and all their transgressions, all their sins; and he shall put them upon the head of the goat, and send him away into the wilderness ... The goat shall bear all their iniquities upon him to a solitary land ...

(Leviticus 16.21–22)

In this ritual it seems that shedding blood is insufficient to deal with 'all their transgressions, all their sins': another animal, usually called a 'scapegoat', must also be used.

Nevertheless, the main emphasis in the ritual of atonement as in the other sacrifices, is on the blood. There are, moreover, strict prohibitions against any Israelite eating or consuming blood themselves. If anyone does so, God says that he will 'set his face' against such a person, 'and will cut him off from among his people'. Blood belongs to God.

For the life of the flesh is in the blood; and I have given it for you upon the altar to make atonement for your souls; for it is the blood that makes atonement.

(Leviticus 17.10–11)

There is, in this set of rules and rituals, continuous public slaughter and bloodshed, and it is directly related to atonement for sin. Why? What sort of a god is being portrayed by these writers and enacted in the cultic system that many Jewish and Christian scholars believe to have been performed in compliance with these instructions? (See Milgrom 1991; Sawyer 1996.) Why should there be so much emphasis on slaughter, sacrifice and bloodshed, from the story of Cain and Abel at the beginning of the Bible to the detailed instructions for ritual sacrifices that were part of Israelite religious observance until the Romans destroyed the Jerusalem Temple in 70 CE?

Scholars have subjected these texts to scrutiny over centuries, and I shall discuss some of their findings briefly below. But I suggest at the outset that as the texts are presented, the emphasis on blood and slaughter is regularly presented in connection with covenant, either in the initial ratification of the covenant, as in the case of Noah, or Abraham with the split carcasses, or Moses reading the 'book of the law' to the Israelites. Now, we have already seen another violent side of the covenant, namely the divine demand for holy war. All other nations who inhabit the land that God promises to the descendents of Abraham are to be exterminated. There is to be bloodshed without exception. Whatever else is going on in these texts, and in whatever ways they can be interpreted, there is a preoccupation with violent bloodshed, focused both externally against 'others' and internally in dealing with the sins and infractions of the community. Death – killing – is to be constantly before the eyes of the Israelites. It is indeed their side of the covenant, the terms under which God will deal with them. The externally directed violence of warfare and the internally oriented violence of slaughter and sacrifice appear in the text as two sides of a coin, both of them crucial to the covenant between Israel and God, a god who is represented as having a virtually insatiable desire for blood.

Sacrifice, purity and patriarchy

It is of course not lost on scholars that many ancient societies practised animal and even human sacrifice. In the Homeric writings sacrifice is taken for granted: Zeus was said to take pleasure in the blood of bulls. In the fifth century BCE when Euripides expressed outrage at the idea of Agamemnon's willingness to sacrifice Iphigenia, his outrage was not against sacrifice in general, but only against the idea that a father would offer his own child. Animal sacrifice was taken for granted. It continued in the Roman Empire: for example a bull would be ritually slaughtered at the time of the election of new consuls.

Nineteenth- and early-twentieth-century anthropologists tried to develop universal or cross-cultural theories of sacrifice, taking into consideration practices of Near Eastern, African and Polynesian societies along with the literary accounts of biblical and classical civilizations. E.B. Tylor, for example, argued that sacrifice could be understood cross-culturally as a gift or tribute to a god (Tylor 1871); Robertson Smith saw it more in terms of a communion meal with the gods (Smith 1889), while Hubert and Mauss, in their influential book on sacrifice (1964, first published in 1898) saw sacrifice as a method or mechanism of contact between sacred and profane worlds, though they did not discuss why it could be assumed that there should be so great a gulf between the two worlds in the first place. J.G. Frazer assembled vast amounts of comparative material, and suggested that sacrifice was used in primitive societies as an attempt to control death (Frazer 1922).

While recognizing the importance of the themes identified in these works, however, more recent scholars have been uncomfortable with some of their underlying assumptions. Many of these scholars held to an idea of progress, a social evolution of religion whereby some cultures and religions are seen as 'primitive' while Western monotheism is 'advanced': such a view has been discredited as Eurocentric prejudice. In addition, the notion that comparisons can be easily drawn between rituals in widely different circumstances to provide a universal cross-cultural theory of sacrifice has come to seem highly doubtful and without much explanatory value. Thus for example René Girard's theory of the scapegoat, discussed in Chapter 2, simply does not fit the practice of sacrifice in African traditional religions (Sundermeier 2002), nor can it account for societies which do not have sacrificial rituals (Jay 1992:131). Similarly general is Walter Burkert's theory that sacrifice is a residue of the aggressive masculine community developed by bands of male hunters: 'community is defined by participation in the bloody work of men' (1972:20). Again, this 'one size fits all' theory is at odds with empirical ethnography (Sered 2002; Sundermeier 2002), which shows many variations on the theme of sacrifice.

Nevertheless, although any theory of sacrifice must be measured against the practices of actual societies, the constellation of ideas around sacrifice developed by these scholars – death, aggression, contact with the gods or gift to them – are valuable in thinking through the significance of sacrifice in biblical writing and its connection with violence and holy war. There is another ingredient as well, which Burkert's theory of aggression and masculine community hints at, namely gender: as Susan Sered has observed, 'cross-culturally, animal sacrifice is one of the most dramatically and consistently gendered ritual constellations'. She continues,

> Sacrifice can be seen to be analogous to gender; both are cultural processes of embodiment and disembodiment in which certain groups or individuals are modified, marked, defined, set off, or classified. Not infrequently, embodied discourses of gender are mapped onto, appropriated by, or mystified via sacrificial rituals; discourses of gender may include thoughts about who is expected to sacrifice what for whom.
>
> (Sered 2002:13–14)

Although there will be variations among societies in the ways that gender, aggression, identity, and links with the sacred find expression in sacrifice, these are themes which emerge as significant.

How, then, is the practice of sacrifice as represented in the Hebrew Bible to be understood in connection with these themes? I begin with the work of Mary Douglas, who was explicitly trying to understand the biblical world from an anthropological perspective. In her book *Purity and Danger* (1966) Douglas famously showed the intense importance of boundaries for societies, a clear sense of what was 'in' and what was 'other'. The 'other' must be carefully excluded. However, any attempt at neat binary classification inevitably leaves anomalies, and these, like the polluting 'other', are threatening sources of anxiety. It is the need to deal with boundary line cases that Douglas sees as the basis of the elaborate divisions into 'clean' and 'unclean' animals and the food laws of the biblical writings, for example. The need for classification and neat lines of demarcation is also Douglas's way of accounting for the purity and defilement laws and the counting up of the 'twelve tribes' in the book of Numbers (Douglas 1993). This tidy universe, Douglas argues,

> was part again of a still larger pattern of social behaviour which used very clear, tight defining lines to distinguish two classes of human beings, the Israelites and the rest.
>
> (Douglas 1975:283)

Societies vary, according to Douglas, but in those societies which feel them-selves under threat and 'surrounded by powerful, rapacious enemies' (305) the boundaries will be drawn most tightly, with no provision made for med-iation or exchange between 'inside' and 'outside'. Douglas does not discuss the geopolitical situation of Israel in the Persian and Hellenistic period when these books of the Bible were probably composed, but we have already noted how the Israelite court and temple would indeed have felt itself under threat from its powerful and hostile neighbours.

But if the boundaries are so tightly drawn between Israel and her neigh-bours, what about between Israel and her god? What sort of mediation is possible here? It is in response to these questions that we can see explicitly the bearing of Douglas's ideas on sacrifice. God and humanity – or more accurately God and the Israelites – are at opposite poles in relation to space and time, the sacred and the profane. God is immortal, humans die. The orderly life of the nation, threatened as it is by external enemies, is under even greater threat from God himself, should they break their covenant with God. As D. Davis has argued,

> The sacred signifies not only God and Temple but also Life, Being, and Order. By contrast the profane is represented by Gentiles, the Wilderness, Death, Nothingness, and Chaos. Between these poles is Israel, its camp and priesthood, and the world of transient experience. In essence the sacred/profane polarity is also the order/chaos polarity; the essential function of ritual is to avert the threat of chaos, and where necessary restore the desired condition of wholeness and order.
>
> (Davis 1977, as discussed in Budd 1989:291–2)

Sacrifice, therefore, allows reality to be classified in an orderly way; and while reinforcing that order it bridges the gap between the two worlds. God can be appeased; his anger can be averted and his assistance sought by an offering of blood. And the careful delineation of boundaries which preserve identity can be reinforced at the same time. The preoccupation with death and violence as expressed in blood sacrifice is thus integral to the self-iden-tity and to the theology of the Israelites at a time when they felt themselves under threat from their powerful neighbours.

Once again, however, while these scholars address the importance of sacrifice for the purity and identity of Israel in relation to God, they ignore gender, effectively equating the identity of Israel with the identity of Israelite *men*. According to the Levitical system, one of the chief sources of pollution was women's blood, especially menstrual blood and the blood of childbirth (Leviticus 15.19–30; 12.1–8). Pollution did not come only from the outside: defilement was an ever present possibility since men who so much as touched a menstruating woman were thereby rendered unclean. Only after a sacrifice of atonement was made for a woman after childbirth (33 days if she had borne a boy, twice that if the baby was a girl) could she again participate in community activities. Moreover, it is precisely a male priest who conducts the atonement ritual; a woman cannot do it for herself. In this respect again, Israelite sacrificial systems conform to Sered's assertion:

> From a gendered perspective, perhaps the most striking observation that can be made about sacrifice, and especially animal sacrifice, is that it is almost always a male dominated and male oriented ritual activity. Furthermore, in a surprisingly wide range of cultural contexts, men's involvement with sacrifice is – implicitly or explicitly – contrasted to women's involvement with childbirth. In other words, in many different cultures men and sacrifice stand in structural tension with, or opposition to, women and childbirth. Usually this tension is expressed in terms of the opposition between life and death.
>
> (Sered 2002:15)

In her perceptive analysis, Sered draws on the path-breaking work of Nancy Jay (1992) who argued that in many societies sacrifice can be seen 'as remedy for having been born of woman' (xxiii). As noted earlier in this chapter, blood sacrifice serves in part to maintain kinship lines between men in a patriarchal society. Jay argues that this kinship, forged between men by means of sacrifice, supersedes the kinship established by birth; the blood of the sacrifice neutralizes the blood of childbirth. Purity, identity, blood kinship and gender come together in the ritual of sacrifice. It is as though sacrifice effects a new birth, a spiritual birth through the agency of men and the Father God: the idea is of course taken up in Christian ideas of being 'born again' (see John 1.13; 3.5), as we will see later in this book.

Not only does sacrifice thus enable men to control life; it enables them also to control death. As Sered argues,

> Through killing the sacrificial victim, the sacrificer demonstrates his power to generate death ... Men are dramatically and ritually gendered as empowered to kill ... This model genders life-taking as a male enterprize.
>
> (Sered 2002:21)

In Israelite society as portrayed in the Bible, therefore, the system of sacrifice which maintained kinship and purity within the community is the counterpart to holy war, which maintains identity and purity over against the external other, and both reinforce the grip of patriarchy.

> Killing, unlike childbirth, grants men wilful control over the processes of nature, and in particular, over the natural processes of life and death ... Men's life-taking, because of its intentionality, becomes a means of

culturally transcending the biological; whereas childbearing, despite values attached to it as a means of perpetuating a social group, remains grounded in the 'naturalness' of women's sexual constitution.

(Rosaldo and Atkinson 1975:70)

Sacrifice, it can be argued, is the most intentional form of life-taking, and gives to its practitioners control not only over the ritual but over life and death in the community, including its involvement in holy war.

Philip Budd, who gives an excellent survey of anthropological ideas of sacrifice and cross-cultural comparisons, points out that much of the work that has been done has focused on the definition or essence of sacrifice rather than on its actual function. As he says,

Much ink has been spilt in attempting to give an 'idealistic' and essentially conceptual meaning to sacrifice; relatively little by contrast on the social operation of the system, its costs to the various strata in society, and its relationship to the exercise of power and the maintenance of status in the community.

(Budd 1989:296)

If, however, we read the biblical narratives of sacrifice and the rules for the conduct of the ritual in the context of the Persian and Hellenistic period, rather than as historical representations of a much earlier period, then its function becomes clearer. At least for the court and temple caste, the rituals of sacrifice and the stories projected into Israel's past would strongly reinforce an ideology of unique identity, a people especially chosen by God, at a time when that identity was felt to be under threat. Along with the rhetoric of holy war, blood sacrifice would be part of the covenant pact that would differentiate Israel from her neighbours by her unique relationship with her Father God. It would also, of course, consolidate patriarchal power, especially that of the priests and the temple. What it did to ordinary people, or how the already poor and oppressed felt about it is another matter; but that sacrifice would function as a technology of patriarchal power can easily be seen.

What this shows, however, is that Israel's auto-narrative is invested at every turn in blood and violent death. Israel, on this reading, constructs itself on necrophilia. But there were other possibilities. As I shall show in the next chapter, the preoccupation with killing, consequent upon interpreting the covenant as exclusion, is not the only alternative. There were voices of protest and dissent, offering a radical counter-narrative which was at least partially sometimes adopted. In terms of the afterlife of the narrative, however, the entanglement of covenant identity with violent bloodshed would have incalculable influence on successive groups – Jews, Christians, Puritans, Afrikaaners, and many more – who deemed themselves the 'chosen people'.

A god of blood

Even if the social role of an ideology of sacrifice begins to emerge from these considerations, however, the theological question remains. What sort of a god is it, who is conceived as always desiring blood? Why is God represented as constantly angry at the sins and impurities of his people – people who he himself, after all, has created finite and imperfect? And if God were angry and/or distant, why would blood sacrifice appease him or bring him nearer? Anthropological comparisons can show that the representations of sacrifice in the Bible are in some respects similar in concept and function to those of other cultures; but insofar as these ideas of sacrifice are theologically significant to Jews and Christians the recognition that other cultures did similar things still leaves us with many questions.

Both Jewish and Christian scholars who try to develop a theology of sacrifice are usually quick to emphasize that in the biblical literature the sacrifices are of animals. Human sacrifice is abhorrent: lambs or bulls or goats might be offered, but not children. In this the Israelites were self-consciously different from their neighbours, who 'burn their sons and their daughters in the fire to their gods' (Deuteronomy 12.31). The god Molech was one who desired such human sacrifice; and Jewish law was emphatic in proscribing it:

> You shall not give any of your children to devote them by fire to Molech, and so profane the name of your God.
>
> (Leviticus 18.21; cf. 20.1–5)

By contrasting Israel's animal sacrifice with the human sacrifice of other societies, it is possible to represent Israel's law as a stage of upward progress in religious development. Thus for example the Jewish scholar Maimonides, in his *Guide of the Perplexed*, writes of God's 'wily graciousness' which did not suddenly prohibit all the things the Israelites were used to sharing with their neighbours, but rather led them forward gradually, in stages, so that they could bear it. Sacrifices were therefore permitted; but they were to be sacrifices to one god only, and offered only in the prescribed place and manner.

> Through this divine ruse it came about that the memory of *idolatry* was effaced and that the grandest and true foundation of our belief – namely the existence and oneness of the deity – was firmly established, while at the same time the souls had no feeling of repugnance and were not repelled because of the abolition of modes of worship to which they were accustomed and than which no other mode of worship was known at that time.
>
> (Maimonides 1963:II.527; *Guide* III.32)

Eventually all of this would be superseded in its turn, but it was a step in the right direction.

Maimonides, writing in the twelfth century CE, was of course assuming a much earlier date for the biblical texts than the sixth century BCE, and accepting as history the stories of the patriarchs and the wilderness wanderings. But even allowing for that assumption, things are much more complicated. In the first place, it has been seriously argued that, far from being a complete contrast, 'Molech' can be read as another name for 'Yahweh' in some biblical texts (Day 1989). Whether or not this is so, the vigour with which the sacrifice of children was proscribed is an indication that it was at the very least a serious temptation for Israelites, and perhaps was actually practised.

Jacob Milgrom, an outstanding scholar of the biblical books of the law, has written a vehement denunciation of those who suggest that child sacrifice was practised, let alone required by God. He says,

> there is no evidence that the firstborn, *except in crisis situations* (e.g. 2 Kings 3.27) were sacrificed; there is no indication that Israel's God ever demanded or sanctioned this practice (*except in popular belief*); and there is no connection between the firstborn and the Molek.
>
> (Milgrom 2002:55, emphasis mine)

But this is far less clear than Milgrom asserts. What counts as a crisis situation? How can clear lines be drawn between 'popular belief' about divine demands and actual divine requirements? Was the story of Abraham and Isaac, for example, merely 'popular belief'? In the story, God requires Abraham to sacrifice his son; and although at the last minute an animal was substituted, it is not for that but for his willingness to slaughter Isaac that Abraham was honoured. There are, in addition, other stories in which children are actually sacrificed by their fathers, as for instance the story of Jephthah and his (unnamed) daughter whose death is, it seems, at least condoned by God.

Most telling of all is the story of the Passover, the founding event in the auto-narrative of the Israelites. According to this story, the people were in Egypt, suffering oppression and servitude to Pharaoh who, in spite of a series of miraculous plagues, would not allow the Israelites their freedom. At last the command of God comes to Moses: on a specified night the Israelites are to sacrifice a lamb per household, and daub the doorposts and lintel of their houses with its blood.

> For I [God] will pass through the land of Egypt that night, and I will smite all the firstborn in the land of Egypt, both man and beast ... The blood [of the sacrificed lamb] shall be a sign for you, upon the houses where you are; and when I see the blood, I will pass over you ...
>
> (Exodus 12.12–13)

And thus it was: in the morning the first born in every house of the Egyptians and among all their cattle was dead, while the Israelites lived and were able to leave Egypt and its bondage. The event is still commemorated by Jews in annual Passover celebrations, and by Christians as part of the rites of Easter. In this story there can be no doubt that it was God himself who demanded blood, that he killed Egyptian children and that the sacrificed lamb was a substitute for the death of the children of Israelites. This story of the Passover and consequent liberation from Egypt is so foundational in the biblical account that it must surely underlie all subsequent laws and rituals of sacrifice. God's demand for blood would never be far from the consciousness of Israelites: if animals were not regularly offered, human life itself must be at risk.

The system of ritual sacrifice thus was central to religious practice and to theological understanding. It is widely accepted that during the Hellenistic and Roman period huge numbers of animals were ritually slaughtered: up to 600,000 lambs at a single celebration of the Passover, for example (*EJ* 'Sacrifice'). The sheer volume of slaughter is similar to that of the Roman games in amphitheatres across the Empire which I discussed in Volume 1, though in these games wild animals and people rather than domestic animals were killed and their purpose had more to do with entertainment than with religion.

But this returns us to the question: what *is* the religious significance of blood sacrifice? What sort of a god is it who requires blood? Why this divine delight in violent death? Jewish and Christian theologians regularly ask about the significance of sacrifice and as regularly turn away from it. Jacob Milgrom, for example, in his careful study of Leviticus (Milgrom 1991), takes the view that sin is a kind of uncleanness or impurity, which accumulates like dirt and has to be purged with blood which acts as a kind of detergent, otherwise God cannot tolerate it. While that is a significant reading of the text, which shows the parallels between various aspects of ritual purity, 'clean' and 'unclean' beasts, and the sacrificial system along lines made familiar by Mary Douglas, it leaves the basic theological question unresolved.

Christian discussions ranging from conservative to liberal similarly turn from the question. Allen Ross, writing on Leviticus for pastors to use as a resource for their sermons, is insistent on the way in which the sacrificial rituals point forward to the Gospel of Christ. He says,

> The Lord accepts with pleasure whoever comes into his presence by substitutionary atonement through the shedding of blood. This was the fundamental truth of the law – as it is, of course, ultimately of the gospel.
> (Ross 2002:95)

Although Brevard Childs writes for a more academic readership, his basic position is hardly distinguishable from that of Ross on the subject of sacrifice:

The priestly institution provided a means of atoning for sins committed within the covenant. It was not a superstitious form of *ex opere operato*, but a profoundly theological interpretation of atonement as a gracious means of access into the presence of God which sin had disrupted.

(Childs 1985:170)

Again there is no comment on why God would delight in bloodshed, or accept it as 'atonement': this is simply taken for granted.

From a very different theological perspective, Gerhard von Rad in his influential *Old Testament Theology* discusses the sacrificial system in terms of 'ideas of gift, of communion, and of atonement' (von Rad 1975:I.254). von Rad is particularly concerned to find the spiritual meaning of the ritual system, and concludes:

Here Jahweh was within reach of Israel's gratitude, here Israel was granted fellowship with him in the sacred meal. Above all, here Israel could be reached by his will for forgiveness. However deep even the most understanding interpretation of the sacrifices in the Old Testament may go, there comes an absolute limit beyond which no further explanation is possible ... There is a realm of silence and secrecy in respect of what God works in sacrifice.

(von Rad 1975:I.260)

This sounds as though von Rad is about to draw a moral or spiritual lesson showing a profound underlying theology: what is this divine silence and secrecy? It is, according to von Rad, that we are not told how God smells the sacrifice! The mystery is not why God should take pleasure in death and blood, but something to do with the divine nose! The whole issue is trivialized.

It is no part of my purpose to supply a theological account of why God should need blood in order to act graciously. My point, rather, is that the representation of a patriarchal god requiring sacrifice is part of the same constellation of ideas in which God's demands for holy war also find a place, ideas which recur in Christendom's notions of Jesus as the 'Lamb of God' and endless warfare, spiritual and literal, against ungodly Others. I shall discuss this further in Part 3.

First, however, I want to show that there was, in the Hebrew Bible, a counter-narrative. Covenant need not be understood in terms of patriarchy, blood sacrifice, and perpetual warfare. Although violence and exclusion are dominant, there are also traces of submerged voices that speak in other tones. Instead of a preoccupation with death, there can be flourishing; instead of violence, beauty.

Chapter 7

Beauty for ashes

The beauty of God

The theme of the beauty or glory of God resonates through the whole of the Hebrew Bible, treated in various ways by the different authors but always taken as central to how the divine should be understood. 'Glory' is an evocative word, often used along with honour and majesty. Beauty is central to its meaning. The glory and beauty of God, and the consequent beauty of all that God makes, is a source of delight and hope to the biblical writers.

Modern biblical commentators, however, whether writing from a Christian perspective of 'Old Testament Theology' or from an effort to read the Bible as literature or as Hebrew scripture, pay only very brief attention to beauty in comparison with other themes like law, covenant, power or holiness.[1] Perhaps nothing is more indicative of the displacement of beauty in the symbolic of Western modernity than the refusal of theologians and scholars of religion to enter into serious engagement with the biblical theme of beauty. I wish to suggest, however, that it is precisely to the marginalized theme of the beauty of the divine, and the resultant beauty of divine creation, that we must look for resources for the transformation of the ugly and sordid violence which takes up such a large part of the Bible itself, and which has so profoundly shaped modernity. Beauty, natality and creativity stand as alternatives to a symbolic obsessed with destruction and death. Although beauty is not a major theme either for biblical writers or for their modern commentators, I suggest that it is a theme of resistance which is always in the margins. When beauty is lifted up, other biblical themes can also be pondered otherwise. Through the divine beauty newness enters the world and makes it sing.

Take for example Moses' encounter with God when he received the ten commandments: endless volumes have been written commenting on this story, and much so-called 'covenant theology' has been based upon it. Yet according to the book of Exodus, this was not how the story began. Earlier in the book there is an account of the people of Israel entering into a covenant with God, during which Moses and some companions are summoned by God.

Then Moses and Aaron, Nadab and Abihu, and seventy of the elders of Israel went up, and they saw the God of Israel; and there was under his feet as it were a pavement of sapphire stone, like the very heaven for clearness.

(Exodus 24.9–10)

What was God like? We are not told. Only the beauty of what is beneath his feet is described; it is as though the author is averting his face from looking upon God. Yet in the story, that is not what the elders of Israel did: 'they beheld God, and ate and drank' (11). Seeing God gave rise to feasting and celebration, though not to detailed description.

Other Hebrew poets and song writers, however, did their best to portray the beauty of God in words. Thus for example the Psalmist writes:

O Lord my God, thou art very great!
Thou art clothed with honour and majesty,
who coverest thyself with light as with a garment,
who hast laid the beams of thy chambers on the waters,
who makest the clouds thy chariot,
who ridest on the wings of the wind,
who makest the winds thy messengers,
fire and flame thy ministers.

(Psalm 104.1–4)

The writer of the Psalm exults in beauty. For him, there is an immediate aesthetic response to the beauty of the world around him and to the beauty of the god who created that world. He stretches language into images that will draw the reader into wonder and worship. The play of light and shade is as a garment for God; the 'wings of the wind' carry the divine in their breath.

The prophet Isaiah also uses vivid imagery as he recounts a vision that set him upon his prophetic path:

I saw the Lord sitting upon a throne, high and lifted up; and his train filled the temple. Above him stood the seraphim ... And one called to another and said:
'Holy, holy, holy is the Lord of hosts;
the whole earth is full of his glory'.

(Isaiah 6.1–3)

It is precisely this vision of the glorious beauty of God that draws Isaiah forward and impels him to offer himself in its service: it is beauty that attracts and inspires. In similar recognition of the attractiveness of divine beauty, another Psalm says,

> One thing have I desired of the Lord,
> that will I seek after;
> that I may dwell in the house of the Lord
> all the days of my life,
> to behold the beauty of the Lord,
> and to inquire in his temple.

(Psalm 27.4)

Again, when Israel celebrated its deliverance from the oppression of Egypt and its safe crossing of the Red Sea, one important aspect of that celebration was delight in their god's beauty and majesty.

> Who is like thee, O Lord, among the gods?
> Who is like thee, majestic in holiness,
> terrible in glorious deeds, doing wonders?

(Exodus 15.11)

Who Indeed? We would look in vain, in the representations of the gods and goddesses of Greece and Rome, for anything to compare with the Hebrew poems in praise of the beauty and glory of God. Zeus/Jupiter is represented as powerful, sometimes even majestic, as he hurls his thunderbolt, but nowhere is there the expression of aesthetic delight for Zeus that we find for God in Hebrew writings. Aphrodite, the goddess of beauty, is praised for her charm and loveliness, but her beauty is construed largely in terms of her sexual attractiveness, an aspect completely absent from biblical representations of the beauty of God. There is plenty in the Homeric writings about the beauty of heroic young warriors; plenty also about the enticement of attractive women like Helen whose beauty precipitated the Trojan War, but not much about the beauty of the gods. Not until Plato's *Symposium*, and the much later *Enneads* of Plotinus, is there consideration of beauty in terms that could suggest divinity; and even here beauty itself is an ideal or form, not a divine person as God is in Hebrew writings.

Even so, there is in the Hebrew Bible much reticence about giving an actual description of the divine beauty. Although it is a persistent theme, the language is oblique, and the imagery usually at a far enough remove to leave no doubt of its metaphorical nature. Perhaps the prohibition against visual portrayal was in some sense taken up into language, so that even poetry represents divine beauty most often not in terms of description but rather in terms of its effects. As Gerhard von Rad puts it in his brief comments on beauty in his *Old Testament Theology*, 'For Israel beauty was something that happened rather than something that existed, because she understood it as the result of God's action and not of God's being' (von Rad 1975.I:368). What does divine beauty do?

Beauty and newness

In the first place, divine beauty creates. It makes a world and its inhabitants, which reflects and manifests the beauty of its creator. Many of the Psalms exult in the beauty of the created world.

> Praise him, sun and moon,
> praise him, all you shining stars! …
> Praise the Lord from the earth,
> you sea monsters and all deeps,
> fire and hail, snow and frost,
> stormy wind fulfilling his command!
> Mountains and hills,
> fruit trees and all cedars!
> Beasts and all cattle,
> creeping things and flying birds! …
> Let them praise the name of the Lord,
> for his name alone is exalted;
> his glory is above earth and heaven.
>
> (Psalm 148.3–4, 7–10, 13)

From the very first line of the Hebrew Bible, there is an answer to the question: how does newness enter the world?

In the beginning God created the heavens and the earth (Genesis 1.1). The divine Spirit broods over the waters, and forms light, sea and land, the heavenly bodies, plants, animals, and finally man and woman.

> And God saw everything that he had made, and behold, it was very good.
>
> (Genesis 1.31)

God is pleased with his work, and calls it 'good', even 'very good'. As previously noted, the Hebrew word is TOB, translated into Greek as καλov: it can mean pleasant, fair, or beautiful as well as good. The Garden of Eden and the world in which it was set was not merely adequate or utilitarian; it was an expression of the glory of God. The beauty of the divine overflows in the work of creation and is revealed in the wonders of the world.

> Who has measured the waters in the hollow of his hand
> and marked off the heavens with a span,
> enclosed the dust of the earth in a measure
> and weighed the mountains in scales
> and the hills in a balance?
> Have you not known? Have you not heard?

Has it not been told you from the beginning?
Have you not understood from the foundations of the earth?

(Isaiah 40.12, 21)

It is God, whose creativity 'has made everything beautiful in its time; also he has put eternity into man's mind, yet so that he cannot find out what God has done from the beginning to the end' (Ecclesiastes 3.11).

The biblical story of creation, and indeed the theme of divine beauty, receives less attention even in the biblical writings themselves than might have been expected: sin, death, war and violence shape most of the narratives, as we shall see; and in the theologies and commentaries of modernity these necrophilic themes are in focus much more prominently than is beauty. Thus for example when the theory of evolution by natural selection replaces the biblical story as the scientific account of the development of life on earth, the change is not only a change of causation. Along with the shift from God as creator to natural selection is a shift towards an emphasis on violence. The development of species of plants and animals is perceived to be a result of struggle for survival, a competitive struggle in which the alternatives are adaptation or death. Although Darwin himself often thought in gentler, less violent terms of the adaptation and development of species, popular perception of its working is one in which death and violence take centre stage.

The contrast is enormous. In the biblical story, newness enters the world by divine creation. There was pleasure and delight when God created the world: 'the morning stars sang together, and all the sons of God shouted for joy' (Job 38.7). In modern thought, all this is gone. Not only does God not have anything to do with the creation of the world, neither does joy or delight. Newness enters the world through death and violence. Species adapt for survival; those lucky enough to mutate in ways that give them an advantage in the struggle will persist; others will become extinct. If by chance the mutation results in something that we humans happen to find beautiful, that is lucky for us, but in no sense can it be said to be the intention or reason for the adaptation.

Fuller discussion of how the preoccupation with death has shaped the science of modernity must be deferred to a later volume. What I want to lift up here is the connection, in biblical thought, between divine creativity and delight, between newness and beauty. Divine beauty itself is celebrated as a well-spring of creativity. Newness is created out of the splendour of divine fecundity, and the result is pronounced to be 'very good'. The nature of the divine, though it is beyond portrayal, is nonetheless shown forth in the beauty of the world. From the perspective of the biblical writers, the capacity of the beauty of nature to give refreshment to humankind, our delight in the delicacy of a primrose or our wonder at the stars, is not a coincidence or a secondary characteristic, as it is in modernity. Rather, the beauty of nature has a capacity to renew us because it is an expression of the divine source of newness. Creation recreates; life and beauty shine with hope.

Moreover, the newness and beauty celebrated in these biblical writings is specific and particular:

> God created the great sea monsters and every living creature that moves, with which the waters swarm, according to their kinds, and every winged bird according to its kind.
>
> (Genesis 1.21)

Plants, fruit trees, stars, animals, man and woman are all particular and individual: 'cattle and creeping things and beasts of the earth according to their kinds', not general but specific. Each thing is pronounced good; each has its own beauty. The beauty celebrated by the biblical writers is not abstract or universal: not the 'open sea of Beauty' of Plato's *Symposium* or 'Beauty Itself' of Plotinus. In relation to Greek writers, a comparison with Sappho would be much more apt: the most beautiful thing is what you love, the individual particular person, 'her lovely way of walking, and the bright radiance of her changing face' (du Bois 1996:80; see Jantzen 2004:62–8). Sappho, however, celebrated individual beauty without reference to creativity or to the divine: in the biblical writings by contrast the particularity of beauty is represented as a direct activity of divine fecundity. In bringing newness and beauty into the world the divine shines forth. Although beauty and its resources for renewal and transformation become a secondary theme in the biblical writers themselves, and peripheral in later commentators, the theme is there on the margins, subverting the imaginary of violence and death which preoccupy the patriarchs.

Beauty and flourishing

In biblical writings, moreover, there is a direct link between divine beauty, creativity, and the flourishing of the world that is brought into being. The beauty of God causes such gladness on earth that it makes the earth respond with fecundity.

> The wilderness and the dry land shall be glad,
> the desert shall rejoice and blossom;
> like the crocus it shall blossom abundantly,
> and rejoice with joy and singing ...
> They shall see the glory of the Lord,
> the majesty of our God.
>
> (Isaiah 35.1–2)

The care of God for his creatures and their direct response to him is the subject of several poems in the Hebrew Bible. In the book of Job, for example, God contrasts his position with Job's by asking rhetorically,

> Can you hunt the prey for the lion,
> or satisfy the appetite of the young lions,
> when they crouch in their dens,
> or lie in wait in their covert? ...
> Do you know when the mountain goats bring forth?
> Do you observe the calving of the hinds? ...
> Is it by your wisdom that the hawk soars,
> and spreads his wings toward the south?
> Is it at your command that the eagle mounts up
> and makes his nest on high?
>
> (Job 38.39–40; 39.1, 26–27)

The Psalmist, similarly, sings of God's care in providing food for people and animals, habitation suitable for their dwelling, and all things needful for their well-being. Everything from the heavenly bodies to the tiniest insects are dependent upon divine generosity.

> These all look to thee,
> to give them their food in due season ...
> When thou hidest thy face, they are dismayed;
> when thou takest away their breath, they die
> and return to their dust.
> When thou sendest forth thy Spirit, they are created;
> and thou renewest the face of the ground.
>
> (Psalm 104.27–30)

In these expressions of the flourishing of all creatures by the hand of God there is no sense of struggle or violence. Divine generosity provides enough for all. Competition is not necessary. All can live together: the flourishing of one is not at the expense of another. The wisdom of the creator has ensured a harmonious world, so that its richness and fecundity is all part of a whole, interdependent and ultimately relying on their creator. It is of course a vision of Utopia – or paradise – but the very possibility of such a vision reveals the contrast with the perception of living things in continuous competitive struggle for survival.

The metaphor of flourishing is used not only for plants and animals but also for people. 'The righteous flourish like the palm tree', says the Psalmist, 'they flourish in the courts of our God' (Psalm 92.12–13). The prophet Hosea extends the metaphor:

> I [God] will be as the dew to Israel;
> he shall blossom as the lily,
> he shall strike root as the poplar;
> his shoots shall spread out;

his beauty shall be like the olive ...
they shall flourish as a garden;
they shall blossom as the vine,
their fragrance shall be like the wine of Lebanon.

(Hosea 14.5–7)

It is a picture of hope and beauty, delight in well-being.

The metaphor of flourishing is significant in the Hebrew Bible, connected with newness of creation and its beauty; but it is displaced, often, with a metaphor of salvation. The two are very different. Flourishing is linked etymologically with flowering and thus with coming to fruition: it is what plants do, naturally and spontaneously, as long as they are not thwarted by external factors. Salvation, on the other hand, is a metaphor that presupposes a situation of threat or danger: to be saved is to be rescued from a situation which without intervention would end in disaster. Salvation implies, moreover, an external saviour, a rescuer who intervenes in a dangerous situation. Flourishing requires no such external intervention: a plant blooms naturally, of itself, without crisis. Flourishing takes place in the context of an interconnected web of life; salvation is the plucking of select individuals from a context of death.

As the biblical writers and their subsequent commentators turned more and more away from creation, newness of life and beauty, and became preoccupied with the deathly themes of sacrifice and war, so the metaphor of salvation predominated over that of flourishing, until in contemporary theological writing 'salvation' is treated as literal rather than metaphorical and 'flourishing' is seldom treated at all. Moreover in keeping with its connection with death, salvation is regularly used in Christendom in relation to life after death: to be 'saved' is to be assured of heaven rather than having to fear damnation to hell fire. None of these concepts arise out of the metaphor of flourishing. Flourishing connotes well-being and fruitfulness in this world, not some other, and the fulfilment of potential. Indeed in the metaphor there is the promise of newness: the flower and the fruit produce the seed for the new plant. The feelings associated with such fulfilment and well-being are attitudes of joy and hope, whereas the feelings associated with salvation are those of relief from fear and danger, accompanied at best with concern for those who are not saved and at worst with gloating over them. We will have occasion later in this volume to revisit the contrasting metaphors of salvation and flourishing, and to see how the entanglement with death and violence displaced beauty and flourishing in Western religious thought. What is important here is to recognize that when creation, beauty, and newness are foregrounded, then life and flourishing, not death and salvation, are the natural metaphors that arise (see Jantzen 1998:156–70).

Indeed it might be held that part of the point of the story, in the context of the book of Exodus, is that visual representation of God is forbidden. It was a sore point. The first two of the famous 'Ten Commandments' prohibit making any statue or image of a deity.

> You shall have no other gods before [besides] me.
>   You shall not make for yourself a graven image, or any likeness of anything that is in heaven above, or that is in the earth beneath ... you shall not bow down to them or serve them ...
>
> (Exodus 20.3–4)

But what did the Israelites do? At first, they entered into covenant with God. No sooner had Moses gone up the mountain for further instruction from God, however, than the Israelites demanded just such a graven image. Moses' brother Aaron asked them for their golden jewellery.

> He received the gold at their hand, and fashioned it with a graving tool, and made a molten calf; and they said, 'These are your gods, O Israel ... '

And he worshipped the calf. It was this that brought Moses down from the mountain in haste, smashing the stone tablets of the law in his rage (Exodus 32). The punishment which followed was intended to teach the Israelites never again to make a visual representation of the divine beauty: any such attempt would be idolatrous.

One of the most insightful commentaries on this passage is written not by a professional theologian but by the composer Arnold Schoenberg in his opera *Moses und Aron*. In Schoenberg's portrayal, Moses represents words, speech, law, whereas Aaron signifies the imagination and the sensory. According to Moses, no sensory image could do justice to the infinite God; no image could portray the divine who is beyond imagination.

> Thou shalt not make for thyself an image! For an
> image reduces, delimits, grasps,
> What should remain unlimited and unimaginable.
> An image wants a name:
> A name can only be taken from what is small;
> You should not worship what is small!
>
> (Schoenberg in Viladesau 1999:42)

When Aaron produces the golden calf, Moses is outraged. How dare Aaron try to represent the unrepresentable in a statue, try to 'contain the Infinite in an image'? Moses destroys the golden calf, seeing it as idolatrous blasphemy. But then Schoenberg uses Aaron to point out that things are more complicated. Does not Moses have the tablets of stone, on which are written the words of God? Do not words, too, convey images of God, conceptual representations if not material ones? If we are to think of God at all, must we not do so in words, concepts and images, finite and inadequate as these inevitably are?

Moses' response is one of despair. He sees that he, too, in his words and mental concepts is creating an image of God.

Unimaginable God!
Inexpressible, many-faceted idea!
… So I too have formed an image for myself: false,
as an image can only be!
So I am stricken.
So all that I thought was madness,
And cannot and must not be spoken!
O word, thou word that I lack!

(Viladesau 1999:47)

Moses smashes the tablets. Their images are conceptual, but they are images nonetheless, and as such they are as idolatrous as the golden calf.

Yet this too ultimately will not do. As Schoenberg finishes the opera – itself an aesthetic representation – he shows that representations are all that humans have. Whether conceptual or sensory, they are finite, and cannot contain infinity; yet they are what we must use to communicate the ungraspable. If they are taken as adequate, then they are idolatrous; but if they are taken as windows for the mind and the imagination, they may extend the human spirit.

Schoenberg's opera is of course a work of modernity; he laboured over it through the Nazi era and it bears the marks of centuries of Jewish and Christian meditation. It is fair to say that many a theologian in modernity has struggled with the same issues, and that so much attention has been paid to the unrepresentability of the divine that there has been less focus on the theme of divine beauty.

Part Three
Early Christianity

Chapter 8

The birth of Christ and early Christianity

Setting the scene

Away in a manger, no crib for his bed,
The little Lord Jesus laid down his sweet head ...

The carol is sung every Christmas; and each year in countless schools and churches the nativity is re-enacted. It was a favourite practice of Francis of Assisi, revered for his love of all creatures; and his example did much to establish the custom in Christendom. According to his early biographer Thomas of Celano, Francis asked that a manger be prepared with hay, and an ox and ass brought to stand near it,

> For I wish to enact the memory of the babe who was born in Bethlehem: to see as much as possible with my own bodily eyes the discomfort of his infant needs, how he lay in a manger, and how, with an ox and an ass standing by, he rested on hay.
>
> (Thomas of Celano 2004:94–5)

The birth of Jesus is the story with which the Gospels begin. They tell of Mary and Joseph and the baby lying in a manger, the angels singing, the shepherds and magi coming to worship. They continue with accounts of his exciting teaching, in stories and parables, and of the way he healed people and gave them new life and hope. Jesus is the icon and the voice of natality, the one who points the way to flourishing.

But Jesus was killed, crucified by the Romans as a criminal. The same Gospels that recount the stories of his birth linger over the events of his death, presenting it in such a way that death becomes their focus. His birth and his life were only a necessary preamble, it may seem; while his death was the means for the salvation of the world. The focus on the death of Jesus in scripture and tradition is, I shall argue, a reflection and a strong reinforcement of the necrophilic preoccupation of the West, sedimented into our consciousness over many centuries. A cross or crucifix is still, in the twenty-first century, the most frequently bought item of jewellery in Europe and the Americas: simultaneously an item of beauty and a symbol of violent death.

Not everyone who wears a cross spends time thinking about its significance, of course. Nevertheless, the ambiguity of its beauty and its violence is suggestive of the ambiguities of Christendom itself, which I shall explore in the chapters that follow: on the one hand, its possibilities for beauty, natality and flourishing, and on the other hand its investment in death and violence. The initial contours of the ambiguities can be quickly sketched. Beginning with beauty, it is evident that Christendom has been the impetus for every variety of artistic expression, from the exquisite mosaics of Venice and Ravenna to the soaring cathedrals of Cologne and Salisbury, from the music of Vivaldi and Bach to the paintings of Giotto and Rembrandt. Our aesthetic sensibilities have been shaped by Christendom. And yet, how important, really, is beauty to Christianity? Though artists express their faith in their work, religious writers and theologians have little to say about beauty. As Edward Farley has observed, with significant exceptions, 'when we closely consult the standard expressions of piety in the prayers, liturgies, sermons, journals and letters of the ages, we find beauty largely absent'. He continues,

> On the whole, beauty is a rarity in 2000 years of the Christian interpretation of the Gospels ... All the types [of theology] (historical, practical, philosophical, systematic) and approaches (neo-Reformation, apologetic, feminist, African-American, liberationist, correlational) share at least one thing in common, a disinterest in beauty.
>
> (Farley 2001:7)

This ambiguity about beauty in Christendom is paralleled by issues of gender. It can hardly be denied that the teaching and practice of the churches has been the most powerful force of patriarchy in the West. Women were seen as the daughters of Eve who brought sin into the world: they were conceptually linked, in theology and in popular story, with the body, sexuality and temptation. Their voices were silenced, their place in society constructed in relation to husband and home. Women were defined, not as people with specific abilities or careers, but in terms of their sexuality: virgin, mother, or whore. Thousands were executed as witches by zealous witch-hunters using criteria set out by monks and theologians. Even today, it is the church – especially the Roman Catholic Church – that resists gender equality and liberation for women, crusading against abortion, contraception, and even the ordination of women to the priesthood. At the same time, masculinity is constructed as dominant and powerful: the male, whether he likes it or not, is to be the head of the household, and the male priest is the representative of Christ on earth.

And yet it is from within Christendom, as well, that women and men have found the resources to fashion gender differently. Women were among the first followers of Jesus. From the early days of Christendom, women and men renounced compulsory heterosexual marriage and childbearing, and chose instead the celibate life of the desert or the monastery: whatever the distortions (and there were many) the convent offered opportunities for empowerment for women like Hildegard of Bingen and Gertrude of Helfta, while men like Francis of Assisi and John of the Cross developed patterns of masculinity quite different from prevalent models of dominance. It was from their religious commitment that early feminists like Elizabeth Cady Stanton and the Pankhurst sisters claimed equality; and it is not in spite of their religious stance but because of it that many women today are working for gender justice in Africa and Latin America, often drawing upon the figure of Mary for inspiration.

Similar ambiguities envelop questions of violence. The Christmas angels sing of 'peace on earth, good will to men'. Jesus is said to be the prince of peace, and the early church was pacifist. Throughout Christian history Christians have drawn on their faith to work for peace, resolution of conflict, and alternatives to violence: Francis of Assisi again is an example, as also are the peace churches of the radical reformation which continue today as Mennonites and Quakers.

Nevertheless, Christendom has been involved in more wars and violence than can be counted. Since Constantine claimed his military victory, armies have marched under the banner of the cross backwards and forwards across Europe and beyond. From the crusaders to the wars of religion, and up to modernity when, in two world wars, both sides claimed divine aid to slaughter one another, the military violence done in the name of the prince of peace is incalculable. Even ostensibly secular societies invoke God's name for their warfare: how many times have American presidents finished their addresses with 'God bless America'? Nor is the violence of Christendom restricted to warfare. Slavery, economic injustice, and colonialism have all been sanctioned by Christendom, as has the domestic violence in which women and children are abused and killed with, often, only muted protest if any at all from the churches.

Now, it is my suggestion, which will be developed in the chapters that follow, that the ambivalences in Christendom towards beauty, gender and violence are all related to one another. The sediments of violence that shape Western consciousness are connected to constructions of masculinity partly inherited from Christendom's Jewish provenance and from classical sources but significantly reshaped into ideals of 'men of God' who 'fight the good fight'. The displacement of beauty, similarly, is connected to the distrust of bodies, especially gendered bodies; and the heart that hardens itself to beauty and its invitations to involvement is a heart whose defensive fear easily turns aggressive. What I want to show is how the foundations for all this were laid in the emergence of Christianity, as the covenant was translated into the kingdom of heaven, sacrifice into the doctrine of atonement, and holy war into the armies of God.

But I want to show, also, how none of this was inevitable. At every turn, choices were made: choices of authority, of interpretation, and of action. These choices could have been made differently: indeed sometimes and by some groups they *were* made differently, so that Christendom itself is the resource for peace, justice, egalitarianism, and beauty. At the present time, when the veneer of secularism which has covered modernity is wearing increasingly thin, these choices must be made again. Will the sediments of fear, defensiveness and violence inherited from centuries of Christendom determine the configuration of the twenty-first century? Or can we work through these afflictions and learn from the narrative of our past and its suppressed voices how to tell our stories differently, with new creativity so that newness can enter the world?

The New Testament as we have it today begins with a story of Jesus' birth and continues, through its first four books, with four accounts of Jesus' life, teachings and death. These four Gospels represent themselves as giving factual narratives based on eye witnesses: they report actual conversations and disputes between Jesus and his followers and enemies, give details of his movements and activities, and include long sermons from the mouth of Jesus himself. It is on the basis of these four Gospels that Christians have taken Jesus as example and Saviour, and that theologians have developed Christian doctrine over centuries.

Yet scholars of the beginning of Christianity, for all their many differences, are in broad agreement that the earliest of the Gospels, Mark, cannot have been written before 70 CE, all four Gospels being completed by the turn of the century. They drew upon earlier sources, oral or written and now lost. There were in addition other Gospels: the Gospel of Thomas, the Gospel of Mary, and so on, which the Christian Church decided not to treat as scripture, thus already demarcating boundaries which could have been drawn otherwise (Robinson 1990). Some of these alternative Gospels present Jesus' activities and his teaching in a quite different light from those which the Church chose to preserve; yet they are hardly known except by specialist scholars, while the four Gospels as we have them have shaped Western consciousness. The point is not that the alternative Gospels would have fostered a less violent or more beautiful world, though it has been argued that they favour more egalitarian gender relations (Pagels 1979). The point, rather, is that Christendom rests from the beginning on a series of choices which could have been made otherwise, starting with which books to treat as authoritative. There was nothing inevitable about the shaping of Western consciousness into its necrophilic preoccupations or its constructions of gender.

In fact, the earliest Christian writing is not the Gospels but some of the letters of Paul, a man who never saw Jesus but who became a Christian about three years after Jesus' death. Paul's letters were written from about 50 CE onwards, to groups of Christians in various parts of the Roman Empire outside of the land where Jesus had lived. Because of the differences between the Gospels and the Pauline writings, and the variations among even those Gospels which the Church preserved, and because of the distance in time that separates all these writings from the time of Jesus, there is much scope for debate about the historical accuracy of the documents and of the meaning of the events and teachings they describe.

This is all the more so because of the dramatic historical events that occurred between the time of Jesus' life and the first writings about him, events which must have influenced the perceptions of the authors. Jesus was probably born in the final years of King Herod, about 4 BCE. Herod was a friend of the Romans, in particular of the current emperor, Caesar Augustus. Palestine had been part of the Roman Empire since 63 BCE, when Pompey conquered Jerusalem and outraged the Jews by pillaging the temple: Herod ruled it as a client king (Richardson 1999). From the time of his death and throughout the lifetime of Jesus there were various arrangements of governance, but always under Roman control. Always, also, there was Jewish resentment and simmering revolt. In 66 CE, that revolt boiled over. But the Jews were no match for the Romans in military terms; and by 70 CE the land had been violently conquered, Jerusalem sacked, and the treasures of the temple carried off as booty to Rome (Horsley 1993, 1995). Even before that, Christians had been persecuted. After the great fire of Rome in 64 CE, Nero blamed the Christians, and executed many of them, probably including Paul and Peter, Jesus' disciples. It was only after all these events that the Gospels were composed.

Although Jesus lived and died before the final tragic conflict with Rome, and that conflict is not directly mentioned in the Gospels, it must have influenced the Gospel writers' perspectives. This is especially so in relation to violence itself and how one should respond to it. After all, one of the few things we know with certainty about Jesus is that he died violently at the hands of the Romans, crucified as a common criminal. Why? Even today, scholars debate the question. Should Jesus be seen as a devout and observant Jew (Vermes 1973), perhaps as one who transformed Judaism (Riches 1980) but somehow fell foul of the authorities (Crossan 1996; Fredriksen 2000)? Was he a political radical, trying to develop a movement of resistance to Roman rule and eventually executed for it (Yoder 1972; Horsley 1993)? Or was he the Son of God, the Second Person of the Trinity, sent by God to die to take away the sins of the world, as enshrined in Christian creed and dogma?

In the following chapters I shall discuss some of these possibilities. My purpose, however, is not to resolve the debate, a task better left to scholars with expertise in the field. Rather, I want to show something of the afterlife of the narratives of Jesus' life and teachings and violent death on the sedimentation of violence in the Western habitus, its gendered nature, and how it interacted with the displacement of beauty. I want also to consider counternarratives, the possibility of other choices. By tracing a genealogy of violence, and by recognizing turning points and deliberate decisions, it is my hope that we can dismantle the destructive violence of our thought and action and learn to live and bring newness into the world.

The scope of this task is as broad as Western history itself, and far too broad for one book. Yet it is urgently important if we are to understand the world we live in and find resources for change. In order to address the issues in a more manageable way, I propose to take the central categories of the previous section: covenant, sacrifice, and holy war, and to see how these are carried forward and modified in the narratives of emerging Christianity. In each case, I shall argue, there is an interaction of violence, gender and beauty; and in each case there are counter-narratives and suppressed voices which, if heeded, can help us to think and live otherwise.

Chapter 9

Covenant in Christendom

At the heart of the communion service, in the prayer of consecration of the bread and wine, the priest rehearses the words attributed in the New Testament to Jesus. Placing his hand on the chalice, the priest says,

> Likewise after supper he took the cup; and, when he had given thanks, he gave it to them, saying, Drink ye all of this; for this is my Blood of the new Covenant, which is shed for you and for many for the remission of sins: Do this as oft as ye shall drink it, in remembrance of me.
> (Liturgy of Holy Communion, citing Matthew 26.27–28 and 1
> Corinthians 11.25)

The communion service, whether it is labelled a mass or a eucharist or a remembrance of the Lord's supper, is held by most Christians to be the most central and solemn rite of Christendom. Few would consciously associate it with violence. Yet in these words of consecration there is overt and deliberate reference to covenant and blood, and implicit reference to violent death. It is, nevertheless, associated with dignity and beauty. In many churches the chalice will be richly jewelled, the priest in finely worked robes, candles lit, and choirs singing. And for most of its history the celebration has been restricted to men: women priests and ministers are relatively recent and still prohibited in the Roman Catholic and Greek Orthodox churches. Whatever the new covenant is, it represents a constellation of violence, gender and beauty re-enacted in every celebration of communion.

In Christianity, Jesus is understood as the one who brought this new covenant, a covenant which fulfilled or transformed the covenant(s) of the Hebrew Bible. It is this covenant which is taken as the foundation for the Christian Church, as the Mosaic covenant was the foundation for Judaism. Even the Bible itself, as Christians have it, is divided into the Old Testament/ Covenant (the Hebrew Bible), and the New Testament/Covenant. Within that New Covenant, moreover, the system of ritual sacrifice becomes a theology of atonement, in which Jesus the Lamb of God is sacrificed for the sins of the world. And the holy war against others and their gods become generalized to a fight against 'the world, the flesh and the devil': the whole life of a Christian is warfare against enemies without and within.

In the following chapters I shall discuss the issues of sacrifice and holy war and their interconnections with gender and beauty in emerging Christendom. In this chapter I wish to concentrate on the idea of covenant, and the way in which that idea was taken up from its Jewish context which I explored in the previous section, and given new life in Christianity through the life and teaching of Jesus and the writings of Paul and other New Testament writers.

The covenant and the kingdom

'Repent, for the kingdom of heaven is at hand' (Matthew 4.17). These are the words with which, according to the Gospel of Matthew, Jesus began his public ministry. In Mark, the saying is slightly expanded:

> Jesus came into Galilee, preaching the gospel of God, and saying, 'The time is fulfilled, and the kingdom of God is at hand; repent, and believe in the gospel'.
>
> (Mark 1.15)

From this point onwards the Gospel writers make much of the idea of the kingdom and of Jesus as king. But what did they mean by it? And what is the relationship between the kingdom of God and the covenant that was formative of the people of Israel?

Whole libraries have been written discussing these questions. My aim is not to come to definitive answers, but to show how certain ideas of the covenant and the kingdom are imbricated in the patterns of violence in Christendom, while alternative interpretations are available for a counter-narrative. There is, however, general agreement about some basic starting points. One is that 'gospel' simply means 'good news'. Whatever Jesus meant by the kingdom that he was announcing, he declared it to be good news for his listeners. A second point of agreement is that Matthew's phrase 'kingdom of heaven' is not something different from Mark's 'kingdom of God'. Rather, it was a conventional circumlocution used by pious Jewish writers who wished to avoid using the name of God. 'Heaven' was used metonymically, the place of God's dwelling standing in for God, in the way that we might use 'the White House says ... ' for 'the president of the USA says ... '.

A third agreement among scholars is that the kingdom of God which Jesus preaches is related to the covenant(s) between God and Israel that was central to Jewish self-understanding. As he is presented in the Gospels, Jesus does not often mention the covenant, the institution of the last supper cited above being the notable exception. It is in the letters of Paul, and those of other New Testament writers (especially the letter to the Hebrews) that the vocabulary of the covenant is once again central. Nevertheless, the kingdom

of God that Jesus preached was meant by the Gospel writers as continuous
with God's covenant in history. As E.P. Sanders puts it,

> They assume that God will do something in *history* that agrees with other
> things he has done ... The God they believed in was the God of Israel,
> the God who called Abraham, gave the law to Moses, and elevated
> David to kingship. That God would now bring his work to fruition.
>
> (Sanders 1993:96)

Why Jesus chose to use the vocabulary of kingdom rather than covenant is a
question I shall leave until later in the chapter.

What, then, was this good news of the kingdom of God which Jesus
preached? According to Luke's representation, Jesus tried to explain it in the
synagogue in Nazareth, his hometown. He read from the book of Isaiah:

> The Spirit of the Lord is upon me,
> because he has anointed me to preach good news to the poor.
> He has sent me to proclaim release to the captives
> and recovering of sight to the blind,
> to set at liberty those who are oppressed,
> to proclaim the acceptable year of the Lord.
>
> (Luke 4.18–19)

As the passage in Isaiah continues, it promises to give comfort to those who
mourn, 'beauty for ashes, the oil of gladness instead of mourning' so that the
ruins of the past could be rebuilt and God's 'everlasting covenant' be
renewed (Isaiah 61.3–8). Jesus' Jewish hearers in the Nazareth synagogue
could have been expected to know the whole passage. No wonder, then, that when
he began his sermon after the reading with the words 'Today this scripture
has been fulfilled in your hearing' (Luke 4.21), they were at first delighted
but then offended: just who did this man Jesus, whom they had known as a
boy in their village, think he was?

That question has of course troubled many from that day to this. The
Gospels do not enter into philosophical arguments about who Jesus was.
Rather, they portray his activity, his teaching, his life and his death, and expect
readers to make up their own minds. As Jesus is represented in the Gospels,
he does not only announce the kingdom of God; he performs it.

> And he went about all Galilee teaching in their synagogues and
> preaching the gospel of the kingdom and healing every disease and every
> infirmity among the people. So his fame spread ... and they brought him
> all the sick, those afflicted with various diseases and pains, demoniacs,
> epileptics, and paralytics, and he healed them.
>
> (Matthew 4.23–24)

There are many stories of individual people whom he healed. Sometimes they were people known to him or his immediate followers, like his disciple Simon's mother-in-law (Luke 4.38). Often they seem to have been strangers to him, like an unnamed blind man whose healing on the Sabbath day caused controversy (John 9). Often, also, the stories portray Jesus healing people with whom a respectable Jewish man would not normally have had dealings. Lepers, for example, were considered ritually unclean and untouchable. Yet

> a leper came to him beseeching him, and kneeling said to him, 'If you will, you can make me clean'. Moved with pity, he stretched out his hand and touched him, and said to him, 'I will; be clean'. And immediately the leprosy left him ...
>
> (Mark 1.40–42)

By reaching out and touching the leper, rather than, say, simply command-ing the leprosy to leave (which Jesus as represented by the Gospel writer would be quite able to do), Jesus was actually sharing the impurity even while healing the man. Incidents such as these reveal the depth of compas-sion and empathy that Jesus indicated to be at the root of the kingdom of God that he announced.

As unexpected as his dealings with lepers was Jesus' response to women. One day when he was hurrying to respond to a summons for help,

> a woman who had suffered from a hemorrhage for twelve years came up behind him and touched the fringe of his garment; for she said to her-self, 'If I only touch his garment, I shall be made well'. Jesus turned, and seeing her he said, 'Take heart, daughter; your faith has made you well'. And instantly the woman was made well.
>
> (Matthew 9.21–22)

Similarly remarkable were his dealings with other women: a Samaritan woman who was living in an adulterous relationship (thus thrice marginal because of her gender, her race and her lifestyle) (John 4); a woman caught in illicit sex (John 8.1–11); a woman who wet Jesus' feet with her tears and dried them with her hair (Luke 7.38). In each case Jesus showed sympathy and understanding to the woman and had harsh words for those who, in their self-righteousness, considered his kindness inappropriate.

Scholars in modernity have made much of these miracle stories, arguing about their plausibility and their implications. Do they violate laws of nature? If so, does that show that they are impossible as stated, and some other interpretation must be found? Alternatively, do they offer proof of Jesus' divinity, showing him to be omnipotent? Whatever answers are given, one thing is clear from the texts of the Gospels: these were not the questions which their authors were concerned with. What mattered to them was the nature of the kingdom of God which they believed Jesus was preaching: the kingdom of God was characterized by healing and well-being for all, even for the outcasts and those on the margins of society. The same is true of the exorcisms which the Gospel writers report. The good news of the kingdom includes triumph over demons and the forces of evil which destroy people's lives. I shall have more to say about Jesus' conflict with Satan and with evil demons when I discuss his attitude to violence; what is important here is that, according to the Gospel writers, one of the signs of the kingdom of God is that people's lives are made whole.

Another indication of the kingdom, for the Gospel writers, is the nature and content of Jesus' teaching. Repeatedly they emphasize that Jesus' hearers 'were astonished at his teaching, for his word was with authority' (Luke 4.32); often this is contrasted with the style of 'the scribes', other teachers in first-century Palestine. Jesus' teaching rang true; his insights had an integrity and accuracy which struck home, so that some were willing to become his disciples while others became his enemies. Jesus' authority did not come from scholarship and he is never represented as engaged in theological discourse. Often the teaching ascribed to him includes pithy sayings:

> What man of you, if his son asks him for bread, will give him a stone? Or if he asks for a fish, will give him a serpent? ... How much more will your Father who is in heaven give good things to those who ask him!
>
> (Matthew 7.9–11)

There are many similar teachings of reassurance of the kindness and generosity of God to those who look to him as to a Father, teachings which would hold appeal and comfort for the poor and simple folk struggling to make a living in the villages of Galilee where Jesus taught.

Often Jesus taught in parables, entertaining stories full of human interest and sometimes humour with a sting in the tail that makes the hearer stop short and reconsider received opinions. There is for instance an account of a lawyer who tried to test Jesus, asking him what he should do to inherit eternal life. When Jesus pointed him to the law of the Mosaic covenant, emphasizing love for God and neighbour, the lawyer 'desiring to justify himself' pressed Jesus further: 'who is my neighbour?' At this point Jesus tells a story of a traveller who was mugged, beaten and left for dead by bandits on the road. Important people – a priest, a Levite, men as important in society as the lawyer himself – saw the injured traveller but hurried by unwilling to get involved.

> But a Samaritan, as he journeyed, came to where he was; and when he saw him, he had compassion, and went to him and bound up his

wounds, pouring in oil and wine; then he set him on his own beast and brought him to an inn, and took care of him.

(Luke 10.33–34)

The lawyer is forced to recognize that it is this Samaritan, a man who would be despised by many Jews because of his race, who was the neighbour to the unfortunate man. Jesus concludes simply, 'Go and do likewise' (Luke 10.37).

The stories of Jesus' teaching and healing make it obvious why he would acquire a popular following, and also how some, especially the self-important, might be offended and become his enemies. To this extent he is like the prophets of the Jewish scriptures, and indeed the Gospel writers frequently portray him as drawing on their words. It is easy to understand Jesus as one who took seriously and literally the prophetic claim that God would renew his covenant with Israel and bring about a time of peace and prosperity, when

> Instead of your shame you shall have a double portion, instead of dis-honour you shall rejoice in your lot; therefore in your land you shall possess a double portion; yours shall be everlasting joy.
>
> (Isaiah 61.7)

The humiliation that Israel had suffered at the hands of oppressing con-querors – the Babylonians, the Greeks under Alexander the Great, the Seleucids, and now the Romans – would be over. God's covenant still held good. The kingdom of God was coming, and Jesus was announcing it. It would be a kingdom of justice and generosity to all, especially good news for the little people who had suffered the most, if more threatening to those of their compatriots who gained positions of importance and benefited from the oppressive regimes.

Thy kingdom come?

But how exactly was this kingdom to arrive, and why was Jesus so confident that it was imminent? What, actually, did Jesus think it would be like: would God literally come and reign on earth? What would happen to the Romans? And what did Jesus' teaching and healing ministry really have to do with so major an event? Parables and healings and charismatic teaching are one thing; all very well, but they hardly amount to establishing the kingdom of God on earth. What did Jesus think his own role was in this new kingdom?

Jesus had dramatic things to say about the coming of the kingdom. As the Gospel writers tell the story, he taught his disciples that there would be a time of great persecution and tribulation for his followers, with conflict and war all around.

Immediately after the tribulation of those days the sun will be darkened, and the moon will not give its light, and the stars will fall from heaven, and the powers of the heavens will be shaken; then will appear the sign of the Son of man in heaven, and then all the tribes of the earth will mourn, and they will see the Son of man coming on the clouds of heaven with power and great glory; and he will send out his angels with a loud trumpet call, and they will gather his elect from the four winds, from one end of the heaven to the other ...

(Matthew 24.29–31; cf. Mark 13.24–27; Luke 21.25–27)

It is a terrifying prospect for all except 'his elect': these, it is promised, will be rescued from the sufferings they have had to endure. 'When these things begin to take place, look up and raise your heads, because your redemption is drawing near' (Luke 21.28).

The tone of all this is quite different from the impression that might be gained from Jesus' teachings of gentleness and compassion. Here there is judgement and retribution for those who oppose the divine kingdom, while those who are included in it receive appropriate rewards. For centuries scholars have been trying to understand what Jesus meant by this dramatic teaching and how it connects with his ministry of healing and kindness. It is not my purpose here to survey all the interpretations let alone to resolve the issue. What I shall do, however, is to select from among relatively recent interpreters a range of positions which demonstrate some of the narrative choices that have been made. What will become clear is that the covenant, the kingdom of God, is inscribed in varying ways in the consciousness of Christendom, some of which valorize death and violence. After considering a range of modern interpretations of Jesus' ideas of how the kingdom would come, I shall return to the question of how early Christendom, starting with Paul, might have understood it.

'The wheel of the world': Schweitzer and Bultmann

All modern interpreters are agreed that Jesus' pronouncements must be understood against a background of apocalyptic or eschatological teaching in previous Jewish literature, that is, teaching which proclaimed that history as we know it is coming to an end through the dramatic intervention of God. The book of Daniel in the Hebrew Bible, for example, looked forward to a similar dramatic moment:

I saw in the night visions,
and behold with the clouds of heaven
there came one like a Son of man ...
and to him was given dominion and glory and kingdom ...

(Daniel 7.13–14)

Early in the twentieth century Albert Schweitzer in his famous book *The Quest of the Historical Jews* (1954; first published in 1906) put forward the view that Jesus, like John the Baptist before him, tried to precipitate that apocalyptic event.

> Jesus ... in the knowledge that he is the coming Son of Man lays hold of the wheel of the world to set it moving on that last revolution which is to bring all ordinary history to a close. It refuses to turn, and he throws himself upon it. Then it does turn; and crushes him.
>
> (Schweitzer 1954:368–9)

Although that was the end of Jesus in physical terms, however, Schweitzer did not consider him a failure. Rather, the very fact that the kingdom of God did not arrive in literal or historical terms reveals that the true message of Jesus transcends such historical limitations.

> That which is eternal in the words of Jesus is due to the very fact that they are based on an eschatological worldview, and contain the expression of a mind for which the contemporary world with its historical and social circumstances no longer had any existence. They are appropriate, therefore, to any world, for in every world they raise the man who dares to meet their challenge, and does not turn and twist them into nothingness, above his world and his time, making him inwardly free, so that he is fitted to be, in his own world and in his own time, a simple channel of the power of Jesus ...
>
> (Schweitzer 1954:400)

As Schweitzer sees it, Jesus was wrong in his expectation of a literal arrival of God on earth to set up his kingdom in accordance with his covenant with Israel. The true covenant was much more profound, reaching not to political realities but to people's hearts. Jesus' message, therefore, although mistaken in its expectations, reaches to the spiritual core of every individual and summons them to follow his example of compassion and love. Schweitzer concludes his book with justly famous lines:

> He comes to us as One unknown, without a name, as of old, by the lakeside, he came to those men who knew him not. He speaks to us the same word: 'Follow thou me!' and sets us to the tasks that he has to fulfil for our time. He commands. And to those who obey, whether they be wise or simple, he will reveal himself in the toils, the conflicts, the sufferings that they shall pass through in his fellowship, and, as an ineffable mystery, they shall learn in their own experience who he is.
>
> (Schweitzer 1954:401)

True to his own insight, Schweitzer then abandoned his career as an academic theologian, trained as a doctor, and spent the rest of his life caring for lepers in Africa.

A rejection of the idea that Jesus' apocalyptic teaching was ever intended as an actual change in the social and political situation prevailing in Palestine during his life was held by Bultmann in the middle of the twentieth century. Like Schweitzer, he argued that the core of Jesus' teaching is ahistorical; indeed it represents the end of history as a significant category for religious believers.

> Jesus' message is connected with the hope ... documented by the apocalyptic literature, a hope which awaits salvation not from a miraculous change in historical (i.e. political and social) conditions, but from a cosmic catastrophe which will do away with all conditions of the present world as it is.
>
> (Bultmann 1951:4)

Accordingly, Jesus' message is not limited to those who lived during his time. Rather, he confronts everyone, even now, with an existential challenge to individual authenticity. Bultmann writes,

> The Kingdom of God ... is that eschatological deliverance which ends everything earthly ... It is wholly supernatural ... Whoever seeks it must realize that he cuts himself off from the world.
>
> (Bultmann 1958:35–7)

Jesus' message is inward and spiritual, coming directly to each unique individual and looking for a change of heart, not a change of the political regime. The change will be supernatural, not social.

What is significant in these interpretations of Jesus' eschatological teaching is the way in which it takes what appears to be good news to the people of Israel that God has not forgotten his covenant with them even though they are at present under Roman domination, and changes it so that it has nothing to do with the Roman regime or even with the people of Israel. Rather, it becomes ahistorical, apolitical, and individualized. Although in the writings of Schweitzer and Bultmann this individual spiritual teaching has ethical implications and in that sense is not wholly removed from this world, it is only a small step from this spiritualizing to the idea that the kingdom of God has nothing to do with this world at all. It is indeed the 'kingdom of heaven': not heaven as a euphemism for God, but heaven as the realm of those who have died. Once this step is taken – and it frequently is, as I shall discuss later – then the whole aim and object of the Christian life is to get to heaven. Life becomes focused on death. Salvation, as we shall see, means everlasting life to which death is the gateway. This world, this life, in its historical and political reality is secondary, at best a means to an end, at worst a distraction.

As an interpretation of Jesus' teaching and of the Jewish apocalyptic literature, however, the positions of Schweitzer and Bultmann run into serious difficulties. There were several strands of Jewish apocalyptic literature, some of them looking for a restored earthly society in which injustice would be abolished while others hoped for an end to earthly history, a resurrection of the dead, and a final judgement. In either case there would be dramatic divine intervention in earthly realities, so that the new world order would be characterized as the reign of God (Hanson 1975; Collins 1999). This intervention was particularly emphasized in some of the Dead Sea Scrolls, writings associated with the Qumran community which lived in the desert south of Jerusalem in the time of Jesus. In these Scrolls we find the idea, already present in earlier apocalyptic writing, that there will be 'an eschatological war in which the heavenly forces help Israel to defeat the nations in a final war in which all evil will be destroyed' (Martínez 1999:191). The kingdom of God is then established on earth. This is not a purely spiritual or individual reality but a social and political transformation in which God is king and his faithful ones reign with him in a world of peace and harmony.

As the Gospels present Jesus, it is clear that this apocalyptic teaching is not far away (Allison 1999). But this does not resolve the question of how his use of it should be understood. To probe the question further, I turn next to more recent scholars of Jesus and the Gospels.

The transformation of Judaism?

John Riches (1980) is among many recent biblical scholars who reject the idea that one can simply lift Jesus' essential teaching out of the social and political context of his time, treating it as ahistorical, spiritual, and addressed to modern individuals without reference to Jesus' own purpose. If Jesus' teaching is 'demythologized', as Bultmann would have it, he may become more congenial to secular modernity, to be sure. But how if his message were precisely one which should make secular modernity *less* comfortable, destabilized in its individualism? Like most other Christian theologians, Riches holds that Jesus' message is indeed relevant for all time, including our own. Nevertheless, unless what he said and did is interpreted in relation to his own time, its continuing relevance cannot be ascertained. Understanding what he said in its historical context does not exhaust its meaning, but it is essential as a basis.

Riches therefore tries to find the import of Jesus' life and teaching by placing it within the Judaism of his time, and showing how he transformed it. All Jewish thought was agreed on the centrality of the covenant which set Israel apart as a chosen nation. Faithfulness to this covenant involved, as discussed in Section 2, the purity of Israel, maintained on the one hand by separation from gentile neighbours and on the other by ritual worship. Riches argues, however, that with the increasing dominance of Hellenistic culture and Roman occupation of Palestine, it became less and less possible or even desirable for Jews to keep themselves strictly separate from gentiles and their ways. At the same time, perhaps partly as compensation, ritual worship and the attendant purity laws become more important.

> The purity regulations become not only a reminder to the Israelites of God's election and separation of them from the nations, they now become, as they are applied to the home and everyday life, a means of preserving that separation in a situation where the land has been extensively infiltrated by the nations.
>
> (Riches 1980:73)

The regulations therefore become more minute and detailed. At the same time, different groups compete with one another as authorities on exactly what the regulations entail and how they are connected with Temple worship: Sadducees, Pharisees, Essenes and Zealots all struggled for control of how Judaism should be defined (83). Basic to all of them, according to Riches, was the premise that God is a god of holiness and justice who expects obedience to his law and will come to the aid of his covenant people, perhaps by violent eschatological intervention, provided that they are faithful to him.

What Jesus did was not to overturn these ideas but to shift them slightly from within so that their meaning was radically transformed. This emphasis was not so much on the demands of God but on God's forgiveness and mercy. He associated with the poor and the outcast, the sick and the ritually unclean, to show that God's love and generosity override concerns for ritual purity. He has dealings with Samaritans and gentiles in an inclusive way; his message is one of love and peace. It is this, not the destruction of enemies, that constitutes the coming kingdom of God: indeed, insofar as they practice this love, Jesus' followers are already in the kingdom. The kingdom of God anticipated in apocalyptic writings is indeed one in which 'God will establish his rule over his people thus fulfilling their deepest hopes' (103); but Jesus looks for a transformation of the hopes themselves. Instead of destruction of their enemies and meticulous observance of ritual, Jesus preaches love that will turn enemies into friends, and freedom that will bring joy rather than duty to religious observance.

> The dominant note of such a proclamation and ministry is joy and confidence ... But such joy in not the joy of the untroubled, of the insouciant. On the contrary those who are invited to share in the kingdom are the oppressed people of Galilee. They are the devout Jews, but also the collaborators and the sinners. What is happening here is a deep

remoulding of the consciousness and experience of Israel. The Jews' experience of oppression, of loss, of deprivation of rights and of their religious heritage, of the long struggle to uphold their traditions, of economic worry and hardship, all this is caught up and *enlarged*.

(109)

The implications of this interpretation of the covenant are profound. It is changed from being an exclusive covenant to being an invitation to all people to join in the generosity of the kingdom of God, a kingdom based on forgiveness and love.

It is an attractive interpretation. However, Riches' argument does not address one glaring question: Why was Jesus crucified? If what Jesus was teaching was love for enemies – including the Romans –, care for the sick and poor, and divine generosity, this might make him more devout than many, but it would hardly make him a criminal. Riches might argue that the various factions of Palestinian society who were competing for control of purity laws and temple worship could have regarded Jesus as a threat or an annoyance. After all, the Gospels are full of Jesus' denunciations of the Pharisees for their hypocrisy and the way they laid extra burdens on already oppressed people. While this is true, however, it is hardly enough to explain why Jesus was crucified, not by the Jews but by the Romans, as a political criminal. As Ed Sanders has argued, Pharisees disagreed amongst themselves about purity laws, sometimes sharply, and they disagreed also with other groups like the Sadducees, 'but people did not kill one another' over these disputes, let alone involve the Romans (Sanders 1993:216). Sanders suggests that Riches has fallen into a 'bad Jesus, good Jesus' syndrome which has all too often played into the anti-Semitic tendencies of Christendom: Jesus transformed Judaism and thus the Church was born (Sanders 1985:218).

In Sanders' view, Jesus was crucified because he was regarded by a group of vocal followers as 'king of the Jews', perhaps regarded himself that way, and had said things about the temple and its destruction which would cause him to be perceived as a trouble maker. Caiaphas, the high priest, was responsible to the Romans to ensure order and good government; it was up to him 'to preserve the peace and to prevent riots and bloodshed' (Sanders 1993:273).

Jesus had alarmed some people by his attack on the Temple and his statement about its destruction ... It is highly probable that Caiaphas was primarily or exclusively concerned with the possibility that Jesus would incite a riot. He sent armed guards to arrest Jesus, he gave him a hearing, and he recommended execution to Pilate, who promptly complied.

(Sanders 1993:269; cf. Frederiksen 1999:234)

Pilate, the Roman governor, had many times shown himself a man who would order executions without a qualm. The life of a poor Jewish peasant was cheap indeed; and if Caiaphas recommended execution Pilate would simply have ordered it to be done.

According to Sanders, the kingdom of God was therefore intended by Jesus and his disciples to be an actual social and political arrangement on this earth, not simply a spiritual or individual summons to authentic living, and 'a good deal more concrete than ... a collection of nice thoughts about grace and forgiveness' (1985:232). But Jesus was not trying to bring it about himself, certainly not by violence or insurrection. Rather, he expected God to intervene; and he was trying to prepare people for that event and live by its promise.

> The kingdom expected by Jesus ... is like the present world – it has a king, leaders, a temple, twelve tribes – but it is not just a rearrangement of the present world. God must step in and provide a new temple, the restored people of Israel, and presumably a new social order, one in which 'sinners' will have a place.
>
> (Sanders 1985:232)

I shall return to the question of violence in a later chapter. The point here is that according to this understanding, Jesus' idea of the kingdom of God, the fulfilment of God's covenant to Israel, was not merely inward or spiritual, nor did it wait until 'heaven' after death, but would come about by God's intervention in the present world.

> Jesus' hope for the kingdom fits into long-standing and deeply held hopes among the Jews, who continued to look for God to redeem his people and constitute a new kingdom, one in which Israel would be secure and peaceful, and one in which Gentiles would serve the God of Israel.
>
> (Sanders 1993:193)

Jesus and empire

If Jesus was executed by Pilate at the behest of Caiaphas on the grounds that he was about to cause trouble, perhaps as a 'messianic pretender' (Frederiksen 1999:234), then if what Jesus was doing was only preparing his people for the coming of God, his execution was a big mistake. Jesus was not out to cause trouble. Christian theology has for centuries understood the death of Jesus as perhaps misguided in human terms but essential in the plan of God for the salvation of the world: I shall discuss this idea of sacrificial atonement and its relation both to the Jewish system of ritual sacrifice and to the violence of Christendom in the next chapter. Here I want to present another way of arguing that Jesus' death was no mistake. Richard Horsley has argued that Jesus was indeed an opponent of the Roman Empire, and that although his methods were non-violent his goals were political. The kingdom of God was in direct opposition to the kingdom of Caesar and his Jewish collaborators.

In a series of books (1993, 1995, 2003) Horsley has made a case against separating narrowly defined religious or spiritual concerns from politics. In particular, he urges that any interpretation of Jesus' teaching of the kingdom of God as the renewal of God's covenant with Israel, must start from the actual political and economic situation that obtained. Palestine had been part of the Roman Empire since 63 BCE, when Pompey captured Jerusalem. It was ruled, first by client kings such as Herod, and then by directly appointed Roman governors like Pontius Pilate, assisted by the Jerusalem Temple hierarchy. Now, E.P. Sanders has argued that, as conquered territories subjected to Rome went, Palestine did not fare too badly (at least not until the revolt of 66–70 CE): it was a province of Rome, but provided it remained quiet and cooperative it was left to follow its own religious and social customs. Roman troops were available should there be any threat to public order (for which the high priest was responsible), but they were normally stationed outside of Jerusalem and required to respect Jewish religious sensitivities. Things could have been worse. Indeed they got worse, much worse, after the revolt of 66 CE; but that was long after the time of Jesus. During his lifetime 'Jewish Palestine was not on the edge of revolt' (Sanders 1993:31).

However, even Sanders recognizes that there was plenty of discontent among the people, both at the Roman rule itself and at the Jewish leaders who served as their subalterns. Horsley makes clear some of the specific reasons for the discontent. Rome did not conquer territories for the good of the territories but for the good of Rome. Grain, taxes, and slaves were all required to satisfy the ever-expanding needs of Rome and the Italian heartlands, and the territories Rome occupied were expected to supply them. In the half century before Jesus' life, many thousands of people had been enslaved and deported from around the Sea of Galilee in northern Palestine. Along with mass enslavements there was also heavy taxation, in grain as well as coin. It is true that some of the profit went to line the pockets of the local leaders as well as the tax farmers and tax gatherers, and never got to Rome; but that would hardly serve to make the taxes (or the tax collectors) more popular. Many of the stories of the Gospels have to do with hunger and poverty; they would have struck an immediate chord with the many whose grain and money were taken as tribute.

Moreover, when there was any form of resistance, the Romans were capable of using harsh measures, including crucifixion, an excruciatingly brutal form of execution. At about the time Jesus was born, for example, about two thousand men were rounded up and crucified (Josephus 1960:474; *Wars* II. V.2). Life was cheap. Although it was more to the advantage of Rome to pacify and subdue the people of their colonies than to annihilate them or have them continually in rebellion, they did not hesitate to use extreme force to terrorize people into subjection. It is not difficult to understand why the people of Palestine would be living in a state of mixed desperation and despair. Open revolt could hardly succeed against the power of Rome, though from time to time attempts were made, only to be ruthlessly suppressed. A few people, mostly the aristocracy, benefited from the Roman occupation and collaborated with it. But the majority of the populace, the peasant farmers and small trades people, would try to keep their heads down and make the best they could of the situation, praying that God would come to their aid.

Into this situation came first John the Baptist and then Jesus, preaching the good news of the coming of the kingdom of God. Pious Jews who believed in the covenant that God had made with Israel were looking for precisely this: 'the expectation was widespread … that in their situation of oppression by foreign empire(s), God would intervene in the near future to judge the empire and to restore the people to independence or sovereignty' (Horsley 2003:82). In such a context it is misguided, Horsley argues, to suppose that Jesus' message was spiritual and apolitical. Such a separation of religion and politics is wrong-headed. Jews believed that it was precisely in religious terms, through divine intervention, that political change would come; but the change they looked for was change in their actual situation, not only change of heart or spiritual renewal, let alone merely the promise of a better life after death.

The question, however, was how this change would take place, and in particular whether there was anything people could do to prepare for the expected divine intervention or even precipitate it. Many of the scribes and scholars believed that there was nothing to do but wait. God would come when God's time was right. In the meantime, God's people must be patient in their sufferings and pray. Others, however, thought that they could form groups of resistance and perhaps open revolt, expecting God to come to their aid if it came to armed conflict. There were several such groups around the time of Jesus; they formed armed bands and looked for the opportunity for effective uprising. When they were caught they were suppressed with typical Roman cruelty (Horsley 2003:36–45; 1993:33–58). Horsley argues that Jesus should be seen as a leader of a similar resistance movement.

> Jesus of Nazareth belongs in the same context with and stands shoulder to shoulder with these other leaders of movements among the Judean and Galilean people, and pursues the same general agenda in parallel paths: independence from Roman imperial rule so that the people can

again be empowered to renew their traditional way of life under the rule
of God.

(Horsley 2003:104)

It is this kingdom of God which Jesus announced, the renewal of the ancient
covenant between God and his people.

Jesus' method, however, was different from that of some of the other leaders
of popular movements of resistance. Yet the question arises as to whether
Jesus could be seen as advocating violence rather than active non-violent
resistance. Horsley argues for the latter; and emphasizes that central to Jesus'
activities was developing communities who lived out their resistance by
engaging in practices of social renewal.

> Jesus acted to heal the effects of empire and to summon people to
> rebuild their community life. In the conviction that the kingdom of God
> was at hand, he pressed a programme of social revolution to re-establish
> just egalitarian and mutually supportive social-economic relations in the
> village communities that constituted the basic form of the people's life.
>
> (Horsley 2003:105)

Thus Jesus healed those who were sick, and expected his disciples to do so
too. He taught them not to copy the behaviour of the wealthy who exploited
them, not to try to be among the great ones of the earth, but to share their
resources with those in need, to help and serve one another. Rather than
indulging in quarrels or jealousy that would fracture community, they were
to show mercy, forgiveness and generosity, building up communities of solidarity and mutual support. Thus they would develop strength to resist the
hopelessness of the situation, and be ready for the day when the imperial
order would be overthrown.

According to Horsley, therefore, the charges against Jesus that led to his
crucifixion were not totally false. He was indeed the leader of a popular
movement of resistance to Roman imperial rule, and the kingdom of God
which he preached was to replace the kingdom of Caesar. Although Jesus'
methods might have been non-violent, not armed rebellion, the Jewish leaders had good reason to fear that his movement was leading to unrest and,
given the harsh climate of the time, it is understandable that he was arrested,
handed over to the Romans and summarily executed.

Be that as it may, Horsley's central point is that the kingdom of God as
Jesus taught it was a kingdom in which the people lived in covenantal communities, where their actual day-to-day lives in their economic and social
relations reflected their covenant with God. This involved radical egalitarianism, both in terms of wealth and in terms of gender. Patriarchal social
relations were not to obtain; the poor and the sick should be given help;
debts should be cancelled; local enmities should be resolved, so that people

could live together in joy and hope rather than deflecting on to one another the oppression they were experiencing at the hands of the occupying power. By the time Jesus had his last meal with his disciples he was aware that his leadership of this movement might well cost him his life. Accordingly, when he took up the cup to share with them, he emphasized again his central message: 'This is the new covenant ... Do this in remembrance of me'.

Summary

Which of these interpretations of Jesus' teaching of the kingdom of God is correct? Was Jesus essentially a teacher of spiritual values of integrity and authenticity, misguided in his eschatological expectations but in spite of that (or because of it) addressing humanity in every age? Did he stand as a reformer of Judaism, recalling a legalistic and exclusivist Judaism to a more merciful and generous understanding of the covenant? Was he the leader of a popular resistance movement against the Roman occupation, encouraging his followers to live in communities of resistance and solidarity? Was his focus on this world, or on another world, inaugurated by divine intervention or entered into through death? Was he preaching personal salvation, or offering a new political and social reality?

The issue for me in the context of this book is not so much which (if any) of these and many more interpretations is the right one. Scholars far more equipped than I in the tools of biblical languages and exegesis have been debating that question for centuries without consensus. What I am after, rather, is the basis upon which the choice of interpretation is made, and the way in which that choice is sedimented into the consciousness of Christendom. If Jesus is seen primarily as a spiritual teacher who left politics to Caesar, then although his ideals of love and compassion set the standards of ethical behaviour, his orientation is other-worldly. The teaching of the kingdom of God transfers the covenant into a heavenly sphere. It is not in this life or in this world that God's people will experience the covenant, except perhaps as a spiritual foretaste. Accordingly, this world is experienced as, at best, the place to prepare for the fullness of the covenant; at worst, it is simply the place where suffering, death and violence hold sway.

Alternatively, if it is accepted that Jesus' teaching must be interpreted in the framework of his social, economic and political context rather than in narrowly theological terms alone, then it has consequences for the material reality of people in this world, in their concrete lived experience. It does not point merely to some heavenly kingdom, with this present world to be endured with patience, but seeks to transform this world into covenant reality. Whether or not Jesus' teaching is plausible or workable is another question, as is also the issue of whether or not or to what extent it could be applied to socio-political contexts besides the one in which he himself was situated. But his teaching is, on this view, not simply teaching about personal salvation or how to get to heaven after death, but about how life should be lived in all its economic and political concreteness.

The point I am making here is that the decision to treat Jesus as a universal spiritual teacher who brings salvation, or alternatively to situate him in his historical context, is precisely that: a *decision.* It is moreover not a decision that can be made on the basis of historical evidence, since an appeal to history is already implicitly a decision (though it is often applied in a highly inconsistent manner). Rather, it is often made on theological or even pre-theological considerations. In the Western societies of modernity it is often held that religion and politics do not mix. Whatever the actual practice (in which it is often obvious that religious considerations are deeply entangled with political), the rhetoric of separation is reinforced by theological emphasis on salvation, where salvation is understood in other-worldly terms. I shall discuss this more fully later. What I want to be clear about here is that the narrative of the historical Jesus as presented in the Gospels has been inscribed into the narrative of Western culture in diverse ways, with implications, in each case, for the understanding of death and violence.

Jesus and gender

The same range of interpretations occur in relation to Jesus and his ideas of gender. With the rise of feminism, recent scholars have often felt it necessary to say something about Jesus' view of women, where earlier scholars avoided the issue altogether. Even those who do comment take very different positions. All are compelled to notice that Jesus as represented in the Gospels was willing to interact with women in his teaching and healing ministry and that they are said to be among his followers. But how important were they? Did Jesus see them as equal to men?

E.P. Sanders, for example, acknowledges that 'women followers play an absolutely essential role in the gospel accounts' (Sanders 1993:124), but that apart from a few incidents we do not know much about them. History was written by men, and 'for the most part women play only supporting roles' (125). However, Sanders argues that there is special significance in the fact that Jesus chose precisely twelve disciples, as these would be the rulers of the twelve tribes of Israel in the coming kingdom of God; and these twelve disciples were all male. Although women were among those who supported Jesus financially and served him in their homes, Sanders says,

> I think it likely that women physically *followed* Jesus only on rare occasions, such as pilgrimages to Jerusalem, when it was generally acceptable for men and women to travel together in groups. If women had actually travelled with Jesus and his disciples on other occasions, and spent the night on the road, there would probably be some echo of criticism of this

scandalous behaviour in the gospels. Female supporters probably played their more traditional role by providing lodging and food.

(Sanders 1993:111)

Richard Horsley, on the other hand, argues that Jesus' efforts at building communities of solidarity involved radical egalitarianism, including non-patriarchal social relations (Horsley 1993:232). Horsley, however, says nothing further about Jesus' treatment of women or women's position among Jesus' disciples: from what Horsley says about Jesus' closest followers we would not guess that women might have been among them. He has a good deal to say about patriarchy, however, as we shall see.

By contrast, Elisabeth Schüssler Fiorenza has worked to reclaim the place of women among Jesus' disciples. She is acutely aware of the ways in which Christendom has presented Jesus as an antithesis to Judaism, and warns against feminists urging a view of Jesus as pro-woman that implicitly denigrates Judaism as misogynist. It is for this reason that Fiorenza opts for an interpretation of Jesus that sees him as bringing about a renewal movement within Judaism.

> The issue is not whether or not Jesus overturned patriarchy but whether Judaism had elements of a critical feminist impulse that came to the fore in the vision and ministry of Jesus ... The praxis and vision of Jesus and his movement is best understood as an inner-Jewish renewal movement that presented an *alternative* option to the dominant patriarchal structures rather than an oppositional formation rejecting the values and praxis of Judaism.
>
> (Fiorenza 1983:107)

The crux of that renewal movement, as Fiorenza sees it, is the wholeness and holiness of all the people of Israel. The kingdom of God is for everyone: women and men, poor and rich, outcasts and sinners as well as Pharisees. Moreover, Jesus' method was not to identify with the wealthy and powerful and work from the top down, but to identify with the poor in 'solidarity from below' (152). Given that this was the case, and given also that women were among the poorest and most oppressed, this means that the 'vision of Jesus calls all women without exception to wholeness and selfhood, as well as to solidarity with those women who are the impoverished, the maimed and outcasts ... ' (153). The Gospels, like other religious and historical documents, were written by men, and often made women marginal or invisible; yet even here we find stories of significant encounters between Jesus and women. Schüssler Fiorenza writes,

> Only when we place the Jesus stories about women into the overall story of Jesus and his movement in Palestine are we able to recognize their

subversive character. In the discipleship of equals the 'role' of women is not peripheral or trivial, but at the centre, and thus of utmost importance to the praxis of 'solidarity from below'.

(Fiorenza 1983:152)

Gender, however, is not only about women. What view did Jesus hold of masculinity, and of the patriarchal social structure of his time? Here again it is possible to assume, with most traditional scholars, that Jesus simply accepted the norms of his time and put his energy into challenging other things: human sinfulness, or deformed Judaism, or Roman oppression. It is also possible, however, to argue with Horsley and Fiorenza that Jesus radically challenged the patriarchy of his society. It is agreed by everyone, for example, that Jesus called God 'Father', and taught his disciples to do so too, especially in prayer: 'Our Father who art in heaven ... ' But how is 'Father' to be understood? Is it to be taken as contrasting with 'Mother', thus implicitly affirming the maleness of God? Or should it be taken to contrast with 'Master' or 'King', thus indicating a relationship of intimacy rather than subservience? Or is it both?

One indication that Jesus opposed the hierarchical structures of his society occurs in connection with his denunciation of Pharisees who 'do all their deeds to be seen of men', love the place of honour at feasts and respectful greetings as they went about in society. In contrast, Jesus says, his disciples are to 'call no man father on earth, for you have one Father, who is in heaven. Neither be called masters ... He who is greatest among you shall be your servant ... ' (Matthew 23.9–11). In this passage it is clear that recognition of God as Father is part of a rejection of rivalry for greatness, and acceptance instead of generosity in dealing with one another. 'You are all brothers', Jesus declares. Thus Fiorenza argues that:

> The 'father' God is invoked here ... not to justify patriarchal structures and relationships in the community of disciples but precisely to reject all such claims, powers, and structures ... The saying of Jesus uses the 'father' name of God not as a legitimization for existing patriarchal structures ... but as a critical subversion of all structures of domination.
> (Fiorenza 1983:150–1)

It is noteworthy, moreover, that Jesus' teaching here echoes the Mosaic covenant, in which the Israelites were forbidden to have a king or the centralized power which kingship represents. Since God was the king of Israel, 'there could be no legitimate human monarch' (Horsley 1993:241). In just the same way, Jesus teaches that since God is the father of all, there could be no legitimate patriarchal social structures.[1]

Such a perspective has a direct bearing on the construction of masculinity. In a society in which men were honoured in part in relation to the sons that they sired, and in which greatness was construed in terms of power and mastery, Jesus' followers were to conduct themselves otherwise. Masculinity was not to be constructed in terms of mastery but in terms of brotherhood, where everyone tried to help one another. If as Horsley argues Jesus was trying to develop communities that could resist the oppression of Rome, then the last thing such communities would need would be men in competition with one another for dominance. The kingdom of God required men who could work together in solidarity and who would not be threatened by taking positions of service or descend into petty squabbling about who was greatest. Although this would not by itself guarantee gender equality, it is obvious that men who do not construe their masculinity in terms of mastery over others are much less inclined to insist upon dominating women and much more open to egalitarian gender relations than are men who feel their man-liness is threatened whenever they are not in a position of power. When this is put together with Jesus' own respectful dealings with women it is clear that the gender relations of the kingdom of God were to be very different from the hierarchical patriarchy and sometimes outright misogyny current in most Mediterranean societies of his time.

The difference in gender construction is brought out further in the ways the Gospel writers represent Jesus' attitudes to the family, the basic kinship unit in Israelite society. There is no indication in the Gospels that Jesus ever married or had children: this in itself would be highly unconventional for a Jewish male. This is not to say that he rejected family life, though he radically reinterpreted it. Thus for example when he was questioned about the legitimacy of divorce, Jesus rejected the current practice which allowed a man to divorce his wife. A divorced woman would be without economic or social resources and might be forced into prostitution; hence 'every one who divorces his wife ... makes her an adulteress' (Matthew 5.32). This was not, however, repudiation of marriage itself; on the contrary, marriage was, according to Jesus, instituted by God at creation, when 'God made them male and female. For this reason a man shall leave his father and mother and be joined to his wife', not to dominate her but as partners in the kingdom of God (Mark 10.7–8).

The Gospel of Mark tells of an occasion when Jesus was teaching in a house, and his mother and brothers arrived. When Jesus was told of it, he said,

> 'Who are my mother and my brothers?' And looking around on those who sat about him, he said, 'Here are my mother and my brothers! Whoever does the will of God is my brother, and sister, and mother'.
>
> (Mark 3.33–35)

The story does not indicate disrespect for his mother and brothers; for all we know they were invited in or Jesus went out to see them. The point rather is that kinship is extended and transformed. The established patriarchal order is subverted, and with it gender constructions of domination and subservience; and in its place is put mutuality and solidarity in the kingdom of God.

If this is a reasonable interpretation of Jesus' (or the Gospels') attitude to gender, however, then two questions arise. First, how was it that Christendom did not maintain such egalitarianism but rather institutiona- lized patriarchy, misogyny and hierarchy throughout the centuries of its existence? The response to that question, and the violence in which the inscription of hierarchical patriarchy is implicated in Christendom will be traced as these volumes proceed.

The second question is this: if indeed Jesus did teach egalitarian relations and constructed gender accordingly, so what? Given that such egalitarianism was not carried forward in the institution of the Christian Church, what does it help that Jesus had a different view? After all, we cannot jump backwards over the centuries to some pristine time with Jesus as though the intervening history never happened. Even if Jesus taught all that a feminist could wish, is it any more than a lovely dream, no longer available? To this I offer two responses. First, there are many Christians, including many of the most conservative, who appeal to Jesus' life and teaching as represented in the Gospels as authoritative for life today. If such an appeal is made, simple consistency requires that Jesus' rejection of relations of power in favour of mutuality in gender relations be taken as seriously as anything else in the Gospels. Second, and more broadly, the very fact that the Gospels offer a possibility of equality and challenge conventional constructions of gender and family shows that such constructions are not inevitable. There is a choice.

Chapter 10

Medieval deaths and delights

Through the long middle ages,[1] these same two strands of necrophilia and natality, the forensic and the organic, intertwined in complicated ways. The emphasis in Christendom on the afterlife, and especially on the terrors of hell, made an obsession with death inevitable, and did much to displace beauty from the earth. Anxieties build up a need for mastery; once again we can see both external representations in the violence of the Crusades and the hunt for heretics, and internal manifestations in the insistence of asceticism, mortification, self-sacrifice, and the invention of purgatory.

On the other hand, there were others, especially among the great mystics and spiritual writers, who were deeply engaged by beauty, both of the world and of God, and who kept alive the choice for flourishing. They looked for alternatives to violence, for social justice rather than holy war, for desire and joy in sanctity and the delights of heaven upon the earth. The two strands were inseparable: one could hardly find a 'pure' example of either, though there are strong differences of emphasis. The point of presenting them as alternatives is not to pretend that historically there were clear contrasts, but rather to show in a schematic fashion how the genealogy of death and the displacement of beauty shifted through the medieval period and bequeathed to modernity its formative choices.

Covenants of death

There were from the early days of Christendom seven sacraments; but always the two central ones were baptism and the eucharist, both of them articulated in the New Testament as covenant, and both of them deeply imbricated in a forensic symbolic of death. In the writings attributed to the apostle Paul the linkage between these rituals and death is lifted up.

> Do you not know that all of us who have been baptized into Christ Jesus were baptized into his death? We were buried therefore with him by baptism into death, so that as Christ was raised from the dead by the glory of God the Father, we too might walk in newness of life.
>
> (Romans 6.3–4).

Paul did not invent baptism, of course. The Gospel writers tell of John the Baptist, preaching repentance and baptizing people in the Jordan River as they confessed their sins; Jesus also was baptized by John. Whatever the significance of this water baptism, and of John's assertion that the one who comes after him will baptize 'with the Holy Ghost', there is no indication in these stories, repeated in all four Gospels, that baptism is preoccupied with death. In a Pauline theology, however, where crucifixion is understood as Christ's substitutionary death for humankind, individual identification with Christ becomes significant, and baptism is a ritual of that identification. As such, it is also then taken up as the ritual of incorporation into Christ's body, the Church. In the Epistle to the Colossians the themes come together of Christ's divinity, individual human incorporation into Christ's death as the means of salvation, the constitution of the Church, the hope of everlasting life, and the consequent exhortation to 'mortify' – literally put to death – bodily desires incompatible with this 'resurrection life':

> In him [i.e. Christ] the whole fullness of deity dwells bodily ... and you were buried with him in baptism ... God having cancelled the bond which stood against us with its legal demands; this he set aside, nailing it to the cross ... Set your minds on things that are above, not on things that are on earth. For you have died, and your life is hid with Christ in God ... Put to death therefore what is earthly in you: fornication, impurity, passion, evil desire ...
>
> (Colossians 2.9–3.5)

It was this conceptual linkage which was to persist through the centuries of Christendom. From early times the baptismal font stood near the entrance of the church. The penitent – later the infant – was baptized, washing away original sin and incorporating him or her into the body of the church, 'christening' them, that is, identifying them with Christ. And this identification was understood simultaneously as enacting a new birth, having nothing to do with mothers or bodies or sexuality, but rather with entrance into the possibility of life in heaven rather than eternal punishment. The significance of the ritual of baptism thus derives from its multiple investment in death and other worlds, an investment whose gendered nature is obvious by the insistence that baptism represents new birth, not of woman but of a Father God and his male ecclesiastical representatives. There were of course shifts in the understanding and practice of baptism through the middle ages, but the symbolism of death to this earthly life and redirection to a life after death remained constant. Each enactment of the ritual repeated and reinscribed its gendered necrophilia.

Something similar is true of the eucharist. Again in the Gospels what is presented is a last meal that Jesus had with his followers, in which he took the opportunity to teach them something about humble service to one another (Luke 22.14–30; John 13.1–30). He talks to them about the death that he foresees at the hands of the authorities; and represents the bread and wine of the meal as his broken body and his blood. In the early Christian community this meal was quickly developed as a ritual which in some sense re-enacted a covenant, and it was incorporated in some writings such as the biblical book of Hebrews into a theology of substitutionary atonement. In such an understanding, which continues to this day, the bread and wine are seen as literally and/or symbolically the body and blood of Christ, ingested by the 'communicant' as, again, uniting them with death to this life, and birth to a life of resurrection. It is a means of grace, a gift of salvation by which one can escape from the hell that would otherwise be waiting. Again the Pauline writings make the connections:

> For as often as you eat this bread and drink this cup, you proclaim the Lord's death until he comes.
>
> (1 Corinthians 11.26)

A return which was expected to be imminent.

However, such a ritual should not be undertaken lightly or without care that the rest of life is brought into accord with the ideals of mortification and self-examination it lifts up, lest it have a baneful effect.

> Let a man examine himself, and so eat of the bread and drink of the cup. For any one who eats and drinks without discerning the body eats and drinks judgment upon himself. That is why many of you are weak and ill, and some have died.
>
> (1 Corinthians 11.28–30)

It is precisely eternal death that the eucharist is meant to repel, leading instead to the heaven of everlasting bliss for which this life is a brief moment of preparation. Again, it is the food and drink of spiritual birth, rejection of the body and blood and food of the mother who gave physical life and celebration instead of the body and blood of Christ which by death overcomes the death to which our mothers bore us. As Philippe Ariès puts it,

> Ever since the risen Christ triumphed over death, the fact of being born into this world is the real death, and physical death is access to eternal life. Thus, the Christian is urged to look forward to death with joy, as if to a new birth.
>
> (Ariès 1981.13)

A new birth symbolically enacted already at baptism.

Vast amounts have been written about these two central sacraments of Christendom, seen by the Church as outward signs or enactments of inward divine grace; and their practice and interpretation has varied across the centuries. But neither the quantity, the variation, nor indeed the familiarity of the rituals should be allowed to obscure the obvious: both these rituals are deeply invested in a gendered celebration of death. Our physical birth, the natality we have through our mothers' labour, is to be overcome by a spiritual birth that requires us to reckon ourselves dead in our natural state and alive only through the enactments of death. Moreover it is only in this way that the sin and guilt which otherwise would merit our eternal punishment can be forgiven.

The depth at which these two central rituals were invested in death can also be seen from the way in which both baptism and the mass were quickly appropriated as rituals *for* the dead. As early as the Pauline writings there is an indication that this was happening. The writer asks of those who are sceptical of the resurrection, 'What do people mean by being baptized on behalf of the dead? If the dead are not raised at all, why are people baptized on their behalf?' (1 Corinthians 15.29). Whatever this might mean, it is phrased as a rhetorical question, as though no one would doubt the efficacy of being baptized for the dead. The connection between baptism and concern for those who have died is assumed.

This is even more evident in the case of the mass. In the Roman Church of late antiquity a central ritual in preparation for death was for the dying person to receive the body and blood of Christ: if the person had already died, it could be placed in the mouth of the corpse. It was called the *viaticum*, literally 'provision for the journey to the other world'; and is reminiscent of the pagan Roman practice of placing a coin in the mouth of the corpse to pay Charon, the shadowy being in charge of the ferry that crossed the river Styx to the underworld. Whether Christians thought of the elements of the mass as payment for the journey of the dead, or as food for that journey, it is clear that the sacrament and death were interlinked in multiple and complex ways. This became even more pronounced in the later middle ages, when regular masses for the dead were said in order to release them from purgatory. Chantry chapels were built and large sums of money left by those who could afford it so that these masses would be many, and the deceased's entry into heaven brought forward. All this rested upon the idea of 'transferable merit' (Levi 2002:3), and thus ultimately on the forensic model of salvation.

In summary, although overtly both baptism and the eucharist are about new birth and entering into life, they are deeply invested in death. The resurrected life *presupposes* death; it arrives only on the other side of death. Our natality, *this* life into which we have been born, must be superseded by a different life, which is available only to those who go through death. The actual death of our bodies is thus seen as the gateway to that life; though we can enter into it in a symbolic and preliminary way if we 'mortify' the desires of a body that has not yet actually died. This life is therefore not to be celebrated for itself, but at most as a basis for that other life which comes through death rather than through birth. As Frederick Paxton observes in this study of death rituals, in the Latin West 'birthday celebrations were replaced by commemorations of the anniversary of a death, which was seen as a new *dies natalis*, a birth into eternal life' (Paxton 1990:26). It is a telling change.

Martyrs, relics and the birth of purgatory

There is a story, recounted by Peter Brown in his account of the development of the cult of the saints, that neatly captures the way in which pre-occupation with death and the afterlife supplanted involvement with this world and its beauty. On an occasion in the fifth century, the country people of the Auvergne were discovered by their bishop holding a three-day festival on a mountain top, on the edge of a marsh formed in its volcanic centre. The bishop was incensed. '*Nulla est religio in stagno*,' he said:

> 'There can be no religion in a swamp. But rather acknowledge God and give veneration to his friends. Adore Saint Hilarius, the bishop of God, whose relics are installed here. He can act as your intercessor for the mercy of God.'
>
> (Brown 1981:125)

We have here, obviously, the bishop's assertion of authority. It will be his word, not the people's, that decrees what religion is. He does not enquire about what they find spiritually nourishing; they must simply change their way of worship. And this way of worship will be the way of a designated site, the church. Living nature will have no place, and true religion will be sharply distinguished from the sacred places, practices and divinities of pagan custom.

In the Europe of late antiquity and the medieval period, Christian priests, bishops and missionaries struggled to eradicate goddess worship, fertility cults, and all forms of paganism. The myths of northern Europe are full of gods and goddesses, portrayed as embodied and located: on a hilltop, at a well or spring, in a grove of trees. They were seen to have power over the sea, crops, cattle, the weather, and above all fertility; and were worshipped in feasts and festivals like Beltane and Samain. But all this was to be eradicated, replaced with radical monotheism.

The implications for the displacement of beauty are enormous. As Edward Farley has pointed out, if the immanent powers within nature – the gods and goddesses of rivers, trees, sun and moon, thunder – are divine, or at least somehow manifest the divine presence, then the beauties of nature are openings to the sacred.

> For most faiths (religions), the world's very coming into being, in meadow and glade, in animal life and starry sky, is itself a manifestation

of immanent divine powers. To be related to the world's particulars is also to be related to the divine powers at work in them ... Beautification is not the only work of the gods, but it is one part of their work as the world is infused with fertility, order, symmetry, differentiation and power.

(Farley 2001:9)

As Farley points out, the peoples who thought of the natural world as imbued with divinity produced artefacts of striking beauty, artefacts which those who insisted on monotheism all too often perceived as idols. For with the triumph of monotheism in the West, there was a rejection of all identification of divinity with the world or with things of nature, a need to eradicate all such imminent deities as false gods, and with that need 'a deep suspicion of their work of beautification' which makes 'nature shimmer' (Farley 2001:10). There can be no religion in a swamp.

Where, then, is religion to be found? In Peter Brown's vignette, it is clear: it is in the church; more precisely, it is in the church which preserves the relics of saints, dead men's bones. The turn from the living beauty of nature to a preoccupation with death could hardly be more stark.

Of bones and beauty

This turn is well illustrated in the change of burial customs. Philippe Ariès has described how, in the pagan cultures of the Mediterranean, cemeteries were kept well away from towns, the dead were separated from the living. Christians, however, wanted to be buried near the 'saints' who had died, especially to the martyrs whom they considered particularly holy. They wanted proximity to the holy dead, whose prayers and succour they desired and for whom also they prayed. Whereas the pagan rites had been such as to help the dead on their way so that their unquiet shades would not molest the living, Christians sought to help the dead partly out of concern for them and partly for the benefits which the dead might confer upon them. There was therefore a much greater sense of continuity between those still alive and those who had died (Ariès 1981.29–30). As Paxton says, Christians did not consider it right to be afraid of a corpse.

> For devout Christians, death was the door to salvation, and the bodies of the dead represented souls that had passed through it. Unlike Jews and pagans both, for whom contact with corpses brought about a state of ritual pollution, Christians regarded the bodies of their dead as sacred and holy, and were urged to handle them freely and without fear.
>
> (Paxton 1990:25)

Not only were dead bodies in general to be regarded as sacred, some bodies were to be regarded as bridging the gap between heaven and earth. These were the bodies of the martyrs, who in imitation of their Lord died violent deaths rather than give up their faith. Already in the catacombs of Rome, the tombs or relics of the martyrs were seen as particularly holy, places of prayer where miracles might happen; and after the conversion of Constantine, relics became essential for the foundation of new churches. The relics might be bits of skin or bones of martyrs or saints, or things particularly holy by association with Jesus or his mother: the wood of the holy cross, for example, or rather generous examples of the virgin's milk. Through the writings of Jerome and Augustine, the cult of relics was given theological justification. Soon there was a roaring trade in relics, often spurious; the Crusaders brought quantities of relics from the Holy Land to Western Europe. Since it was held that God was specially present through these relics of his people, it was expected that miracles would occur where relics were venerated. And since relics were believed to be particularly holy (and valuable), it became usual to house them either in the altar itself, or in magnificent reliquaries, as costly and beautiful as could be made: gold, chased silver, precious stones – the cathedral museums of Europe are full of the most intricate and fabulously expensive reliquaries housing dead bones. Art – beauty – is bent to the service of death.

Some of the places where relics were kept became famous sites of pilgrimage: Walsingham in England, for example, and Santiago Compostela in Spain are especially noteworthy; but many a little church or shrine, housing its minor relic in its altar, might hope that it would be a place where prayers would be answered and healings would occur. It was of course not lost on the ecclesiastical hierarchy that relics would bring pilgrims, and their money with them; and along with genuine devotion there was also bare-faced exploitation of relics for power and profit. It was such abuse that in due time called forth the sarcasm of Erasmus and the denunciations of Luther and Calvin. But throughout the middle ages, the cult of relics shows again the preoccupation with death; the production of priceless reliquaries is a signal example of artistic beauty given over to its celebration.

And after death the judgement

Above the central portal of the west front of the Cathedral at Autun, built in the twelfth century, is a huge rendition in stone of the final judgement. Christ in glory sits on his throne, surrounded by his apostles. At the bottom of the scene, the dead rise from their graves, snakes clawing after them. Their souls are weighed in a balance: devils and angels pull at either side of the scale. The saved grip the hem of the angels' garments and are taken by them to heaven; grinning devils with savage mouths and furry tails seize the damned. Their place for all eternity will be hellfire: a hellfire both infinite in duration and unbearable in the intensity of its physical pain.

It is a scene repeated with variations on any number of medieval cathedrals. It is frequently depicted on the tympanum of the west portal – in other words, directly above the doorway through which ordinary people would enter the church. Anyone entering the cathedral, reading this 'sermon in stone', would be reminded, if they needed reminding, that after death comes the judgement, and that the torments of hell await those who are not redeemed by the mercy of Christ through the church, the ark of salvation.

Four hundred years later Michelangelo completed his painting of the Sistine Chapel, again with a scene of the last judgement. Here too we have the risen Christ as judge, the dead rising from their graves at the angels' trumpet call, the saved going up to heaven and the damned being beaten down to hell by grinning demons coiled about with snakes. But in the Michelangelo painting, something else is happening as well. The Virgin Mary, often represented in medieval renditions of the judgement on a throne assisting Christ, is twisted away from him as though she cannot bear to look at what is happening. Not only the damned are dismayed. The saints and the saved, forming a circle around Christ, are depicted as full of anxiety. These are not people who are easy about the judgement or confident of their own salvation. The idea of the judgement arouses trepidation in everyone, even those bound for heaven.

In the contrast between the two renditions is an indication of the deepening anxiety about death and judgement through the middle ages and into the renaissance, the emergence of what Jean Delumeau has called 'a western guilt culture' (Delumeau 1990). It is part of the development of forensic theology, and with it the focus on sin, confession, penance and mortification. Delumeau traces the growing sense of fear and preoccupation with sin: sin was sorted into categories of 'deadly' and 'venial'; examination of conscience, confessors' handbooks and penitential regimes became standard. Augustine's doctrines of original sin and predestination were interpreted and reinterpreted until in the reformation they were at the root of Luther's despair and Calvin's teaching of total depravity and the idea that some were elect from all eternity for salvation and all others for damnation.

All these preoccupations are of course based upon forensic theology. The covenant must be kept; departure from it will result in punishment. There is no escape from this. It is deemed essential to the holiness and justice of God, even though in Christian theology, Jesus bears the punishment for those who are saved. In contrast to Jewish thinking, which had not placed much emphasis on life after death, Christians through the middle ages were increasingly preoccupied with what would happen to them after the final judgement. Thus for instance Dante's *Divine Comedy* enthusiastically depicted the several punishments of each circle of hell and purgatory, and (perhaps with less vividness) the joys of the circles of heaven. Indeed the doctrine of purgatory became much more prominent from the twelfth century onward: Jacques Le Goff goes so far as to argue that purgatory was 'born' during this period (Le Goff 1984; see also Bremmer 2002). Contempt for the world and 'celebrations' of the *danse macabre* became part of the means of dealing with the anxieties of death. But above all the church gained power over the lives and thinking of people, a power whose technology rested at least in large part on guilt and fear, the central ingredients of the forensic theology of the middle ages. It would lead to the despair of Luther and the eruption of his teaching of '*sola gratia*': rejection of all the church's proffered means of grace, and the hope of salvation only through faith in the unmerited mercy of God through the sacrifice of Christ. Yet immense as this change was, the theology of the reformation was built no less firmly upon the forensic model than the 'Catholic' system which it sought to replace, as we shall see.

A persecuting society

The anxieties of the covenant, the fears of judgement and the guilt of sin led once again, inevitably, to efforts of mastery, and thus to both externalized and internalized violence. The most famous form of the externalized violence is the 'holy war' which Christendom fought against the 'infidel', the series of Crusades from about 1071 to 1291. There were many motivations for the Crusades: military, economic, religious and political; and scholars continue to debate their history and influence (see for example Richard 1999; Tyerman 2004). Whatever the detail, however, it is clear that the Crusades represent an enormous investment in death. Not only were there the deaths of innumerable soldiers and civilians of both sides, but also the motivation for the Christian soldier engaging in the war in the first place was regularly represented in terms of ensuring a place in heaven. Christopher Tyerman cites the instance of one Jakelin de Mailly, killed by Muslims in Galilee in 1187, whose chronicler wrote of him,

> He was not afraid to die for Christ. At long last, crushed rather than conquered by spears, stones and lances, he sank to the ground and joyfully passed to heaven with the martyr's crown, triumphant. It was indeed a gentle death with no place for sorrow, when one man's sword had constructed such a great crown for himself from the crowd laid all around him. Death is sweet when the victor lies encircled by the impious people he has slain with his victorious right hand ...
>
> (Tyerman 2004:1–2)

Whether Jakelin's death was indeed 'gentle' or 'sweet' may, given the circumstances, be doubted; but that is not the point. The main object of the chronicler's representation is that death earned by the slaughter of 'Christ's enemies' is a death that earns immediate entry into heaven. No one who has given himself to this enterprise need fear hell fire or even a long stay in purgatory: he will have instead the 'martyr's crown'.

Whatever other motivations may also have prompted the Crusades, successive popes urged the faithful to join the armies of Christ by promising that if they did so they would be granted indulgences, years off purgatory for their service. There is of course no way of knowing whether people would have enlisted anyway. Clearly, however, the dread of judgement and the idea of merit gained by participating in the recapture of the holy places of Jerusalem – especially the scenes of Christ's own death, and the relics associated with it – were significant in the rhetoric and probably the reality of motivation.

Once again, the forensic model of merit and judgement is central; without it the history of the Crusades could not get underway. The covenant and its implied courtroom externalized itself in violence. It was a violence which Steven Runciman, foremost Western historian of the Crusades, has described as 'one long act of intolerance in the name of God which is the sin against the Holy Ghost' (from Tyerman 2004.15) and whose echoes resonate around and poison relationships between Muslims and the 'Christian' West to this day.

The violence was not only directed against the 'infidel'. R.I. Moore has shown how, from the tenth to the thirteenth centuries, Western Christendom developed attitudes of intolerance which were expressed in violent persecution of 'others'. Those who were considered deviant – Jews, lepers, sodomites or heretics – became the objects of religiously sanctioned attack.

> Persecution became habitual. That is not to say simply that individuals were subject to violence, but that deliberate and socially sanctioned violence began to be directed, *through established governmental, judicial and social institutions,* against groups of people defined by general characteristics such as race, religion or way of life; and that membership of such groups in itself came to be regarded as justifying these attacks.
>
> (Moore 1987:5)

If the judgement of God and the threat of damnation hung over those who did not keep themselves pure, then it was of the first importance that the impure be found out and exterminated from the community, lest all be condemned together. As Moore shows, there had of course been heretics, Jews, lepers and the rest from very early times; but it was during this period of heightened anxiety about death and the judgement that the attitudes of a persecuting society were etched into the consciousness of Western Christendom. The Crusades ... [2]

Chapter 11

A reconfiguration of desire

Reading medieval mystics in postmodernity

By the grace of God ... I conceived a great desire ... of longing with my will for God.

(Julian of Norwich 1978:179)

My love is as a fever, longing still
For that which longer nurseth the disease ...
My reason, the physician to my love ...
Hath left me, and I desperate now approve
Desire is death ...
Past cure I am, now reason is past care,
And frantic-mad with evermore unrest ...

(Shakespeare 1980: *Sonnet* #147)

What is desire? Is desire conceived 'by the grace of God'? Or is desire death, 'frantic-mad' in tormented restlessness? Or is it both? How does a configuration of desire affect the representation of what it is to be a person? – a woman? Feminists have worked hard to reconfigure and reclaim desire. But desire does not stand alone: it is interconnected with other key ingredients of the masculinist cultural symbolic. In this chapter I wish to outline a way of reconfiguring desire by drawing on the work of Julian of Norwich and other writers in the Christian mystical tradition that shows it not to be deathly but central to human flourishing. By this appropriation of Julian's teaching I shall illustrate how religion can be a significant resource for feminist philosophical thought. I am inviting feminists who have dismissed religion as patriarchal and unhelpful to think again, and not to assume that religion is antithetical to critical and progressive thinking. But I am also challenging philosophers of religion, especially those of the Anglo-American analytic persuasion, not to suppose that feminist engagement will permit business as usual. Boundaries, methods, and aims are all redrawn when philosophy of religion is approached from a feminist perspective (Jantzen 1998).

Whose desire?

'Desire is death'. Shakespeare's expression is extreme, but the constellation of death and desire and its contrast with truth and rationality is a common-place of the Western symbolic. So also is the implicit gender construction: reason, the physician, is male; and the object of desire is presumed female. Many go further than Shakespeare and figure the woman not only as the object but also as the cause of desire, the temptress, and hence the target of blame. Desire is premised upon a lack, a lack configured female and asso-ciated with death. There are many variations on this theme: in the seven-teenth century, John Donne bemoaned the sexual arousal women caused him, 'since each such act, they say, diminisheth the length of life a day' (Hollander 1973:543); in Freud, woman-who-lacks-a-penis is associated with castration, which in turn is a sign/threat of death. The theme of desire, lack, death and the female runs with a few exceptions through Western culture from Plato to Lacan (Dollimore 1998; Schrift 2000).

The voice of desire in Shakespeare's 'Sonnet' is obviously a male voice; the desire is masculine desire. So also, though much more subtly, is the desire for beauty and goodness of the aspiring philosopher in Plato's *Symposium*: the object of his love and of his desire is whatever he isn't, or whatever he hasn't got – that is to say, whatever he is lacking in, 'he who has turned away from woman and procreancy of the body and joined himself instead to a male friend for procreancy of the spirit rather than the flesh' (*Symposium* 200c, 209a). The gender of desire is not often emphasized in the writings of phi-losophers, but insofar as they take the masculine position as universal and normative, they also take for granted that their (masculine) account of desire is universal.

But what would happen if a woman voiced desire? How might her desire be configured? Women are of course not supposed to desire: good women are configured as the submissive receptacles of male desire, a representation of women which fits neatly with the configuration of desire as lack. Yet there do exist women's voices waiting to be heard, voices which speak of desire but do so in a different register. In the following section I shall listen closely to one of them: the voice of Julian of Norwich, a fourteenth-century English mystic and theologian. I shall explore her configuration of desire, showing that it is based not on lack but on plenitude and delight. Desire here is not linked with death and madness and 'evermore unrest', nor is woman seen as either passive receptacle or treacherous temptress. Instead, desire is linked with natality and flourishing, beauty and creativity; and women and men equally can be full of grace.

I think that it is no coincidence that a major voice offering an alternative configuration of desire is that of a woman. Nevertheless it would be wrong to give an impression of exact gender mapping. Julian's configuration of desire rests on a tradition of Christian spirituality heavily dependent on that of Augustine, as I shall show – though her emphasis often falls differently. Moreover, there have been modern secular male writers – Spinoza, Nietzsche, Deleuze – who reject the idea of desire as premised upon a lack; contrariwise, there are women writers who fall in with the idea. Nevertheless, I believe that the resources for reconfiguration offered in the writings of Julian enable us to see how desire and gender can be thought together in a way that is positive for both women and men, rather than at women's expense.

Julian of Norwich: Desire reduplicated

The famous *Showings* of Julian of Norwich, the book in which she recounts her experience of God in a period of acute illness, is permeated with desire. The theme of longing runs throughout the book; indeed the actual word 'desire' is among the most prominent in her text. In the early chapters, where she gives some background to her experiences, she emphasizes that her youth had been filled with longing. She 'desired three graces by the gift of God', namely, recollection of the Passion of Christ, a bodily illness, and most importantly, three 'wounds': 'contrition, compassion, and longing with the will for God'. The prayers are unusual, as she herself clearly recognized. What is important for this chapter is that she makes plain that all are subsumed in the final one, longing with the will for God. This request (but not the others) she continues to make 'urgently' and 'without any condition' (1978:178–9). There is, here, a doubling of desire. Julian prays for longing for God: her desire is to be given desire; she longs to long. Throughout her text this desire for the reduplication of longing is repeated with gentle insistence, not in the fever or frenzy of Shakespeare's 'Sonnet', but nevertheless forming a steady undercurrent of the work.

Now, there is something very strange going on here if we assume the symbolic of desire as indicating lack. Obviously Julian would not pray urgently for something unless she desired it; yet what she is praying for is the desire itself. So she already has what she asks for; indeed unless she already had it she could not ask for it. How, then, is her prayer, her desire for desire, to *be* interpreted?

Readers of Julian's *Showings* cannot help but be struck by the spectacular visions she had of the dying Christ. In analytic philosophy of religion, the mystical visions of a range of figures are often lumped together without much reference to historical or textual context and discussed in relation to questions about the evidential value of 'mystical experience' for claims for the existence of God. Moreover, the god whose existence is thus discussed, is assumed to be the omni-everything patriarch of 'classical theism' (Swinburne 1977; Davis 1989; Alston 1991; Pike 1992). I do not think feminists should have much patience with these discussions; certainly they are nowhere near Julian's focus. Even the visions themselves were not her primary interest.

Important though they were, for her they were a means to an end, and that end was increasing love and desire for God, the desire she desired. Julian is emphatic that 'I am not good because of the revelations, but only if I love God better ... for I am sure that there are many who never had revelations or visions ... who love God better than I' (1978:191).

The visions do not satiate Julian's desire for God. Rather, they serve to answer her prayer for desire; they reduplicate her longing even while also satisfying it. Throughout her text Julian's desire continually increases even while it is being fulfilled. In her account of her second revelation she puts it vividly:

> For I saw him and sought him ... And when by his grace we see something of him, then we are moved by the same grace to seek with great desire to see him for our greater joy. So I saw him and sought him, and I had him and lacked him; and this is and should be our ordinary undertaking in this life ...
>
> (193)

'When we see him' and therefore our desire is fulfilled, *then* 'we are moved to seek with great desire to see him'. It is the fulfilment of desire that motivates desire.

Now, from a post-Freudian perspective all of this could be read as thinly disguised eroticism, where sexual desire is increased precisely by its satisfaction. It is not enough if God the divine lover gives himself to her once: indeed, one encounter inflames the desire for more. Moreover, Julian does here explicitly use the language of lack; and taking this passage on its own, it would seem to fit snugly into the Western trajectory of desire modelled upon sexuality and premised upon a lack: a gentler, less tormented version than we find in Shakespeare's 'Sonnet' but part of the same pattern. I want to argue, however, that this is not the case. Rather, I believe that Julian fundamentally rejects the binary: lack *or* fulfilment, desire *or* satisfaction, just as she can also be shown to reject other binaries such as 'body *or* soul', 'God *or* world', 'Father *or* Mother'. As I shall show, in Julian's text it is not only lack upon which desire is based, but also plenitude; indeed without plenitude the lack does not appear.

The reciprocity of desire

To support these suggestions, an initial step is to investigate the work of longing in Julian's text. The first thing that becomes obvious is that in her view, Julian's longing for God is reciprocated by – indeed is a reflection of – God's longing for her, and for all of humanity. The divine desire, the love that longs for reciprocation, is at the heart of the love of God which Julian experiences; Jesus, she says, stands 'moaning and mourning' until we receive divine love, and desire it in our turn. So important is this reciprocity of desire that it could stand as the theme of her whole book: 'Love was his meaning', as she sums it up (342). Perhaps nowhere is the theme of divine desire more explicit than in that part of her vision where she sees the drying wind blowing on Jesus as he hung crucified, and the great thirst which this caused him: this thirst she interprets as 'his longing in love for us'. Nor did this come to an end when at last he died. Rather,

> he still has that same thirst and longing which he had upon the Cross, which desire, longing and thirst, as I see it, were in him from without beginning; and he will have this until the time that the last soul which will be saved has come up into his bliss.
>
> (230–1)

The thirst of Christ is interpreted as an unquenchable desire for human salvation and bliss, a longing rooted in divine love and generosity. Few of us now, whether religious or not, would be comfortable with the conventional religious worldview or the cosmology of heaven and hell that Julian takes for granted, or with what seems to be a valorization of suffering. However, I propose to stick with the discomfort for a bit longer in order to get clearer on Julian's configuration of desire. As I hope will become clear, this configuration is not dependent on the cosmology out of which it arises, and offers a significant alternative to the idea of desire premised on a lack.

The important point here is that in Julian's teaching, human longing for God, the desire for desire, is a response to divine longing illustrated in the thirst of Christ. It is not self-generated. As she puts it,

> ... truly is there in God a quality of thirst and longing; and the power of this longing in Christ enables us to respond to his longing. ... And this quality of longing and thirst comes from God's everlasting goodness ...
>
> (231)

Human desire for God is a reciprocation and mimesis of divine desire. Mimetic desire, in Julian's terms, has its source in the divine.

The reciprocity of desire is nowhere more clearly presented than in Julian's teaching on prayer, where she says that 'Our Lord God is following us, helping our desire' (254). She claims this insight on the basis of her fourteenth revelation, where Christ says to her in very strong terms, 'I am the ground of your beseeching. First, it is my will that you should have it, and then I make you to wish it, and then I make you to beseech it' (248). This being the case, it is to be expected that desire – including desire for desire – will continually increase even while it is being fulfilled, as already discussed. But this is not a matter, in Julian, of 'the more you get, the more you want' in a Lacanian sense, of ever-shifting desire whose satiation only escalates the lack. Julian puts it much more in terms of growing fulfilment and flourishing. In her words,

> And then we can do no more than contemplate him and rejoice, with a great and compelling desire to be wholly united with him, and attend to his motion and rejoice in his love and delight in his goodness ...
>
> (255)

At this point, standard moves in the philosophy of religion would be either to analyse Julian's account of her experience and its evidential value for the credibility of theism, as already mentioned, or to begin to ask questions about the consistency of the concept of God or the coherence of the theism that Julian presupposes. Is the idea of divine desire compatible with a doctrine of God's impassibility? If God is in need of nothing, is it coherent to speak of divine desire? But these are not the questions that I want to pursue, or at least not in the terms in which analytic philosophy of religion pursues them. In the first place, I find them philosophically and religiously flat footed, as though what is of deepest significance could be captured in neat little analytical or dogmatic boxes. Moreover, most feminists, myself included, do not find conventional theology congenial anyway. If we ever held to it (and I did), we have rejected it, for a range of moral, intellectual, and social/political reasons. Even if its consistency and coherence could be shown, so what? But third, and most importantly, these analytical moves distract attention away from what I find to be far more interesting and pertinent questions, in this instance the question of how desire can be reconfigured. Partly because of the sterility of analytic philosophy of religion, and partly because many feminists adopt the secularism of modernity as completely and unthinkingly as our forebears adopted Christendom, the resources of religion are often untapped for their fascinating promptings as to how to rethink the discourses and practices of post/modernity. The discourse of desire, important in itself, is I believe (but cannot be shown in one essay) only one instance of many more of the central and problematic discourses of modernity where the resources of religious texts (perhaps especially texts by women) indicate how we might think otherwise.

Plenitude and lack

For Julian the desire for God is the most fundamental of all human desires. If this is mimetic – if the desire *of* the divine is always already the ground of desire *for* the divine – then to understand human desire it is necessary to understand divine desire. This opens two possibilities: either human desire is not premised upon a lack, or else even God is characterized by that lack. Yet it would appear that neither of these options would be theologically acceptable to Julian, given that she wished to remain loyal to the teachings of 'holy Church'. The first alternative seems at odds with the teaching that humans need God, and indeed contrary to the whole doctrine of sin, whereby humankind is perceived as alienated from God and thereby in a state of fundamental lack. The second is firmly contradicted by the medieval doctrine that there is no lack in God; God is all plenitude. But then how can God desire? And in what sense could human desire, mired in sin and lack, be mimetic of divine desire? Was Julian just muddled? – a beautiful mystic, perhaps, but theologically confused? (She was, after all, 'only a woman': how much can we expect?!) (Cf. Vandenbrouke 1968:425, 363.)

I think not. In the first place, the theme and the vocabulary of desire, while central to Julian, is by no means unique to her. On the contrary, it was integral to the tradition of spirituality in Christendom from late antiquity onwards, which taught that human longing for God is and can only be a response to God's prior longing for humanity. A pivotal example for Christendom in this regard is Augustine of Hippo. Augustine has been much castigated, rightly, for the ways in which his emphasis on the desire of and for God led him to denigrate other forms of human desire, especially sexual desire. At his influential worst, he separated spiritual desires from physical ones, and fostered a misogynist suspicion of the body that has done incalculable harm as it resonated through the Christian centuries. But there is more to Augustine. In his *Confessions*, from first to last he represents his increasing longing for God in terms of God's desire for him. He exclaims, addressing God:

> You called me; you cried aloud to me; you broke my barrier of deafness. You shone upon me; your radiance enveloped me; you put my blindness to flight. You shed your fragrance about me; I drew breath and now I gasp for your sweet odour. I tasted you, and now I hunger and thirst for you. You touched me, and I am inflamed with love of your peace.
>
> (X.27; 1961:232)

When Julian says that she finds in herself 'desire, which was that I might see him more and more; understanding and knowing that we shall never have perfect rest until we see him clearly and truly in heaven' (1978:261), she is echoing Augustine's famous words: 'You have made us for yourself, and our hearts can find no rest until they rest in you' (1.1; 1961).

Julian and Augustine do indeed acknowledge lack, in fact the urgency of their desire (though not the frenzy) compares to that in Shakespeare's 'Sonnet'; it would be foolish and pointless for anyone to pretend they were without needs. Julian says so explicitly: 'I had him and lacked him'. Augustine uses metaphors of extreme need: blindness, deafness, gasping for breath, hunger and thirst. But the important question is: where do these needs come from? How do they arise? In Julian, as we have seen, desire for God is responsive; the longing to long is already divine grace. Thus it is not the need that initiates the desire. Rather, desire is generated, paradoxically, by its fulfilment. Lack is the premise of desire only in a secondary sense; at bottom desire is premised on plenitude. Only when she already has God can she want God.

In the Christendom upon which Julian drew, God lacks nothing. God's desire is construed not as need but as the overflow of divine love and goodness; the theological term is 'grace'. God's longing for humanity is understood not as a manifestation of divine need – God is complete in God's self – but as generosity. It is a longing better characterized in terms of fecundity and overflowing joy and abundance than in terms of lack or scarcity. Creation is the central symbol of such divine fecundity: the Spirit of God brooding over chaos like a hen over her eggs, bringing forth abundance and variety. Thus in Julian's text, immediately after her expression of desire for God and her prayer for the reduplication of that desire, she continues, 'for [God's] goodness fills all creatures and all his blessed works full, and endlessly overflows in them' (1978:184). God is addressed as the one whose love and desire for humankind is an overflowing of generous plenitude. God is understood as wholly self-sufficient; and God's desire for the world and for humankind is sheer gift of divine abundance.

Death and natality

Julian is greatly preoccupied with sin in much of her text, precisely because she sees it as separating humankind from God, creating absence and lack. She wonders why 'the beginning of sin was not prevented' (224), and considers sin the 'sharpest scourge' that can strike anyone. Sin, in Christendom, is understood at least in part precisely as desire, *evil* desire, desire for what will actually harm ourselves and/or others: thus Shakespeare's tormented 'desire is death'. From this it might be thought that it is sin that generates human need for salvation; sin therefore that lies at the basis of desire for God. But Julian sees it otherwise. In her view, sin and its distortions of the individual and society are precisely what *block* desire, not what produce it.

One way of blocking desire is of course to deflect its passion into inappropriate and unfulfilling channels; hence again Shakespeare's 'fever, longing still for that which longer nurseth the disease'. But it would be misguided to make such distorted desire the paradigm by which desire itself should be understood. As we have seen, in Julian's terms desire for God – and all good desire – arise not out of sin or need but out of response to divine desire; if lack in itself could never produce desire, sin is even less likely to do so. Had there been no sin, all our desire would be for the good; our desire for God would be based on unimpeded response to divine presence, not on lack or divine absence. A consequence of this view is that our desires need to be healed and trained away from their harmful and alienating distortions; we need a therapy of desire. But that is very different from seeing desire as death, or wishing that it could be eradicated.

Julian presents a striking image which makes her meaning clearer. She writes:

> And in this time I saw a body lying on the earth, which appeared oppressive and fearsome and without shape and form, as it were a devouring pit of stinking mud; and suddenly out of this body there sprang a most beautiful creature, a little child, fully shaped and formed, swift and lively and whiter than the lily, which quickly glided up to heaven.
>
> (306)

In the immediate context, Julian elaborates this in terms of a contrast between a foul body and a beautiful soul. But as I have argued elsewhere (2000:138–40), contrary to appearances, this is not another example of the body-hating dualism for which Christendom is notorious: Julian's overall acceptance and delight in the body and its functions puts her well beyond such dualism. Rather, we have here a recognition (paralleled by Julian's parable of the servant who falls into a ditch and becomes utterly befouled while attempting to do his lord's bidding) that the filth and grime are only 'skin deep'; they can be washed away. The contrast is that between a clay doll, which no matter how much it is cleaned still remains clay until it is washed away without remainder, and a lovely child who has fallen into the mud and needs a thorough cleaning to be restored to beauty, but it is not mud through and through. In this image I believe Julian's anthropology is encapsulated, and with it her account of sin and desire.

Now, what becomes clear is that an account such as Julian's offers possibilities for a reconfiguration of desire that is not dependent upon the conventional Christendom in which Julian couches it. To draw the contrast, we might think, for instance, of Freudian–Lacanian psychoanalytic theory. Here we find that desire is paradigmatically deathly; as Freud presents it in the (highly gendered) account of the *'Fort-Da'* game in *Beyond the Pleasure Principle* (Freud [1920] 1984), desire seeks repetition, but repetition always looks to stasis and is ultimately connected with the death drive. Or in more Lacanian terms, desire is founded on the loss of the (m)other and the fragmented 'self' that tries to hold itself together by aggressivity and violence, while all the while, the (m)other for which the self yearns (and by which it is threatened) is configured as lack and linked with death. Desire *itself* – not just distorted or alienated desire – is deathly (cf. Lacan 1977:8–29; Rose 1993).

But I want to challenge that view. The theme of death and mortality, no less than the theme of desire as premised upon a lack (and linked with it), runs through the Western cultural symbolic as an existential and philosophical category, to the virtual exclusion of what is surely at least as important: that we are natals. It is as necessary for us to ponder the implications of the fact that we were born as it is to ponder the fact that we will die. Our natality signals that we are creatures with beginnings, and indicates the possibility of newness, creativity; I shall return to this below. It signals also the inescapability of our gendered bodiliness: everyone who is born is born of a woman's body and is in turn a gendered body, not a sexless soul. Moreover, by the *fact* of our natality we are connected with other bodies, first with our mother and ultimately with the whole web of life on earth. We are not atomistic individuals, sprung like mushrooms out of the ground as Hobbes once fantasized; without a supportive interconnected network we would not have survived. The fact of our natality thus has ethical and political consequences as surely as does the fact that we will die. For every Plato who ponders death as the release of the soul from the prison-house of the body, and for every Heidegger who sees confrontation with mortality as freeing us for authenticity, there is a gap in the tradition for a philosopher who ponders our gendered, interconnected embodiment and all its creative potential.

I have discussed this in more detail elsewhere (1998:Chapter 7). What I want to highlight here is the importance of natality for the representation of desire. What if we were to take a leaf from Julian's book, and reject the idea that we are mud through and through, pondering instead the beautiful child? I suggest that such consideration of natality leads to rethinking the characterization of desire as metonymous death.

To begin with the process of birth itself: in psychoanalytic literature, the birth of an infant is treated as *expulsion* from the womb, as faeces are expelled in defecation, or as Adam and Eve are expelled from the Garden of Eden in punishment for sin. The impetus comes from the mother, who gets rid of the foetus. But surely we should stop and think about this model of expulsion. It is certainly true that during the period of labour, especially in its late stages, 'expulsion' is exactly what the woman wants; to that extent the model is accurate. But that is where its accuracy ends. A baby is not a piece of shit, nor is it being punished for wrong-doing. Rather, it is welcomed as new life. And is the infant reluctant to be born? Does it want to stay in the womb? Whatever the answer (and it is not obvious how an answer could be established) it is certainly the case that from the time a baby is born it responds with increasing eagerness to stimulation from the world around it, grasping for new experiences, desiring life and responding to all its wonder. Desire, surely, is here premised on possibility and the active grasp of the newness and creative impulse inherent in natality. My point is not to deny the reality of the death drive, let alone the struggle and cost involved for an infant in the will to life, even in highly privileged material and social circumstances. But to characterize the infant as *only* passive or reluctant, or to make the death drive the paradigm of *all* desire, seems to me wrong. It is rather like assimilating a beautiful child who has fallen in the mud with a clay figure, which may be prettily dressed but actually is mud all the way through.

Creativity

The theme of enthusiasm for life which emerges when we take natality as seriously as mortality thus invites a different configuration of desire than that which is central to psychoanalytic theory, or indeed to much of the trajectory of Western philosophical thought. I wish now to go further, and consider what this active desire comes to, and in what terms its activity can be understood.

In the writings of Julian, and the Augustinian tradition of which she is a part, divine plenitude is closely linked with creativity. Thus in a famous passage of the *Confessions*, Augustine asks repeatedly, 'What do I love when I love my God?' What is it that draws this responsive desire from me? He questions a range of physical things: the sea and its creatures, the winds and sky and stars, the earth and its wonders, and asks of each one: 'But what is my God?' In turn they reply, 'We are not your God'. Augustine persists, and at last his answer comes: 'Clear and loud they answered, "God is he who made us". I asked these questions simply by gazing at these things, and their beauty was all the answer they gave' (X.6; 1961:212).

I shall return below to the centrality of beauty for active desire. Here I wish first to consider what is involved in creativity. In Augustine and Julian, and the tradition of spirituality of which they form a part, creation and re-creation is fundamental to the configuration of desire, both divine and human. As already mentioned, God's good abundance is expressed in the created world; and human desire for God is a response based on our status as created beings, made in such a way that responsive desire is part of our nature. As Julian has it, 'our natural will is to have God, and God's good will is to have us' (1978:185). And Augustine, placing similar weight on responsive desire, further emphasizes that divine creativity does not rely for resources on anything that exists already. He says,

> But by what means did you make heaven and earth? What tool did you use for this vast work? You did not work as a human craftsman does, making one thing out of something else as his mind directs. Nor did you have in your hand any matter from which you could make heaven and earth, for where could you have obtained matter which you had not yet created, in order to use it as material for making something else? Does anything exist by any other cause than that you exist?
>
> (XI.5; 1961:257)

In Augustine and in Christian theology following his thought, this is an expression of the doctrine of *creatio ex nihilo*, creation out of nothing. More properly, it is creation out of the plenitude of the creator. It is not that there is something called 'nothing' out of which God creates, but rather that the resources for creation are not external to God but are part of the divine fullness.

Although Augustine is here contrasting divine with human creativity, the contrast actually only works on the basis of a presumed underlying parallel: both the divine creator and human creators are makers of the new. To be creative is to be innovative. It is not simply to repeat what already exists. Creativity is thus related to natality, the birth of something that has not existed before. The contrast between divine and human creation is not that only God can make the new, but that only God can make the new out of materials that did not already exist. Unlike God, human creators use existing materials, and are influenced by what has gone before. Nonetheless creation is not repetition; it is the emergence of the new.

Now, few of us would accept the Bible story of creation, or even Augustine's sophisticated rendition of it, as a factual account of the origin of the universe. Nevertheless, I suggest that these theological articulations of creativity repay reconsideration in relation to natality and desire. What motivates human creators, and from where do they get their resources? Good biographies of artistic creators try to discover the influences on their lives and art: their childhood background and traumas, previous works in their field, their cultural and personal history and its painful and resourceful stimulation. All of these are of course illuminating for an understanding of their work. Yet in case after case their biographers recognize in these giants of human creativity an overwhelming desire, almost a compulsion to create, in the most adverse circumstances imaginable, of poverty, isolation or illness. They paint and write and compose out of the fullness of their hearts and minds, out of their plenitude. Their urgent desire is to create, to make the new. Moreover, it is not to create in the abstract, but to paint *this* picture, compose *this* symphony, influenced by the past but also unlike anything there has been before. Is their desire best characterized as premised upon a lack?

I suggest that it is not. Although it is always possible to find in the biography and psychology of creative women and men lacks which have deeply affected their creativity for good or ill, their creative work, their making of newness and their desire to create cannot be *reduced* to lack. It is rather out of the fullness of their hearts and minds – a fullness often developed by long years of hard work and practice – that they find both the resources and the desire to create. Human creativity arises (as does divine creativity in Augustinian theology) out of overflowing plenitude, a plenitude which cannot be denied its creative desire and whose greatest fulfilment is the making of something new. There is no need to romanticize this; there is much hard work as well. Moreover, motivation is always complex. But that very complexity is undervalued if plenitude is ignored and desire is linked exclusively with lack and death.

Beauty

The configuration of desire developed up to this point in this paper, from a rereading of Julian of Norwich and the tradition of Christian spirituality in which she stands, has shown that not only divine desire but human desire too can be the out-flowing of inner resources; the theological model is helpful not as a literalistic account of divine desire but as a different approach to human longing. But then how is desire mimetic? Is there a way of interpreting this mimesis which goes beyond the theological pieties out of which it emerges?

Another way of asking these questions is to probe creativity more deeply. If creativity – of art or music or thought or human relationship – arises out of fullness rather than emptiness, where does that plenitude come from? What are the resources for the fullness that eventually overflows in the making of the new? It may not be the case that 'desire is death'; indeed I am arguing that desire may be rooted in natality. But where desire is in fact premised on a lack, and coupled with fear, greed and insecurity, it is assuredly death-dealing; we need to ask not only about the subjects of desire but also about its victims. Who pays the price for the satisfaction of Western desires? When we turn the question around like that, it becomes urgent to find ways of entertaining desires that bring creativity and flourishing rather than destruction. It is also obvious that desire has been thought in the West to be the prerogative of privileged men; and that women, colonized peoples, and the earth itself have too often paid the price of those desires. Indeed, the configuration of desire as death – the death and loss of the (male) subject of desire – can be seen for what it is: a classic case of guilty projection, in which the perpetrators of death configure themselves as its victims.

Neither feminists nor philosophers of religion have shown much interest in examining the sources of human creativity. When the topic has been discussed in modernity it has usually fallen under the rubric of aesthetic theory, which has focused on such terms as 'genius' or 'hero of the imagination'. Of whatever dubious use such terms may be, they do not provide much insight into the question of the source of plenitude for creativity. To be more accurate, they shut down such questions by suggesting that the plenitude is innate or just given, a rare but natural quality which we must respect or even treat with awe. But might we not rather explain creativity and foster its resources in a way that would enhance its availability for the transformation of post/ modern culture, fixated as it is on lack, competition and violence?

I suggest that once again suggestions emerge from religious writers like Julian and Augustine who configure desire differently and who place plenitude and creativity at its centre. What do they see as the source of creativity? What exactly is it that evokes their response? In Julian of Norwich, beauty (or 'loveliness' as she often has it) is central to responsive desire. Though she does not select beauty as a separate theme for discussion, it forms a steady undercurrent in her book. Perhaps the best-known illustration is that part of the vision in which she is given the whole universe like a hazelnut to hold in the palm of her hand. She is amazed at its fragile beauty, concerned about how it can last; and she is given the assurance of God's tender care for it (1978:183). In her visions of Jesus on the cross, she makes much of the beauty of his *face*, 'the fairest of heaven, the flower of earth' (194), and sees it as a revelation of divine beauty, marred and discoloured by the sufferings of the crucifixion. She responds to the loveliness of his face – 'lovely' both in the sense of 'loving' and in the sense of beautiful. Indeed, it is precisely this loveliness that evokes the reduplication of her desire. The divine plenitude that calls for her mimetic desire is experienced by Julian as loveliness.

The privileging of beauty in Julian's writings echoes that in the Augustinian tradition of spirituality in which she stands. I have already quoted Augustine's account of the answer of the earth and sky and stars to his question about their creator: 'Clear and loud they answered, "God is he who made us". I asked these questions simply by gazing at these things, and their *beauty* was all the answer they gave' (X.6; 1961:212; emphasis mine). For Augustine, the overflowing creative plenitude of the divine is expressly characterized as beauty; and it is this beauty which evokes his response. Time and again he returns to the theme.

> But what do I love when I love my God? Not material beauty or beauty of a temporal order; not the brilliance of earthly light, so welcome to our eyes; not the sweet melody of harmony and song; not the fragrance of flowers, perfumes and spices; not manna or honey; not limbs such as the body delights to embrace. ... And yet, when I love him, it is true that I love a light of a certain kind, a voice, a perfume, a food, an embrace ...
>
> (X.6; 211)

These words have often been read as denoting a sharp division between the physical and the spiritual, with the admonition that physical things of beauty are to be rejected for some spiritualized or other-worldly beauty. There is much in Augustine that lends itself to such a dualistic interpretation and its fateful and misogynist consequences for Western culture. But I believe that a more generous reading is also called for, one which recognizes how Augustine is struggling to come to terms with the heartfelt intensity of his own response to beauty. As he says in a later passage,

> The eyes delight in beautiful shapes of different sorts and bright and attractive colours. I would not have these things take possession of my soul. Let God possess it, he who made them all. ... Yet those who have learnt to praise you for this as well as for your other gifts, O God, Maker of all things, sing you a hymn of praise for it.
>
> (X.34; 239–40)

The beauties Augustine finds in the world around him, in music, and even in erotic attraction, are not themselves gods. Therefore to stop at them would be to stop short, to make them into idols. Nevertheless, they are beautiful, and their beauty is a reflection of divine beauty. Augustine's rejection of their divinity is not a rejection of their beauty; rather he responds to them, and through them to God their maker. Their beauty tells him about the divine beauty. As he says later on, 'It was you, then, O Lord, who made them, you who are beautiful, for they too are beautiful' (XI.4; 256). And from the depths of his being he cries out, 'Late have I loved you, O Beauty so ancient and so new, late have I loved you!' (X.27).

Moreover, Augustine is clear that human creativity is mimetic desire, response to the beauty of divine creation. The makers of the new are able to be creative because of this divine plenitude with which they are filled. He says,

> the beauty which flows through men's minds into their skillful hands comes from that Beauty which is above their souls and for which my soul sighs all day and night. And it is from this same supreme Beauty that men who make things of beauty and love it in its outward forms derive the principle by which they judge it.
>
> (X.34; 240)

The resources that enable creativity, the desire to make something new out of overflowing inner plenitude, are nurtured by beauty; it is as a response to beauty that creativity can be set free.

Perhaps the reason that desire has been so persistently configured as a lack in the Western symbolic is that symbolic has been preoccupied with truth (and with good) and has very largely ignored beauty and its resources. But the writers of the spiritual tradition in Christendom have much to say that cuts the other way. In their view, it is the beauty of holiness that evokes a response of desire and yearning at its attractiveness. It thereby helps to form the character of the one who responds to it, drawing them also to be makers of the new, whether in artefact or in the shape of their lives and actions.

There is of course also much in Christendom, even in the writers I have cited, that is contrary to this theme of delighted and creative human response to beauty. There is a rejection of the material world, a disparagement of its pleasures, a fear of its delights. The beauty of the human body, of sexuality, particularly of women, is often represented as temptation or evil rather than as the outpouring of divine desire. There is also the use of beauty for display and ostentation; the magnificence of medieval cathedrals and their contents, for example, can be read as expressions of piety and mimetic creativity, but also as technologies of power. And always there is the question: what counts as beauty; and who is doing the counting?

All of that being granted, it remains the case that there is in this emphasis on beauty that we find in the writers of Christian spirituality something crucial to a reconfiguration of desire. It is the insistence that beauty evokes longing, desire is ignited by loveliness, and responds creatively. It is engaged with natality, the making of the new, not out of preoccupation with death but as a mimetic response to overflowing resources. This is a responsive desire, not self-generated; but it is desire premised on plenitude rather than on a lack, on overflowing generosity rather than scarcity, on creativity rather than on exclusionary violence and death. Indeed, it is through such engagement with beauty and natality that lack and death themselves can be better understood, so that they stand not as binary opposites to plenitude and life but as elements within them, never denied or without value, but taking their appropriate, secondary, place.

My argument is *not* that the cosmology or the doctrines of early Christendom are necessary for this reconfiguration of desire; quite the reverse. In fact, even in the ordinary experiences of our lives we can observe the relationship between beauty, creative plenitude, and mimetic desire. The sight of the clouds hanging in a mountain valley or a tree turning to burnished red makes us wish we could paint, or take a good photograph, or at least send a postcard, partly to preserve it in memory and partly to share it with others who would have a similar creative response: 'I wish you were here; you'd love this'. The makers of the new in art and music and writing nourish themselves with beauty and in their turn overflow with creative desire (Scarry 1999:6).

But although the reconfiguration of desire is not logically dependent upon Christendom, nevertheless the resources of its spirituality can serve as a reminder of a countervailing strand in the Western symbolic to the more usual theme that desire is death. In thinkers like Julian of Norwich and Augustine we can discern ways of thinking otherwise, recognizing desire as an aspect of our natality and mimetic creativity. I would not wish to be understood as advocating a business-as-usual approach to theological orthodoxy; and I hope I have made plain my rejection of the usual boundaries of the philosophy of religion. However, I contend that if feminists adopt an unquestioning secularism which rejects as valueless the resources of spirituality, we lose more than we gain. It is necessary, as Luce Irigaray has said, to 'rethink religion' – and, I suggest, to rethink secularism too, in order not to acquiesce in the symbolic of lack and death in which post/modern desire is invested. That such a reconfiguration of desire will also require a revolution in psychoanalytic theory, not to mention a restructuring of social and political thought and practice, can hardly be denied. What is at issue is nothing less than a transformation of the world from a self-perpetuating fixation on death to an opening of natality. But then, transformation is what feminism – and religion – are all about.

Chapter 12

Feminism and flourishing

Gender and metaphor in feminist theology

I will heal their faithlessness; I will love them freely,
for my anger has turned from them.
I will be as the dew to Israel;
he shall blossom as the lily,
he shall strike root as the poplar;
his shoots shall spread out;
his beauty shall be like the olive, and his fragrance like Lebanon.
They shall return and dwell beneath my shadow,
they shall flourish as a garden;
they shall blossom as the vine,
their fragrance shall be like the wine of Lebanon.

(Hos. 14.3–7)

The promise of the love of God for Israel as it comes to Hosea the prophet is a
promise of flourishing. God's beneficence is not niggardly; Israel will 'dwell
beneath God's shadow' and will 'flourish as a garden'. The same promise of
flourishing is made repeatedly in the Wisdom literature: 'The tent of the righteous shall flourish' (Prov. 14.11); 'The righteous flourish like the palm tree' (Ps.
92.12) or 'like a green leaf' (Prov. 11.28). To be sure, the wicked also are said to
flourish 'like a green bay tree' (Ps. 37.35); but their flourishing does not last: 'I
went by, and lo, he was gone: I sought him, but his place could nowhere be
found' (Ps. 37.36). By contrast, 'the steadfast love of the Lord is from everlasting
to everlasting upon those who fear him, and his righteousness to children's children' (Ps. 103.17). The prophet Zechariah, looking forward to a golden future,
specifically includes both women and men in the expected flourishing:

On that day the Lord their God will save them
for they are the flock of his people;
for like the jewels of a crown they shall shine on his land.
Yea, how good and how fair it shall be!
Grain shall make the young men flourish,
and new wine the maidens.

(Zech. 9.16–17)

In New Testament writings the vocabulary of flourishing has all but disappeared. Nevertheless, parallel concepts can be found, as for instance in the ideas of fullness and abundance, which, though they are not exactly the same as the concept of flourishing, nevertheless express many similar ideas. The great prayer of the writer of Ephesians, for example, expresses the desire that 'you ... may be filled with all the fullness of God', and continues with an exultation in God 'who by the power at work within us is able to do far more abundantly than all that we ask or think' (Eph. 3.19–20). In 2 Corinthians, where the context is an exhortation to generous giving to the poor, the writer assures his readers that 'God is able to provide you with every blessing in abundance, so that you may always have enough of everything and may provide in abundance for every good work' (9.8). Perhaps the most central of all the 'abundance' sayings is the one attributed to Jesus in the Fourth Gospel in which he speaks of himself as the good shepherd of the sheep, in contrast to thieves and robbers: 'The thief comes only to steal and kill and destroy; I have come that they may have life, and have it abundantly' (Jn 10.10).

In spite of this biblical emphasis, Christian theology since the Reformation has paid relatively little attention to the ideas of flourishing and abundance, focusing far more on the concept of salvation. It would be a strange theological dictionary or encyclopaedia that did not have substantial entries on 'salvation'; whereas few carry more than a passing reference to 'flourishing'.[1] The same is true of major theological writers. Karl Barth, for example, devotes the whole five volumes of Book IV of the *Church Dogmatics* to a discussion of the doctrine of reconciliation, within which the concept of salvation is central. 'Flourishing' or 'abundance' are not so much as mentioned in the index; and while it would be unfair to conclude from that that Barth had nothing to say about flourishing, it is obvious that its place in his thinking is far subsidiary to that of salvation (Barth 1977). The significant exceptions to the emphasis on salvation rather than flourishing are the theologians of liberation, whether Latin American, Black, or feminist, all of whom see flourishing as far more central to the Christian message than do traditional Eurocentric theologians. In Christian theology in Western modernity, 'salvation' has been a key term; 'flourishing' has not.

Why not? My intention in this chapter is not to trace out what theologians have to say about either salvation or flourishing, but rather to ask why it should be that one has received so much less attention than the other. I wish to examine some of the contrasting ingredients of the concepts of salvation and flourishing, and in so doing, point to some of the reasons why the former has been more congenial to theologians of modernity than the latter. My thesis is that the concept of salvation has been developed in a manner which marches in lockstep with the social and political projects of modernity, from colonialism to capitalism; whereas the concept of flourishing would challenge those projects. Furthermore, I will show that the contrast between salvation and flourishing is a gendered contrast; and that while I do not claim a one-to-one gender mapping, the emphasis on salvation rather than flourishing discloses and perpetuates the masculinist bias of Western theology.

As long ago as 1960, Valerie Saiving pointed to the gendered nature of theological reflection about sin and salvation. In an essay that proved to be a landmark for feminist theology, she showed that whereas theology had spoken of 'the human situation' in what we would now call a totalizing manner, gender differences need to be taken into account. In particular, the sins and temptations to which men are prone, especially pride and the will to power, are different from those which beset women, who are much more likely to be tempted by inadequate self-esteem and underdevelopment (Saiving 1979:37). Subsequent feminist theologians have built on Saiving's work, pointing out that, as Daphne Hampson puts it, 'the conception which is held as to what constitutes salvation presumably relates to the conception which is held of sin' (Hampson 1990:126). Thus if women are more in need of self-esteem and learning to take ourselves seriously, Hampson suggests that a concept of salvation as healing may be more helpful than a concept of salvation as the breaking of overweening pride or shattering the sinful ego.

This recognition of the significance of salvation as healing (rather than, for example, as destruction of the ego) is of enormous importance; indeed, if carried to its logical conclusion, especially if it were seen in global as well as individualistic terms, I believe that it would subvert many of the unhelpful conceptualizations of salvation which I will outline below. It may be possible (and some of the feminist writings already cited go some way towards this) to reform the doctrine of salvation in such a way that it could become liberating. But it may also be useful to attempt another approach altogether, namely to see how things would be different if, instead of (or in addition to) a theology of salvation, we were to develop a theology of flourishing. How would that change our theological perspective, not least in relation to the gendered social and political context in which theology is done?

It is useful to begin with some definitions. The word 'flourish' is etymologically linked with flowers, with blossoming. It is related to the Middle English *florir* and the Latin *florere*, which mean 'to flower'; perhaps it is not insignificant that the word 'flower' in Latin is in the feminine. As a noun form, a 'flourish' is the mass of flowers on a fruit tree, or the bloom of luxuriant, verdant growth. In the more common verb form, to flourish is to blossom, to thrive, to throw out leaves and shoots, growing vigorously and luxuriantly. In the human sphere it denotes abundance, overflowing with vigour and energy and productiveness, prosperity, success and good health. The concept of flourishing is a strongly positive concept; one who flourishes is going from strength to strength.

'Salvation', on the other hand, is a term which denotes rescue. One is saved *from* something: from drowning, from calamity, from loss. These have negative connotations; it would be an odd turn of phrase to say that one had been saved from something desirable. To be saved means to be delivered from a situation which was problematic or even intolerable; there is a sense of crisis and of rescue from danger which is wholly absent from the notion of flourishing. It is only in an extended sense that one could speak of salvation in terms of healing, and it would necessitate seeing the 'illness' in terms of a crisis or an intolerable situation. 'Salvation' implies that there has been need of an urgent rescue, or calamity would befall.

Moreover, the concepts of flourishing and salvation, respectively, imply a different source or impetus. Salvation normally implies rescue by someone; there is a *saviour*. The remedy for the negative situation must come from outside the situation itself; the people who need to be saved cannot normally save themselves from drowning or disaster. By contrast, flourishing occurs from an inner dynamic of growth, with no need for interference from the outside. A plant left to itself in appropriate conditions will of its own nature grow and flower and bear fruit; in normal circumstances the idea of rescue would be inappropriate. There is a luxuriant self-sufficiency implied in the notion of flourishing, an inner impetus of natural energy and overflowing vigour. A movement or a person 'in full flourish' is vibrant and creative, blossoming and developing and coming to fruition. Although such flourishing of course draws upon external sources as a plant draws on the nutrients of the earth and air and water, this sort of continuing interdependence within the natural order is of an utterly different kind than the desperate need of someone in crisis for an external saviour or rescuer.

It is important to recognize that both 'salvation' and 'flourishing' are metaphors. Human beings are not literally plants which can thrive with luxuriant growth, and blossom and bear fruit. Neither, however, are human beings literally drowning, or in an immediately life-threatening crisis from which we must be rescued. In both cases, the words must be understood as depicting not a literal situation, but rather a way of understanding ourselves in relation to God and the world. As Janet Martin Soskice has emphasized, metaphors such as salvation and flourishing operate as models, opening out to disclose new possibilities of thought (Soskice 1985:114). But a metaphor used as a model may distort as well as disclose, especially if its metaphorical status is forgotten and it is not balanced by other, corrective models.

The language of salvation is so thoroughly ingrained into Christian theological thinking that we scarcely recognize that we are working with an extended metaphor; it has come to seem like literal theological truth. But when we contrast it with the metaphor of flourishing, we can begin to see that if we developed a theology around that model instead of (or as well as) the model of salvation, we would be led to quite a different account of the human condition and our relation to one another and to God, as I shall outline. It is of course not the case that there is equal support in Scripture (let alone tradition) for a theology based on the metaphor of flourishing as there is for a metaphor of salvation; developing such a theology requires the same 'search for lost coins'[2] that is typical of any theology of liberation which is working with the texts and traditions of the dominant discourse. Furthermore, though the language of salvation is more pervasive, there is at least *considerable* scriptural warrant for a theology of flourishing, as I have already pointed out and as will become more evident below. It therefore follows that theological concentration on the metaphor of salvation to the virtual exclusion of metaphors of flourishing represents a series of *choices*, whether conscious or unconscious, on the part of theologians. These choices, I wish to argue, are choices which can be seen to have at least as much to do with the social and political agendas of modernity as with specifically scriptural or religious requirements.

Fundamentally, the choice of the language of salvation rather than the language of flourishing in Christian theology both denotes and reinforces an anthropology of a very particular kind. If we think in terms of salvation, then the human condition must be conceptualized as a problematic state, a state in which human beings need urgent rescue, or calamity will befall. The human situation is a negative one, out of which we need to be delivered. In Christian theology, this obviously links with the idea of a divine saviour, and hence with Christology and with the doctrine of the incarnation and the trinity. But how would we characterize the human situation in all its diversity if we used instead the model of flourishing? We could then see human beings as having natural inner capacity and dynamic, able to draw on inner resources and interconnection with one another, and potential to develop into great fruitfulness. Whereas with the metaphor of salvation God is seen as the Saviour who intervenes from outside the calamitous situation to bring about a rescue, the metaphor of flourishing would lead instead to an idea of the divine source and ground, the one in whom we are 'rooted and grounded in love', in whom we 'live and move and have our being', the vine of whom we are the branches and can bring forth much fruit. The biblical references are deliberate; they show again that there is ample scriptural warrant for developing a theology of flourishing, of growth and fruition from an inner creative and healthy dynamic, rather than a theology which begins from the premise that the human condition is a negative condition or crisis from which we must be rescued by an external saviour. Of course, the concept of the divine would then also necessarily be much less deistic; God would not be thought of as a being external to the world, but rather as its source and wellspring; Jesus would not be envisaged as the heroic saviour entering human history from outside, but rather as one who manifests what it may mean to live fully and naturally in the creative justice of God. Concentration on the model of salvation to the virtual exclusion of the model of flourishing has meant that such balancing perspectives have to a large extent been eliminated from theological thought.

This imbalance is, I suggest, riddled with gender implications. In the first place, it is by now very well known that women have been identified with nature and the body, while men have been identified with culture and spirit.[3] Furthermore, sin and temptation have often been seen in Christian history as emanating from the physical, the body, especially from sexuality; as Eve was the mother of sin, so the body, associated with woman, continues to be its cause. It is of course true that there is plenty of scriptural warrant to reject this facile identification of sin with the body; the biblical concept of the flesh does not map onto the physical body nearly as neatly as Augustinian thinkers would have it do throughout the centuries of Christendom. Most theologians now would be embarrassed by Tertullian's thunderings that each woman is another Eve: 'You are the devil's gateway ... you are the first deserter of the divine law: you are she who persuaded him whom the devil was not valiant enough to attack'.[4] Biblical accuracy notwithstanding, however, in popular and even scholarly theological thinking, sin has been closely linked with bodiliness, especially with sexuality, and hence with woman.

All this is well known. What is not so often recognized is how this reinforces the patriarchal dimensions of the concept of salvation, and how disruptive of it the alternative model of flourishing would be. If we are working with the metaphor of salvation, then, as already noted, the human condition must be seen as sinful, broken, in crisis; this is our natural state, out of which we need to be rescued. However, if we think instead in terms of flourishing, then the natural condition of humanity is good; we need only to be allowed to develop normally. But this would entail a radical rethinking of the underlying assumptions about gender. If the female continues to be linked with nature, then contrary to tradition, the female must be linked with goodness, with the natural ability to flourish. Alternatively, if the male continues to be linked with goodness, then the male must now be linked with nature rather than with spirit or culture, that which stands over against nature, since it is from within nature, rather than from some external 'spiritual' source, that flourishing occurs. Or, even more radically, the whole millennia-old linkage of the male with spirit and goodness and the female with nature and sinfulness could be disrupted altogether. Whereas the model of salvation coheres unproblematically with a patriarchal structuring of society, a whole new theology of gender relations would be prompted by a theology modelled instead on flourishing.

Moreover, the alternative possibilities for conceptualizing Christ in a theology of flourishing would be highly congenial to feminist concerns. Many feminists have been deeply troubled by the masculinity of Christ; as Rosemary Radford Ruether put it, 'can a male saviour save women?' (Ruether 1983:116). In the struggle to retain both the understanding of Christ as Saviour and the historically undeniable maleness of Jesus, feminists have found themselves in a conundrum, sometimes suggesting an androgynous Christology (Ruether 1975:135) or a Christa figure, at other times trying to develop an account of salvation which is independent of the sex (or race or colour) of the saviour.[5] What none of these sufficiently recognizes, however, is that the idea of a saviour is a metaphor, part of the whole model of salvation. It is that model which requires a rescuer from outside the situation, and which constructs Jesus as the rescuer. Once again, the picture of a heroic figure swooping in to rescue the damsel in distress is all too reminiscent of familiar male fantasies. Such a picture would be a wild caricature of contemporary Christologies; but it does point to the ease with which the idea of a male saviour resonates with popular gender stereotypes. It would be of considerable value to feminist theology to develop as a counterbalance a theology of flourishing, in which the idea of a heroic saviour does not get a purchase. Instead, Jesus could be seen as the one who manifests what human flourishing can be, passionate for justice, full of humour and wisdom and insight, with the integrity of compassion taken to its furthest extent; such understandings of Jesus have indeed already been developed within feminist and womanist theology, though not explicitly in connection with a theology of flourishing.[6] Even those who wish to retain a traditional doctrine of trinity and incarnation can hardly deny that this is a much neglected understanding of Christology for which there is considerable scriptural warrant. Many, especially feminists, will want to go beyond this, and argue that the traditional doctrines should not merely be counterbalanced but should be replaced. I shall not argue for either position here, but simply point to the fruitfulness of the model of flourishing as against the model that calls for a heroic saviour.

Another highly significant aspect of the salvation model, from which much else follows, is that salvation is individualistic. A particular individual can be saved, singled out for rescue, though all others around perish. The combined influence of Luther and Calvin on Protestant theology has made this individualized aspect of salvation central to much subsequent theological thought. Luther, agonizing about the state of his soul and his eternal destiny, could not be content to accept that he was right with God in virtue of his membership of the Roman Church or even as a brother in the Augustinian monastery. Something else was necessary, something special, namely the grace of God to himself personally, appropriated by faith. No one could have faith for him; he himself must put his trust in God, and God would save him, Martin Luther, though all others should perish. And having thus committed himself to the grace of God by faith he was assured of his own salvation while the Pope and all the Roman Church were consigned to hell. Again, Calvinistic theology, with its vocabulary of election, invited people to ponder their personal eternal destiny, and ask themselves whether they were indeed among the elect, and whether this was confirmed in their lives. John Bunyan's *Pilgrim's Progress* is only one of many spiritual autobiographies of the early modern period which reveal the grip of this individualized, subjectivized understanding of salvation, in which the grace of God was observed at work in the inner self, the soul standing naked and alone before God, rescued by divine grace from eternal catastrophe and fleeing all companionship to undertake a spiritual journey to the celestial city (Bunyan 1967).

There have been many studies which have discussed the convoluted connections between these Protestant conceptions of personal salvation and the rise of capitalism and individualistic liberalism.[7] Without rehearsing them, I wish to point out two things. The first is that such individualism would be impossible in a theology built upon the model of flourishing rather than upon the model of salvation. The idea that one could flourish by oneself alone can get no purchase. Although Hobbes had a fantasy of men springing up as mushrooms out of the ground, 'come to full maturity without all kind of engagement to each other' (Hobbes 1841:109), his fantasy bears no relation to reality; every child is brought into the world in relation to people, and it is only through nurturing and care that a child can survive and thrive. It is within a nexus of relationships that we develop into personhood, learning to laugh and play and speak and think. At the most basic physical and psychological levels, human flourishing requires interconnection, not isolation.[8] The atomistic individualism upon which Western modernity is built is consistent with a theology modelled on the metaphor of salvation in a way in which it could never be consistent with a theology modelled on a metaphor of flourishing. Again, this is not to say that all those who develop a theology of salvation do so in individualistic terms. However, when the understanding of salvation is extended from particular individuals who are saved to larger aggregates or even to global salvation, then it is necessary either that these groups (or the world itself) be seen in peril or crisis and in need of rescue, or else the concept of salvation is stretched in ways that take it so far beyond the basic metaphor that clarity of meaning is lost.

A theology of flourishing would pre-empt some of these problems. Many of the biblical references to flourishing refer explicitly to the flourishing of the nation or community; indeed, the anthropology of atomistic individuals would be abhorrent to the mentality of the biblical prophets. In the sayings of Jesus, such as that of the vine and the branches, it is again implied that there are many branches, in relation with one another as well as with the vine. The model of flourishing is one which assumes the interconnectedness of people, and indeed of the ecosystem; flourishing is impossible by oneself alone. It is therefore a helpful model to set over against the competitive individualism which can easily be reinforced by the model of personal salvation.

However, it would not be correct to suppose that the metaphor of flourishing connotes a community romantically free from all ills. In fact, one of the questions which demands attention if one is thinking in terms of flourishing is the question of *who* flourishes, and at whose expense? In a world in which the North devours the labour of the South, with a huge flow of cash and goods from the poor to the rich, it is obvious that at least in economic terms it is possible for some groups to flourish off the backs of others, though their humanity may be stunted by it (George 1988). Indeed, Darwinian theories of natural selection have sometimes been used as a legitimation of such competition; after all, if the world is one in which only the fittest survive, then is it not the case that cut-throat competition is the law of survival even in the natural world? But this is to misrepresent the situation. Ecologists are tireless in reminding us of the interconnectedness of the ecosystem, the dependence of each form of life on all the others in the biosphere. Though Darwin drew the language of competitiveness from the capitalist economics of his time, even a moderate understanding of the interdependence of plant and animal life makes obvious how misplaced such language is as an overall account of their adaptation and flourishing. The metaphor of flourishing carries with it an idea of connectedness which contrasts with the individualism of the metaphor of salvation. In the former, the question 'who benefits and who loses?' is insistent and demands to be addressed: who is labouring and suffering in order that I may flourish? In the latter, it can get no purchase: unless one had the idea that only a certain number of people could be saved, the question of who was damned because of my salvation would not arise. A theology of flourishing, therefore, lends itself readily to a politicized theology of justice and protest; while a theology of salvation easily becomes introverted and depoliticized – which of course means that it supports the status quo.

If the first point about the particularist tendencies of a theology of salvation is that it easily falls in with the competitive individualism of global capitalism, the second is that such competitive disconnectedness is strongly gender-bound. It is a fundamental premise of psychoanalytic theory, whether Freudian or Lacanian, that a person is individuated by differentiation from their primary care-giver, a differentiation which also involves sexual self-identification. When, as in Western societies, masculinity is constructed as other than and oppositional to femininity, the consequence is that whereas a little girl can differentiate herself from her mother without developing an antagonism towards her, thereby retaining connectedness while still establishing her own identity, a little boy must pull himself away from his mother, and see himself in oppositional terms as a disconnected individual.[9] The interconnections between the construction of masculinity and the socio-economic system of competitive individualism have received much attention. What has been less frequently noted is how neatly it coheres with a theology built on the model of personal salvation.

This is all the more true because salvation has regularly been held to be of the soul. Whatever the state of the physical body and its material conditions, the soul could be saved by the gracious intervention of God. Such concepts are obviously part of the thinking of 'born again' Christian fundamentalists, but the inward turn has a long history also in liberal and neo-orthodox Christianity since Schleiermacher and Kierkegaard, respectively. Schleiermacher in *Speeches* insists that true religion is not the outward form of doctrine or morality, but is 'essentially contemplative … to have life and to know life in immediate feeling' (Schleiermacher 1958:36). Though Schleiermacher's account of the saviour is more in terms of manifestation and mediation than in terms of a divine rescue, his emphasis on inwardness and individual subjectivity is much to the fore. Similarly, Kierkegaard rejects the objectivity of the intellectual enterprise of theology and declares that truth is subjectivity, that it is in inwardness where authenticity and hence salvation are to be found (Kierkegaard 1941:169–224). Though there are of course huge differences between Schleiermacher and Kierkegaard, their agreed insistence on the priority of the inward over the outward is to that extent consistent with the dualism which has dogged Christianity ever since its affair with Platonism in the early years of Christendom.

According to a dualist conception, it is the soul which must be saved, while the flesh – too often equated with the body and particularly with sexuality – must be mortified, put to death, as the enemy of the soul. There are obvious connections here with the gendered understanding of material nature as against the cultural or spiritual, as discussed above. I have written elsewhere about the pervasiveness and theological perversity of dualism[10] and its connection with the construction of the male as spirit and the female as material[11]; it is in any case a well-rehearsed theme.[12] What I wish to emphasize here is, once again, the contrast that arises if, instead of a theology of salvation, we were to consider a theology of flourishing. The notion of flourishing does not begin to make sense unless bodiliness is taken into account; dualism is ruled out from the start. The concept of flourishing is one which involves thriving, luxuriant growth, obvious and exuberant good health; all of these are rooted in bodily well-being, including both physical health and adequate material provision. Sick people, starving people, people whose existence is miserable because they lack the necessities of physical and psychological well-being, cannot be said to be flourishing; the biblical writer connects flourishing with abundance of grain and wine. Of course it is sometimes possible that a person who falls ill can nevertheless flourish in mind or spirit for a time, just as a person kept in solitary confinement can sometimes rise above it and flourish inwardly; but these are occasions for wonder, for amazement, exceptions to our normal expectations. They should not therefore be seen as counter-examples to the idea that flourishing involves connectedness, adequate physical and psychological rootedness to support the blossoming and fruitfulness which grows out of that nourishing ground. A theology built on the model of flourishing, therefore, would be unable to ignore the physical and material realities of people, their bodiliness and their physical and psychological well-being, in the way that a theology built on the model of salvation of souls has sometimes done.

Closely connected with this is the other-worldly orientation of salvation. From very early in the Christian era, arguably from the biblical sources themselves, the idea of salvation was connected with the idea of eternal destiny. The opposite of salvation was damnation. Medieval sculpture and paintings are replete with portrayals of final judgements, in which the 'saved' are escorted by gentle angelic arms to heaven, while the 'damned' are given over to voraciously grinning demons, who whip them into the jaws of hell. Indeed, the crisis, the impending catastrophe from which one is saved is precisely damnation to hell; this is where the rhetoric of salvation gets its grip, especially in popular imagination. And once it is also accepted that 'outside the church there is no salvation', then not only is the authority of the church absolute, but the metaphor of salvation as a theological model has obtained hegemonic status.

Yet even in the biblical writings there is strong reason to question such an understanding. The sayings attributed to Jesus in the Fourth Gospel, for example, speak of eternal life not as a blissful state at which one could arrive after death, having been saved from hell by divine intervention, but rather as a present quality of life. Whoever believes in him, Jesus says, *has* eternal life; whoever does not is 'condemned already', not merely in the sense that there is some catastrophe awaiting of which this person is as yet not aware, but in the sense that such a person is already dealing in death, loving 'darkness rather than the light' (Jn 3.18, 19, 36). Such teachings of eternal life as a present quality of life rather than a future state are in obvious tension with the many other biblical passages which speak in terms of a destiny after death, and though they have usually been reconciled by means of the teaching that the future state is conditional on the present, it is clear that even in Scripture eternal life is not seen strictly in other-worldly terms. An emphasis on flourishing would obviously bring it even more firmly down to earth. It is not a heavenly kingdom to which the Hebrew prophets looked, but the flourishing of the theocracy in the land of Israel. Nor is the abundant life spoken of in the New Testament a life reserved for some future scenario, but a fruitful life in the present, 'rooted and grounded in Love'. This is not incompatible with the possibility of a future heavenly state, but the orientation is not toward death and what happens after death, but toward life in this world.

Philosophers of religion have been much preoccupied with questions of religious pluralism. Can there, after all, be salvation outside the church – or even outside belief in Christ? Can religious traditions other than Christianity be salvific? In the past, these discussions have often gone on as though the concept of salvation itself were unproblematic, and that it was not to be understood literally rather than as a theological model. That is, it was assumed (often without being explicit about it) that there are two alternative possibilities after death, and the question is whether people who are not Christians are automatically consigned to hell, or whether 'we' (!) might meet them in heaven because they had somehow been rescued from that fate ('saved'). The arrogance of such a view has become obvious; and many philosophers are willing to recognize that traditions other than Christianity offer 'salvific possibilities'; yet the language of salvation remains largely in place.

Such language, however, becomes increasingly problematic as one moves from a traditional Christian notion of salvation as rescue from eternal damnation to an idea of the 'universal salvific will of God', to use the terms made popular by the work of John Hick.[13] Part of the problem is that 'salvation' is a concept which is specific to Christianity. Buddhists, for instance, do not look forward to salvation but to nirvana. For a Christian to say that Buddhists will nevertheless be 'saved' seems to imply that Buddhists will find themselves, after death, in a heavenly place ruled over by Jesus – hardly something they would see as desirable. Of course, if the alternative is to burn in hell for all eternity, then even Buddhists would be glad of salvation; but that is hardly the point. Rather, if the idea of religious pluralism is taken seriously, then the question of whether there is any future state at all, and how it should be characterized if there is, is itself part of the investigation; and this means that the language of salvation, with its Christian connotations, becomes stretched to breaking point. What is one saved *from*, and by *whom*? Why should such language any longer be used?

The work of John Hick provides a fascinating case study of how the language of salvation becomes elasticized. In his early thought he held to the idea of heaven and hell, and 'assumed it to be a central Christian position that salvation is through Christ alone, and therefore that those who do not respond to God through Christ are not saved but, presumably, damned or lost' (Hick 1973:121). The more he entered into the idea of the 'universal salvific will of God', however, the more he extended the possibility of salvation to those outside the Christian faith; but he continued to think of salvation in terms of eternal destiny in an other-worldly state after bodily death. In his most recent work, in which he takes his pluralist insight fully seriously, he glosses the term 'salvation' as 'liberation' or 'human transformation', and speaks not in terms of heaven and hell, but in terms of a shift from self-centredness to reality-centredness (Hick 1989:36). Nevertheless, he continues to insist on 'the *soteriological* character of religion' (Hick 1989:21) as his starting point, though the concept of salvation is now far removed from anything to do with a saviour or a crisis or catastrophe from which people need to be rescued.

What Hick never considers is the fact that 'salvation' is itself a metaphor, and that it is not the only metaphor which could be chosen. In fact, the metaphor of flourishing would provide him with a model much more congenial to his recent work, since it is a model which not only reveals the obvious inappropriateness of individualistic self-centredness, as we have seen, but which also carries within it the ideas of liberation from conditions of oppression which render flourishing impossible. Part of the reason why discussions of religious pluralism tend to get bogged down is, I suggest, because of the fixation on the model of salvation as though it were fully literal, without the recognition that, like any model, it has limitations, and needs to be counterbalanced by other models, among which flourishing is a significant option. Even philosophers who, like Hick, find the idea of eternal damnation for many or even some of humanity morally abhorrent, continue to cling to the vocabulary of salvation as though that were the only one available, even though it now has to be glossed in ways which are at variance with its central connotations of rescue, and continue to a large extent to think in terms of other worlds, worlds beyond death, as part of what salvation involves.

The French philosopher and psychoanalyst Luce Irigaray has pointed out a significant gender linkage in the preoccupation with other worlds. She points out that while on the one hand the project of modernity has been the mastery of the material world, which is in itself a highly gendered project, on the other hand the identification of reality and goodness with spirit has meant that there is also an element of scorn for the material world and an effort to escape from it. In her words,

> The patriarchal order is based upon worlds of the beyond: worlds of before birth and especially of the afterlife, other planets to be discovered and exploited for survival, etc. It doesn't appreciate the real value of the world we have and draws up its often bankrupt blueprints on the basis of hypothetical worlds.
>
> (Irigaray 1993:27)

Whether in the Platonic form of the philosophical life 'with one foot in the grave', seeking escape from the body through self-mastery, or in the traditional religious form of looking to heaven and trying to live in its light while mortifying the flesh, or in the secular form of space flights and telescopes, or even in the intellectual form of preoccupation with the possible worlds of modal logic, all this attention to the 'worlds of the beyond' distracts attention from the actual world in which we live, and our relationships and responsibilities to it and to one another. When this is coupled with the age-old linkage of the female with matter and the male with spirit, the sexist nature of the desire to master and ultimately to escape from matter becomes all the more evident. To the extent that a theology of salvation is couched in terms which implicitly despise this world and look for another, better one, such a theology colludes with attitudes which are interlocked with structures of domination. Taking a pluralist position here, arguing that salvation is universal, does not meet this point, since the implication is still that this world is one from which one must be saved.

Such a position is foreclosed if the model of flourishing is used instead. It is not possible to emphasize flourishing without emphasizing also the material conditions of people's lives. Indeed, while it is possible to be 'saved' while leaving everything else as it is, this is by no means the case with flourishing. Since flourishing involves the physical and communal realities of a person's life, as already discussed, a theology of flourishing could not content itself with looking piously to an afterlife where present injustices will be abolished, while doing nothing in the struggle for their abolition here and now. For this reason a theology of flourishing would not be able to avoid confrontation with issues of domination, whether in terms of poverty, class, race, sex, or any other form of injustice, since these are the things which prevent people and communities from flourishing. A theology built on the model of flourishing would necessarily be a political theology which confronted social and economic issues not as marginal theological interests but as central to theological thought.

From this perspective it becomes possible to see that a theology based on the model of salvation is no less a political theology, but the underlying political stance has become invisible, often even (or especially) to those who develop such theologies. Any theology – indeed any intellectual stance – which does not recognize and challenge the present political and social injustices thereby implicitly condones them. When salvation is taken as a root metaphor for theology, it is easy to suppose that this is a 'religious' concept, removed from political involvement. But any such removal of the religious from the contemporary world is in the service of the status quo, whatever the intentions of the practitioners. The temptation to remove theology from social and political engagement is to a considerable extent foreclosed if one begins with the model of flourishing rather than the model of salvation. Whereas the rhetoric of salvation lends itself as a tool for those who wish to ensure that religion does not meddle in politics or get seriously involved in struggles against social injustices, the vocabulary of flourishing does not allow for such privatized and depoliticized religion.[14]

For spirituality, too there are implications. From what I have said above, it might seem as though the model of flourishing would lead one to emphasize only the public and the political at the expense of the private and inner life. Closer attention to the metaphor, however, shows that that would not be the case. A plant which flourishes does so from its own inner life, 'rooted and grounded' in its source. If that inner life is gone, the plant withers and dries up, no matter how good its external circumstances. What is different from the model of salvation, however, is that the inner and the outer are not separable; there is no flourishing 'soul' of the plant while its 'body' withers in intolerable material conditions. A theology built on the model of flourishing is one whose spirituality is holistic, rather than the privatized, subjectivized spirituality so characteristic of contemporary Christianity.[15] As such, it is highly congenial to feminists, for whom, in spite of backlash, the personal continues to be the political.

Notes

Preface

1 Within this series she also jointly wrote, with Hanneke Canters, *Forever Fluid: A Reading of Luce Irigaray's 'Elemental Passions'* (Manchester, 2005).
2 Jeremy Carrette has sought to map out the theme of Grace Jantzen's proposed fifth volume *The Desire of Psychoanalysis* in his memorial article 'In the Name of Life! Psychoanalysis and Grace Jantzen's Critique of Philosophy'. This will appear in a forthcoming volume, edited by Elaine Graham, from a memorial conference held in Grace Jantzen's honour.

1 Violence, desire and creation

1 For an excellent discussion of this theme of desire and recognition in Hegel, and its reception via Kojève in twentieth-century France, see Butler 1999.
2 Girard rejects out of hand feminist critics of his theory, suggesting that they simply 'want now to join the power games of the males' and thereby lose 'their real moral superiority' (Girard 1996:275; cf. 226–7). But this misses the point that violence is always already involved in gender construction, and that Girard's analysis of violence cannot account for it, thereby omitting a huge dimension of what it purports to explain.
3 See my discussion of this in Jantzen 2004:222–45.

2 Imagining natality: Narrative and Utopia

1 I discussed this in relation to death in Jantzen 2004:29–34.
2 Though her account cries out for it, Arendt had little to say about gender. Cf. Honig 1995.
3 The example of Oedipus is central to the discussion in Cavarero 2000.

4 The chosen ones: Death and the covenant

1 For a review of Christian scholarship see Nicholson 1986, Davidson 1989; for Jewish scholarship see Sperling (ed.) 1992.
2 Thus for example a standard textbook introduction to the Hebrew Bible which has gone through many editions and reprintings is called simply *People of the Covenant* (Flanders *et al.* 1996).
3 These may of course be two variations of the same tale; but the compilers/writers of Genesis present it as two separate occasions in the narrative which we now have.

5 'I am a jealous god': Monotheism and holy war

1 Lori Rowlett (1996) dates the book of Joshua – and indeed the whole Deuteronomistic history – somewhat earlier, to the so-called Josian reforms of the seventh century BCE; but this is still many centuries later than the events it purports to relate, and the same issues arise.

6 'When I see the blood': Sacrifice ...

1 See for example R. Wilkin, who points out that 'Origen, writing in the early third century, devoted a large section of his homilies on Genesis to the figure of Abraham; Ambrose in the fourth century wrote two books on him; Gregory of Nyssa, Chrysostom, and others preached about him regularly; Cyril of Alexandria in the early fifth century discusses him extensively in a book on Genesis and in an Easter sermon; Augustine devotes a dozen chapters to him in *The City of God,* and numerous other writers hold him up as a model and example for Christians' (Wilkin 1972:724). See also Martin Luther's extensive discussion of Abraham and his relation to Jesus in Pelikan (1964).

7 Beauty for ashes

1 Thus for example Gerhard von Rad devotes two pages of his two-volume *Old Testament Theology* to a consideration of divine beauty (1975.I.367–8); Walter Brueggemann (1997) hardly mentions it. Neither does Karl Rahner in his *Foundations of Christian Faith* (1978), written from a Catholic perspective, nor does Paul Tillich in his three-volume *Systematic Theology* (1951) (from a Protestant perspective) in spite of his interest in aesthetics. The exception is Karl Barth, who meditates on the beauty and glory of God in his massive *Church Dogmatics* (see Vol.II.i.324f; 650f), though his emphasis is more on caution about the sensory and bodily nature of beauty and the problems of aestheticism than on the theological richness of the theme.

9 Covenant in Christendom

1 Duling (1995) is among modern scholars who interpret this passage in the context of the Matthean 'church' some time after the death of Jesus. The anti-patriarchal point, however, remains unchanged.

10 Medieval deaths and delights

1 The terms 'middle ages' and 'medieval' are of course artificial as markers of discreet historical periods. I am using them as shorthand for roughly the era between Constantine and Erasmus.

2 Editorial note: this chapter was unfinished with a final incomplete sentence 'The crusades ... ' We felt that we would retain the chapter without attempting to add additional material.

12 Feminism and flourishing: Gender and metaphor in feminist theology

1 For example, A. Richardson and J. Bowden (eds.) (1983) devote a relatively long article to 'salvation', but 'flourishing' does not appear at all.

2 The biblical phrase is used as the title of Ann Loades's collection of articles in feminist theology, *Searching for Lost Coins: Explorations in Christianity and Feminism* (1987).

3 For two books among many which establish the connection, see Margaret Miles (1989) and Rosemary Ruether (1975).

4 Tertullian, in B.J. MacHaffie (ed.) (1992), p. 27.

5 For a useful discussion of some of these, see Hampson (1990:50–79).

6 See, among others, Carter Heyward (1989) and Dolores S. Williams (1993).

7 Two of the most notable are Max Weber (1930) and R.H. Tawney (1926).

8 I have discussed this in greater detail in my 'Connection or Competition: Identity and Personhood in Feminist Ethics' (1992).

9 For a full discussion of this, see Nancy Chodorow (1978). Chodorow has been criticized for not paying enough attention to differences among women, and for a deterministic tendency; but her basic analysis of the formation of differential gender identity is widely accepted.

10 G.M. Jantzen, *God's World God's Body* (London: DLT, 1984).

11 G.M. Jantzen, *Power, Gender and Christian Mysticism.*

12 For a thorough discussion of its trajectory through Western philosophy, see Charles Taylor (1989).

13 Among Hick's many writings, see especially *God and the Universe of Faiths* (1973) and *God has Many Names* (1982).

14 A notable example of this is the response of the Roman Catholic Church to the liberation theology of the Medellin Conference; the Church's position was that priests should occupy themselves with the salvation of the people, and not get involved in the political situation. See R. McAfee Brown (1990).

15 For a discussion of how such privatized spirituality feeds the political status quo, see my 'Spirituality and the Status Quo' (1990) and Kenneth Leech (1992).

Bibliography

Abusch, Tzvi. (2002) 'Sacrifice in Mesopotamia', in Albert I. Baumgarten, ed. *Sacrifice in Religious Experience*, Leiden: Brill. pp. 39–48.

Ackroyd, Peter (1983) 'Goddesses, Women and Jezebel', in A. Cameron and A. Kuhrt, eds. *Images of Women in Antiquity*, London: Croom Helm.

Aeschylus (1977) *The Oresteia*, trans. Robert Fagles, Harmondsworth: Penguin.

Aho, James A. (1981) *Religious Mythology and the Art of War: Comparative Religious Symbolisms of Military Violence*, London: Aldwych Press.

Albright, W.F. (1957) *From the Stone Age to Christianity: Monotheism and the Historical Process*, New York: Doubleday.

Allison, Dale C. Jr. (1999) 'The Eschatology of Jesus', in *The Encyclopedia of Apocalypticism: Volume I The Origins of Apocalypticism in Judaism and Christianity*, New York: Continuum.

Alston, William P. (1991) *Perceiving God: The Epistemology of Religious Experience*, Ithaca, NY: Cornell University Press.

Alt, Albrecht (1966) *Essays on Old Testament History and Religion*, Oxford: Blackwell.

Alter, Robert (1981) *The Art of Biblical Narrative*, New York: Basic Books.

Alter, Robert (1998) 'The Poetic and Wisdom Books', in John Barton, ed. *The Cambridge Companion to Biblical Interpretation*, Cambridge: Cambridge University Press.

Arendt, Hannah (1958) *The Human Condition*, Chicago: University of Chicago Press.

Ariès, Philippe (1981) *The Hour of Our Death*, New York: Alfred A. Knopf.

Auerbach, Erich (1968) *Mimesis*, Princeton: Princeton University Press.

Augustine (1961) *Confessions*, trans. R.S. Pine-Coffin, London: Penguin.

Bal, Mieke (1988) *Death and Dissymmetry: The Politics of Coherence in the Book of Judges*, Chicago: University of Chicago Press.

Barr, James (2000) *History and Ideology in the Old Testament: Biblical Studies at the End of a Millennium*, Oxford: Oxford University Press.

Barth, Karl (1968) *The Epistle to the Romans*, trans. Edwyn C. Hoskyns, Oxford: Oxford University Press.

—— (1977) *Church Dogmatics*, Volume IV, Books 1–5 and Index Volume. Edinburgh: T. & T. Clark.

Barton, John (1997) *The Spirit and the Letter*, London: SPCK.

—— (ed.) (1998) *Cambridge Companion to Biblical Interpretation*, Cambridge: Cambridge University Press.

Bauman, Zygmunt (1989) *Modernity and the Holocaust*, Cambridge: Polity.

Baumgarten, Albert I., ed. (2002) *Sacrifice in Religious Experience*, Leiden: Brill.

Beach, Eleanor Ferris (1997) 'Transforming Goddess Iconography in Hebrew Narrative', in Karen King, ed. *Women and Goddess Traditions in Antiquity and Today*, Minneapolis: Augsburg Fortress.

Beal, Timothy K. (2002) *Religion and its Monsters*, New York and London: Routledge.

Binger, Tilde (1997) *Asherah: Goddesses in Ugarit, Israel and the Old Testament*, Journal for the Study of the Old Testament Supplement Series 232, Sheffield: Sheffield Academic Press.

Blenkinsopp, Joseph (1998) 'The Pentateuch', in John Barton, ed. *The Cambridge Companion to Biblical Interpretation*, Cambridge: Cambridge University Press.

Bloch-Smith, Elizabeth (1992) *Judahite Burial Practices and Beliefs about the Dead*, Journal for the Study of Old Testament Supplement Series 123, Sheffield: Sheffield Academic Press.

Bolin, Thomas M. (2002) 'Warfare', in John Barton, ed. *The Biblical World*, Vol. 2, London and New York: Routledge.

Bourdieu, Pierre (1990) *The Logic of Practice*, trans. Richard Nice, Cambridge: Polity.

Bowman, Charles H.O. (2003) *The Goddess Anatu in the Ancient Near East*, Graduate Theological Union, Berkeley, PhD 1978, Ann Arbor, MI: University Microfilms Inc.

Bremmer, J.N. (2002) *The Rise and Fall of the Afterlife*, London and New York: Routledge.

Brennan, Teresa (1993) *History after Lacan*, London and New York: Routledge.

Brown, Peter (1981) *The Cult of Saints: Its Rise and Function in Latin Christianity*, Chicago: University of Chicago Press.

Brown, R. McAfee (1990) *Gustavo Gutierrez: An Introduction to Liberation Theology*, New York: Orbis Books.

Brueggemann, Walter (1982) *Genesis: Interpretation: A Bible Commentary for Teaching and Preaching*, Atlanta: John Knox Press.

—— (1997) *Theology of the Old Testament: Testimony, Dispute, Advocacy*, Minneapolis: Fortress Press.

Budd, Philip J. (1989) 'Holiness and Cult', in R.E. Clements, ed. *The World of Ancient Israel*, Cambridge: Cambridge University Press.

Bultmann, Rudolph (1951–55) *New Testament Theology*, Two Volumes, New York: Scribners.

—— (1958) *Jesus and the Word*, New York: Scribners.

Bunyan, John (1967) *The Pilgrim's Progress from this World to that Which is to Come*, ed. J.B. Wharey and R. Sharrock, London: Penguin.

Burkert, W. [1972] (1983) *Homo Necans: The Anthropology of Ancient Greek Sacrificial Religion and Myth*, Berkeley: University of California Press.

Butler, Judith (1999) *Subjects of Desire: Hegelian Reflections in Twentieth-Century France*, New York: Columbia University Press.

Cavarero, Adriana (2000) *Relating Narratives: Storytelling and Selfhood*, trans. Paul A. Kottman, London and New York: Routledge.

Childs, Brevard (1974) *Exodus: A Commentary*, Old Testament Library, London: SCM Press.

—— (1979) *Introduction to the Old Testament as Scripture*, Philadelphia: Fortress Press.

—— (1985) *Old Testament Theology in a Canonical Context*, Philadelphia: Fortress Press.

—— (1992) *Biblical Theology of the Old and New Testaments*, Minneapolis: Fortress Press.

Chodorow, Nancy (1978) *The Reproduction of Mothering: Psychoanalysis and the Sociology of Gender*, Berkeley: University of California Press.

Christ, Carol P. (1991) 'Mircea Eliade and the Feminist Paradigm Shift', *Journal of Feminist Studies in Religion* 7, no. 2.

Clements, R.E., ed. (1989) *The World of Ancient Israel: Sociological, Anthropological and Political Perspectives*, Cambridge: Cambridge University Press.

Clines, David J.A. (1995) *Interested Parties: The Ideology of Writers and Readers of the Hebrew Bible*, Journal for the Study of the Old Testament Supplement Series 205, Sheffield: Sheffield Academic Press.

Collins, John J. (1999) 'From Prophecy to Apocalypticism: The Expectation of the End', in John J. Collins, ed. *The Encyclopedia of Apocalypticism*, Vol. 1. *The Origins of Apocalypticism in Judaism and Christianity*, New York: Continuum.

—— (2002) 'Death and Afterlife', in John Barton, ed. *The Biblical World*, Vol. 2, London and New York: Routledge.

Condren, Mary (1989) *The Serpent and the Goddess: Women, Religion and Power in Celtic Ireland*, San Francisco: Harper and Row.

Crossan, John Dominic (1991) *The Historical Jesus: The Life of a Mediterranean Jewish Peasant*, San Francisco: Harper.

—— (1996) *Who is Jesus? Answers to Your Questions about the Historical Jesus*, Knoxville: Westminster/John Knox Press.

Curtis, A. (1994) 'The Psalms since Dahood', *Ugarit and the Bible: Proceedings of the International Symposium on Uarit and the Bible, Manchester, September 1992*, Ugarit-Velag, pp. 1–10.

Dalley, Stephanie, ed. (2000) *Myths from Mesopotamia: Creation, the Flood, Gilgamesh and Others*, revised edition, Oxford: Oxford University Press.

Davidson, Robert (1989) 'Covenant Ideology in Ancient Israel', in R.E. Clements, ed. *The World of Ancient Israel*, Cambridge: Cambridge University Press.

Davies, D. (1985) 'An Interpretation of Sacrifice in Leviticus', in B. Lang, ed. *Anthropological Approaches to the Old Testament*, London: SPCK.

Davies, Philip R. (1992) *In Search of 'Ancient Israel'*, Journal for the Study of the Old Testament Supplement Series 148, Sheffield: Sheffield Academic Press.

Davis, Caroline Franks (1989) *The Evidential Force of Religious Experience*, Oxford: Clarendon.

Day, John (1985) *God's Conflict with the Dragon and the Sea: Echoes of a Canaanite Myth in the Old Testament*, Cambridge: Cambridge University Press.

—— (1989) *Molech: A God of Human Sacrifice in the Old Testament*, Cambridge: Cambridge University Press.

—— (2000) *Yahweh and the Gods and Goddesses of Canaan*, Journal for the Study of the Old Testament Supplement Series 265, Sheffield: Sheffield Academic Press.

De Lauretis, Teresa (1987) *Technologies of Gender: Essays on Theory, Film and Fiction*, Bloomington, IN: Indiana University Press.

de Moor, J.C. (1997) *The Rise of Yahwism: The Roots of Israelite Monotheism*, revised edition, Leuven: University Press.

de Vries, Hent (1995) 'Adieu, à dieu, a-Dieu', in Adriaan Peperzak, ed. *Ethics as First Philosophy*, New York and London: Routledge.

—— (2002) *Religion and Violence: Philosophical Perspectives from Kant to Derrida*, Baltimore and London: The Johns Hopkins University Press.

Delaney, Carol (1998) *Abraham on Trial: The Social Legacy of Biblical Myth*, Princeton: Princeton University Press.

Delumeau, Jean (1990) *Sin and Guilt: the Emergence of Western Guilt Culture*, New York: St. Martin's Press.

Derrida, Jacques (1978) *Writing and Difference*, trans. Alan Bass, London: Routledge.

Dever, William G. (2001) *What did the Biblical Writers Know and When did they Know it? What archaeology can Tell us about the Reality of Ancient Israel*, Grand Rapids, MI and Cambridge: William B. Eerdmans.

Dollimore, Jonathan (1998) *Death, Desire and Loss in Western Culture*, New York: Routledge.

Douglas, Mary (1966) *Purity and Danger: An Analysis of the Concepts of Pollution and Taboo*, London and New York: Routledge.

—— (1975) *Implicit Meanings: Essays in Anthropology*, London and New York: Routledge.

—— (1993) *In the Wilderness: The Doctrine of Defilement in the Book of Numbers*, Journal for the Study of the Old Testament Supplement Series 158, Sheffield: Sheffield Academic Press.

du Bois, Page (1995) *Sappho is Burning*, Chicago and London: University of Chicago Press.

Duling, Dennis C. (1995) 'The Matthean Brotherhood and Marginal Scribal Leadership', in Philip E. Esler, ed. *Modelling Early Christianity: Social Scientific Studies of the New Testament in its Context*, London: Routledge.

Eaton, Alfred Wade (1969) *The Goddess Anat: The History of her Cult, Her Mythology and her Iconography*, Yale University PhD 1964, Ann Arbor, MI: University Microfilms Inc.

Eichrodt, Walther (1961, 1967) *Theology of the Old Testament*, 2 vols. Philadelphia: Westminster Press.

Eilberg-Schwartz, Howard (1990) *The Savage in Judaism: An Anthropology of Israelite Religion and Ancient Judaism*, Bloomington, IN: Indiana University Press.

Eisenstein, Zillah (2004) *Against Empire: Feminisms, Racism, and the West*, London and New York: Zed Books.

Eliade, Mircea (1978) *A History of Religious Ideas*, three volumes, trans. Willard R. Trask, Chicago: University of Chicago Press.

Emmerson, Grace I. (1989) 'Women in Ancient Israel', in R.E. Clements, ed. *The World of Ancient Israel*, Cambridge: Cambridge University Press.

Encyclopaedia Judaica (2004) CD-ROM edition @ Jewish Multimedia (Israel) Ltd.

Euripides (1953) *Alcestis, Hippolytus, Iphigenia in Tauris*, trans. Philip Vellacott, Harmondsworth: Penguin.

—— (1963) *Medea and Other Plays*, trans. Philip Vellacott, London: Penguin.

—— (1972) *Orestes and Other Plays*, trans. Philip Vellacott, London: Penguin.

Farley, Edward (2001) *Faith and Beauty: A Theological Aesthetic*, Aldershot: Ashgate.

Finkelstein, I. and N. Na'aman, eds. (1994) *From Nomadism to Monarchy. Archaeological and Historical Aspects of Early Israel*, Jerusalem: Israel Exploration Society.

Fiorenza, Elisabeth Schüssler (1983) *In Memory of Her: A Feminist Theological Reconstruction of Christian Origins*, New York: Crossroad.

Flanders, Henry Jackson Jr., Robert Wilson Crapps, and David Anthony Smith (1996) *People of the Covenant: An Introduction to the Hebrew Bible*, fourth edition, New York and Oxford: Oxford University Press.

Foucault, Michel (1977) *Language, Counter-Memory, Practice: Selected Essays and Interviews*, ed. D.F. Bouchard, Ithaca, NY: Cornell University Press.

—— (1978) *The History of Sexuality: An Introduction*, trans. Robert Hurley, London: Penguin.

—— [Maurice Florence] (1994) 'Foucault, Michel, 1926 –', in Gary Gutting, ed. *The Cambridge Companion to Michel Foucault*, Cambridge: Cambridge University Press.

Frazer, J.G. (1922) *The Golden Bough: A Study in Magic and Religion*, abridged edition, London: Macmillan.

Frederiksen, P. (1999) *Jesus of Nazareth, King of the Jews: A Jewish Life and the Beginnings of Christianity*, New York: Alfred A. Knopf.

Fredriksen, Paula (2000) *From Jesus to Christ*, New Haven, CT: Yale University Press.

Frei, Hans W. (1974) *The Eclipse of Biblical Narrative: A Study in Eighteenth and Nineteenth Century Hermeneutics*, New Haven, CT: Yale University Press.

Frend, W.H.C. (1984) *The Rise of Christianity*, Philadelphia: Fortress Press.

Freud, Sigmund ([1920] 1984) 'Beyond the Pleasure Principle', in S. Freud. *On Metapsychology*, The Penguin Freud Library, Vol. 11, trans. J. Strachey and A. Richards, eds, Harmondsworth: Penguin.

Freyne, Sean (2004) *Jesus, A Jewish Galilean: A New Reading of the Jesus Story*, London and New York: T & T Clark.

Friedland, Roger and Richard Hicht (2000) *To Rule Jerusalem*, Berkeley and London: University of California Press.

George, Andrew (trans. and intro.) (1999) *The Epic of Gilgamesh: A New Translation*, London: Penguin.

George, Susan (1988) *A Fate Worse Than Debt*, London: Penguin.

Girard, René (1977) *Violence and the Sacred*, trans. Patrick Gregory, Baltimore: John Hopkins University Press.

—— (1986) *The Scapegoat*, trans. Yvonne Freccero, Baltimore: John Hopkins University Press.

—— (1987) *Things Hidden Since the Foundation of the World*, trans. Stephen Bann and Michael Metteer, Stanford: Stanford University Press.

—— (1996) *The Girard Reader*, ed. James G. Williams, New York: Crossroad.

Gottwald, Norman K. (1980) *The Tribes of Yahweh: A Sociology of the Religion of Liberated Israel 1250–1050 BCE*, London: SCM.

—— (1993) *The Hebrew Bible in its Social World and in Ours*, Atlanta: Scholars Press.

—— (2001) *The Politics of Ancient Israel*, Louisville, KY: Westminster/John Knox Press.

Gray, John (2003) *Al Qaeda and What it Means to be Modern*, London: Faber and Faber.

Gunn, David M., and Fewell, Danna N. (1993) *Narrative in the Hebrew Bible*, Oxford: Oxford University Press.

Hamerton-Kelly, Robert G. (1992) *Sacred Violence: Paul's Hermeneutic of the Cross*, Minneapolis: Fortress Press.

Hampson, Daphne (1990) *Theology and Feminism*, Oxford: Blackwell.

Hanson, Paul (1975) *The Dawn of Apocalyptic*, Philadelphia, PA: Fortress Press.

Hegel, G.W.F. (1977) *Phenomenology of Spirit*, trans. A. V. Miller, Oxford: Oxford University Press (originally published 1807).

Heyward, Carter (1989) *Speaking of Christ: A Lesbian Feminist Voice*, New York: Pilgrim Press.

Hick, John (1973) *God and the Universe of Faiths*, London: Macmillan.

—— (1982) *God has Many Names*, London: Macmillan.

—— (1989) *An Interpretation of Religion: Humanity's Varied Response to the Transcendent*, London: Macmillan.

Hill, C. (1988) *A Turbulent, Seditious, and Factious People: John Bunyan and His Church*, Oxford: Oxford University Press.

Hobbes, Thomas (1841) *Philosophical Rudiments Concerning Government and Society* [*De Cive*] in *The English Works of Thomas Hobbes of Malmesbury*, II. London.

Hollander, John, and Kermode, Frank, eds. (1973) *The Literature of Renaissance England*, Oxford: Oxford University Press.

Homer (1996) *The Odyssey*, trans. Robert Fagles, New York and London: Penguin.

Honig, Bonnie (1995) 'Toward an Agonistic Feminism: Hannah Arendt and the Politics of Identity', in Bonnie King, ed. *Feminist Interpretations of Hannah Arendt*, University Park, PA: Pennsylvania State University Press.

Horsley, Richard A. (1993) *The Sociology of the Jesus Movement*, New York: Crossroad.

—— (1995) *Galilee: History, Politics, People*, Philadelphia: Trinity Press International.

—— (2003) *Jesus and Empire: The Kingdom of God and the New World Disorder*, Minneapolis: Fortress Press.

Hubert, Henri and Marcel Mauss (1964) *Sacrifice: Its Nature and Function*, trans. W. D. Halls, London: Cohen & West.

Huttgård, Anders (1999) 'Persian Apocalypticism', in John J. Collins, ed. *The Encyclopedia of Apocalypticism: Volume I. The Origins of Apocalypticism in Judaism and Christianity*, New York: Continuum.

Irigaray, Luce (1993) *Je, tu, nous: Towards a Culture of Difference*, trans. A. Martin, London: Routledge.

Jacobsen, Thorkild (1976) *The Treasures of Darkness: A History of Mesopotamian Religion*, New Haven and London: Yale University Press.

Jantzen, Grace M. (1984) *God's World God's Body*, London: DLT.

—— (1990) 'Spirituality and the Status Quo', *King's Theological Review* 13.1.

—— (1992) 'Connection or Competition: Identity and Personhood in Feminist Ethics', *Studies in Christian Ethics* 5.1.

—— (1995) *Power, Gender and Christian Mysticism*, Cambridge: Cambridge University Press.

—— (1998) *Becoming Divine: Towards a Feminist Philosophy of Religion*, Manchester: Manchester University Press, and Bloomington, IN: Indiana University Press.

—— (2000) *Julian of Norwich: Mystic and Theologian*, 2nd ed., London: SPCK, and New York: Paulist Press.

—— (2004) *Foundations of Violence: Death and the Displacement of Beauty Volume One*, London and New York: Routledge.

Jay, Nancy (1992) *Throughout Your Generations Forever: Sacrifice, Religion and Paternity*, Chicago: University of Chicago Press.

Jones, G.H. (1989) 'The Concept of Holy War', in R.E. Clements, ed. *The World of Ancient Israel*, Cambridge: Cambridge University Press.

Josephus, F. (1960). *The Great Roman-Jewish War*, New York: Harper & Brothers.

Joy, Morny (1993) 'Levinas: Atterity, the Feminine and Women – A Meditation', in *Studies in Religion/Sciences Religieuses*, 22, no. 4.

Julian of Norwich (1978) 'Showings', in J. Walsh and E. Colledge, eds. *Classics of Western Spirituality*, London: SPCK, and New York: Paulist Press.

Kaufman, Y. (1972) *The Religion of Israel from its Beginnings to the Babylonian Exile*, trans. M. Greenberg, New York: Schocken Books.

Keel, Othmar, and Christoph Uehlinger (1998) *Gods, Goddesses, and Images of God in Ancient Israel*, trans. Thomas H. Trapp, Edinburgh: T&T Clark.

Kierkegaard, Søren (1941) 'Truth is Subjectivity', in his *Concluding Unscientific Postscript*, Princeton: Princeton University Press.

—— (1983) *Fear and Trembling* and *Repetition*, trans. Howard V. Hong and Edna H. Hong, Princeton, NJ and London: Princeton University Press.

Lacan, Jacques (1977) *Ecrits: A Selection*, trans. A. Sheridan, London: Tavistock/Routledge.

Le Goff, Jacques (1984) *The Birth of Purgatory*, Chicago: University of Chicago Press.

Leech, Kenneth (1992) *The Eye of the Storm: Spiritual Resources for the Pursuit of Justice*, London: DLT.

Lemche, Niels Peter (1988) *Ancient History: A New History of Israelite Society*, Journal for the Study of the Old Testament Supplement Series No. 5, Sheffield: Sheffield Academic Press.

—— (1990) *The Canaanites and their Land: The Tradition of the Canaanites*, Journal for the Study of the Old Testament Supplement Series No. 110, Sheffield: Sheffield Academic Press.

Levi, A. (2002) *Renaissance and Reformation: The Intellectual Genesis*, New Haven and London: Yale University Press.

Levinas, Emmanuel (1969) *Totality and Infinity: An Essay on Exteriority*, trans. Alphonso Lingis, Pittsburgh: Duquesne University Press.

—— (1985) *Ethics and Infinity: Coversations with Philippe Nemo*, trans. Richard A. Cohen, Pittsburg: Duquesne University Press.

—— (1989) *The Levinas Reader*, ed. Séan Hand, Oxford: Blackwell.

—— (1996) *Basic Philosophical Writings*, eds. Adriaan T. Peperzak, Simon Critchley and Robert Bernasconi, Bloomington: Indiana University Press.

Lindbeck, George (1984) *The Nature of Doctrine: Religion and Theology in a Postliberal Age*, London: SPCK.

Loades, Ann (1987) *Searching for Lost Coins: Explorations in Christianity and Feminism*, London: SPCK.

Long, Asphodel P. (1992) *In a Chariot Drawn by Lions: The Search for the Female in Deity*, London: Women's Press.

Lyotard, Jean François (1984) *The Postmodern Condition: A Report on Knowledge*, trans. Geoff Bennington and Brian Massumi, Manchester: Manchester University Press, and Minneapolis: University of Minnesota Press.

Maccoby, Hyam (1982) *The Sacred Executioner: Human Sacrifice and the Legacy of Guilt*, London: Thames and Hudson.

MacHaffie, Barbara J., ed. (1992) *Readings in Her Story: Women in Christian Tradition*, Minneapolis: Augsburg Fortress.

Maimonides, Moses (1963) *The Guide of the Perplexed*, Two Volumes, trans. Schlomo Pines, Chicago and London: University of Chicago Press.

Martínez, García (1999) 'Apocalypticism in the Dead Sea Scrolls', in *The Encyclopedia of Apocalypticism: Volume I. The Origins of Apocalypticism in Judaism and Christianity*, New York: Continuum.

Mendenhall, George (1954) *Law and Covenant in Israel and the Ancient Near East*, Pittsburgh: Biblical Colloquium.

Miles, Margaret (1988) *The Image and Practice of Holiness: A Critique of the Classic Manuals of Devotion*, London: SCM Press.

—— (1989) *Carnal Knowing: Female Nakedness and Religious Meaning in the Christian West*, London: Burns & Oates.

Milgrom, J. (1991) *Leviticus: A New Translation with Introduction and Commentary*, Anchor Bible 3, Garden City, New York: Doubleday.

—— (2002) 'Were the Firstborn Sacrificed to YHWH? To Molek? Popular Practice or Divine Demand?', in Albert I. Baumgarten, ed. *Sacrifice in Religious Experience*, Leiden: Brill.

Miller, Patrick D. (1973) *The Divine Warrior in Early Israel*, Cambridge: Harvard University Press.

Mills, Mary E. (1999) *Historical Israel: Biblical Israel: Studying Joshua to 2 Kings*, London and New York: Cassell.

Moore, Robert Ian (1987) *The Formation of a Persecuting Society: Power and Deviance in Western Europe 950–1250 A.D.* Oxford: Blackwell.

Mowinckel, Sigmund (1962) *The Psalms in Israel's Worship*, Oxford: Oxford University Press.

Nicholson, Ernest W. (1986) *God and His People: Covenant and Theology in the Old Testament*, Oxford: Clarendon Press.

Nielsen, Edvard (1968) *The Ten Commandments in New Perspective: A Traditio-Historical Approach*, Studies in Biblical Theology 2/7, London: SCM Press.

Norwich, John Julius (2003) *A History of Venice*, London: Penguin.

Noth, Martin (1960) *The History of Israel*, 2nd English ed., trans. P.R. Ackroyd, London: Adam and Charles Black.

Olyan, Saul M. (1988) *Asherah and the Cult of Yahweh in Israel*, Society of Biblical Literature Monograph 34, Atlanta, GA: Scholars Press.

Oppenheim, A.L. (1977) *Ancient Mesopotamia: Portrait of a Dead Civilization*, 2nd revised edition. Chicago University Press.

Ostriker, Alicia Suskin (1993) *Feminist Revision and the Bible*, Cambridge, MA and Oxford: Blackwell.

—— (1994) *The Nakedness of the Fathers: Biblical Visions and Revisions*, New Brunswick, NJ: Rutgers University Press.

Pagels, Elaine (1979) *The Gnostic Gospels*, London: Penguin.

Paxton, Frederick S. (1990) *Christianizing Death: The Creation of a Ritual Process in Early Medieval Europe*, Ithaca, NY: Cornell University Press.

Pelikan, J., ed. (1964) *Luther's Works*, St. Louis: Concordia Publishing House.

Peperzak, Adriaan (1997) *Beyond: The Philosophy of Emmanuel Levinas*, Evanston, IL: Northwestern University Press.

——, ed. (1995) *Ethics as First Philosophy: The Significance of Emmanuel Levinas for Philosophy, Literature and Religion*, New York and London: Routledge.

Perdue, Leo G. (1994) *The Collapse of History: Reconstructing Old Testament Theology*, Minneapolis: Fortress Press.

Pike, Nelson (1992) *Mystic Union: An Essay in the Phenomenology of Mysticism*, Ithaca, NY: Cornell University Press.

Plaskow, Judith (1990) *Standing Again at Sinai: Judaism from a Feminist Perspective*, San Francisco: Harper Collins.

Plato (1961) *The Collected Dialogues of Plato*, E. Hamilton and Huntington Cairns, eds. Princeton: Princeton University Press.

Provan, Iain (1998) 'The Historical Books of the Old Testament', in John Barton, ed. *The Cambridge Companion to Biblical Interpretation*, Cambridge: Cambridge University Press.

Rahner, Karl (1978) *Foundations of Christian Faith: An Introduction to the Idea of Christianity*, trans. Willliam V. Dyck, London: Darton, Longman & Todd.

Redekop, Vern Neufeld (2002) *From Violence to Blessing: How an Understanding of Deep-Rooted Conflict Can Open Paths to Reconciliation*, Ottawa: Novalis.

Reventlow, Henning Graf (1984) *The Authority of the Bible and the Rise of the Modern World*, trans. John Bowden, London: SCM Press.

Richard, Jean (1999) *Crusades c.1071–c.1291*, Cambridge: Cambridge University Press.

Richardson, Alan, and John Bowden, eds. (1983) *A New Dictionary of Christian Theology*, London: SCM Press.

Richardson, Peter (1999) *Herod: King of the Jews and Friend of the Romans*, Minneapolis: Fortress Press.

Riches, John (1980) *Jesus and the Transformation of Judaism*, London: Darton, Longman and Todd.

Ricoeur, Paul (1965) *History and Truth*, trans. Charles A. Kelbley, Evanston, IL: Northwestern University Press.

—— (1986) *Lectures on Ideology and Utopia*, ed. George H. Taylor, New York: Columbia University Press.

Robinson, James M., ed. (1990) *The Nag Hammadi Library*, revised edition, San Francisco: Harper Collins.

Rosaldo, M., and Atkinson, J. (1975) 'Man the Hunter and Woman: Metaphors for the Sexes in Ilongot Magical Spells', in R. Willis, ed. *The Interpretation of Symbolism*, New York: John Wiley, pp. 43–75.

Rose, Jacqueline (1993) *Why War?* Oxford: Blackwell.

Rosenberg, Roy A. (1965) 'Jesus, Isaac and the "Suffering Servant"' in *Journal of Biblical Literature*, 84, no. 4, pp. 381–388.

Ross, Allen P. (2002) *Holiness to the Lord: A Guide to the Exposition of the Book of Leviticus*, Grand Rapids, MI: Baker Academic.

Rowlett, Lori L. (1996) *Joshua and the Rhetoric of Violence: A New Historicist Analysis*, Journal for the Study of the Old Testament Supplement Series 226, Sheffield: Sheffield Academic Press.

Rowley, H.H. (1956) *The Faith of Israel: Aspects of Old Testament Thought*, London: SCM.

Ruether, Rosemary R. (1975) *New Woman/New Earth: Sexist Ideologies and Human Liberation*, San Francisco: Harper & Row.

—— (1983) *Sexism and God-Talk: Towards a Feminist Theology*, London: SCM Press.

Sacchi, Paolo (2004) *The History of the Second Temple Period*, London and New York: T & T Clark/Continuum.

Saggs, H.W.F. (1999) *The Babylonians: A Survey of the Ancient Civilization of the Tigris – Euphrates Valley*, London: Folio Society.

Said, Edward (1994) *The Politics of Dispossession: The Struggle for Palestinian Self-determination, 1969–1994*, London: Chatto & Windus.

Saiving, Valerie (1979) 'The Human Situation: A Feminine View', in C.P. Christ and J. Plaskow, eds. *Womanspirit Rising: A Feminist Reader in Religion*, San Francisco: Harper & Row.

Sanders, E.P. (1985) *Jesus and Judaism*, Minneapolis: Fortress Press.

—— (1993) *The Historical Figure of Jesus*, London: Penguin.

Sawyer, John F.A., ed. (1996) *Reading Leviticus: A Conversation with Mary Douglas*, Journal for the Study of the Old Testament Supplement Series 227, Sheffield: Sheffield Academic Press.

Scarry, Elaine (1999) *On Beauty and Being Just*, Princeton: Princeton University Press.

Schleiermacher, Friedrich (1958) *On Religion: Speeches to its Cultured Despisers*, trans. J. Oman, New York: Harper & Row.

Schmidt, Brian B. (1994) *Israel's Beneficent Dead: Ancestor Cult and Necromancy in Ancient Israelite Religion and Tradition*, Tübingen: J.C.B. Mohr (Paul Siebeck).

Scholder, K. (1990) *The Birth of Modern Critical Theology*, London: SCM.

Schrift, Alan (2000) 'Spinoza, Nietzsche, and Deleuze: An Other Discourse of Desire', in H. Silverman, ed. *Philosophy and Desire*, 173–85. New York and London: Routledge.

Schwartz, Regina M. (1997) *The Curse of Cain: The Violent Legacy of Monotheism*, Chicago: University of Chicago Press.

Schweitzer, Albert (1954) *The Quest of the Historical Jesus: A Critical Study of its Progress from Reimarus to Wrede*, trans. W. Montgomery, London: SCM.

Sered, Susan (2002) 'Towards a Gendered Typology of Sacrifice: Women and Feasting, Men and Death in an Okinawan Village' Sacrifice in Religious Experience (Studies in the History of Religions), in Albert I. Baumgarten, ed. *Sacrifice in Religious Experience*, Leiden: Brill.

Shakespeare, William (1980) *The Complete Works*, ed. J. D. Wilson, London: Octopus.

Shlaim, Avi (2000) *The Iron Wall: Israel and the Arab World*, London: Penguin.

Smend, Rudolph (1970) *Yahweh War and Tribal Confederation: Reflections upon Israel's Earliest History*, trans. Max Gray Rogers, Nashville, TN: Abingdon Press.

Smith, Mark S. (2001) *The Origins of Biblical Monotheism: Israel's Polytheistic Background and the Ugaritic Texts*, Oxford: Oxford University Press.

Smith, Robertson W. (1889) *Lectures on the Religion of the Semites*, London: Black.

Sophocles (1953) *Electra and Other Plays*, trans. E.F. Watling, Harmondsworth: Penguin.

Soskice, Janet M. (1985) *Metaphor and Religious Language*, Oxford: Clarendon Press.

Sperling, S.D., ed. (1992) *Students of the Covenant. A History of Jewish Biblical Scholarship in North America*, Confessional Perspectives Series, Atlanta, GA: Scholars Press.

Spiegel, Shalom (1969) *The Last Trial*, trans. Judah Goldin, New York: Schocken Books.

Spronk, Klaas (1986) *Beatific Afterlife in Ancient Israel and in the Ancient Near East*, Neukirchen-Vluyn: Neukirchener Verlag, Butzon & Bercker Kevelaer.

Stanton, Elizabeth Cady, and the Revising Committee (1974) *The Woman's Bible*, Seattle: Coalition on Women and Religion.

Stillman, Edmund, and William Pfaff (1964) *The Politics of Hysteria: The Sources of Twentieth Century Conflict*, London: Victor Gollancz.

Stroup, George W. (1981) *The Promise of Narrative Theology*, Atlanta: John Knox.

Sundermeier, Theo. (2002) 'Sacrifice in African Traditional Religions', in Albert I. Baumgarten, ed. *Sacrifice in Religious Experience*, Leiden: Brill, pp. 3–12.

Swinburne, Richard (1977) *The Coherence of Theism*, Oxford: Clarendon Press.

Tawney, R.H. (1926) *Religion and the Rise of Capitalism*, London: Penguin.

Taylor, Charles (1989) *Sources of the Self: The Making of the Modern Identity*, Cambridge: Cambridge University Press.

Taylor, Mark C., ed. (1998) *Critical Terms for Religious Studies*, Chicago and London: University of Chicago Press.

Tertullian (1992) 'On the Apparel of Women', in B.J. MacHaffie, ed. *Readings in Her Story: Women in Christian Tradition*, Minneapolis: Augsburg Fortress.

Teubal, Savina J. (1993) 'Sarah and Hagar: Matriarchs and Visionaries', in Athalya Brenner, ed. *A Feminist Companion to Genesis*, Sheffield: Sheffield Academic Press.

Thomas of Celano (2004) *The Francis Trilogy*, ed. Regis J. Armstrong, New York: New York City Press.

Tillich, Paul (1951) *Systematic Theology*, Vols. 1–3, Chicago: University of Chicago Press.

Tracy, David (1998) 'Writing', in *Critical Terms for Religious Studies*, Chicago: University of Chicago Press.

Trible, Phyllis (1984) *Texts of Terror: Literary-Feminist Readings of Biblical Narratives*, Philadelphia: Fortress Press.

Tromp, Nicholas J. (1969) *Primitive Conceptions of Death and the Nether World in the Old Testament*, Rome: Pontifical Biblical Institute.

Tyerman, Christopher (2004) *Fighting for Christendom: Holy War and the Crusades*, Oxford: Oxford University Press.

Tylor, E.B. (1871) *Primitive Culture: Researches into the Development of Mythology, Philosophy, Religion, Art and Custom*, London: Murray.

Vandenbrouke, F. (1968) 'New Milieux, New Problems', Part II, in J. Leclercq, F. Vandenbrouke and L. Bouyer, eds. *A History of Christian Spirituality, Vol. II. The Spirituality of the Middle Ages*, New York: Seabury.

Vermès, Géza (1973) *Jesus the Jew: A Historian's Reading of the Gospels*, Minneapolis: Fortress Press.

—— (1987) *The Dead Sea Scrolls in English*, third edition, London: Penguin.

Viladesau, Richard (1999) *Theological Aesthetics: God in Imagination, Beauty, and Art*, Oxford: Oxford University Press.

Von Rad, Gerhard (1975) *Old Testament Theology*, Vols. I & II, trans. D.M.G. Stalker, London: SCM.

—— (1991) *Holy War in Ancient Israel*, trans. Marva J. Dawn, Grand Rapids, MI: Eerdmans.

Walls, Neal (2001) *Desire, Discord and Death: Approaches to Ancient Near Eastern Myth*, Boston: American Schools of Oriental Research.

Weber, Max (1930) *The Protestant Ethic and the Spirit of Capitalism*, London: Unwin University Books.

Weinfeld, Moshe (1990) 'The Uniqueness of the Decalogue', in Ben-Zion Segal, ed. *The Ten Commandments in History and Tradition*, Jerusalem: Magnes Press.

Wellhausen, Julius (1884) *Skizzen und Vorarbeiten 1*, Berlin: G. Reimer.

Whitelam, Keith W. (1996) *The Invention of Ancient Israel: The Silencing of Palestinian History*, London and New York: Routledge.

Wilken, R.L. (1972) *The Myth of Christian Beginnings: History's Impact on Belief*, Garden City, NY: Doubleday.

Williams, Dolores S. (1993) *Sisters in the Wilderness: The Challenge of Womanist God-Talk*, New York: Orbis Books.

Wilson, Robert R. (1998) 'The Prophetic Books', in John Barton, ed. *The Cambridge Companion to Biblical Interpretation*, Cambridge: Cambridge University Press.

Wolff, Hans Walter (1974) *Anthropology of the Old Testament*, London: SCM.

Wright, G.E. (1960) 'The Old Testament', in G.E. Wright and R.H. Fuller, eds. *The Book of the Acts of God: Christian Scholarship Interprets the Bible*, London: Duckworth.

Yoder, John Howard (1972) *The Politics of Jesus: Vicit Agnus Noster*, Grand Rapids, MI: Eerdmans.

Zunes, Stephen (2003) *Tinderbox: U.S. Middle East Policy and the Roots of Terrorism*, London: Zed Books.

Index